SECRETS
OF SILICON VALLEY

SECRETS
OF SILICON VALLEY

WHAT EVERYONE ELSE CAN LEARN FROM
THE INNOVATION CAPITAL OF THE WORLD

DEBORAH PERRY PISCIONE

palgrave
macmillan

First published in 2013 by PALGRAVE MACMILLAN® in the U.S.—
a division of St. Martin's Press LLC, 175 Fifth Avenue, New York, NY
10010.

Where this book is distributed in the UK, Europe and the rest of the
world, this is by Palgrave Macmillan, a division of Macmillan Publishers
Limited, registered in England, company number 785998, of Houndmills,
Basingstoke, Hampshire RG21 6XS.

Palgrave Macmillan is the global academic imprint of the above
companies and has companies and representatives throughout the world.

Palgrave® and Macmillan® are registered trademarks in the United
States, the United Kingdom, Europe and other countries.

ISBN: 978-0-230-34211-8

Library of Congress Cataloging-in-Publication Data

Piscione, Deborah Perry.
    Secrets of Silicon Valley : what everyone else can learn from the
innovation capital of the world / Deborah Perry Piscione.
       p.   cm.
    1. Santa Clara Valley (Santa Clara County, Calif.)—Economic
conditions. 2. High technology industries—California—Santa Clara
County. 3. Technological innovations—California—Santa Clara County.
I. Title.
HC107.C22S3957   2013
330.9794'74—dc23
                                                              2012038481

A catalogue record of the book is available from the British Library.

Design by Letra Libre, Inc.

First edition: April 2013

10 9 8 7 6 5 4 3 2

Printed in the United States of America.

CONTENTS

PART I
AN EAST COASTER GOES WEST

Los Altos Hills, California

A little over six years ago, my husband persuaded me to jettison our political lifestyle in Washington, DC, for California, the land of better weather.

I had spent nearly 18 years in the nation's capital, and much of my identity was wrapped up in the city. On January 3, 1989, the first day of my Capitol Hill job, I sat in the fourth row of President George

H.W. Bush's inauguration with my colleague, David Rivera, who later became a member of Congress, and a powerful donor from Florida. That weekend, I attended my very first inaugural ball and none other than then-Secretary of State James Baker walked up and shook my hand before meeting with U.S. Senator Connie Mack, for whom I worked, to congratulate him on his election victory. In the following weeks, icons like Robert Redford, Shirley Temple Black, and a handful of Fortune 500 executives visited our office to meet with the senator. I was lucky to meet them all. For someone just starting out their career, it was exhilarating.

As an undergraduate student I had spent a semester in London and became intrigued by the political dynamics of foreign policy, so when Rep. Ileana Ros-Lehtinen won a special election in the then-eighteenth congressional district of Florida and vied for a seat on the coveted House Foreign Affairs Committee, it didn't take much convincing for me to move over from the U.S. Senate to the U.S. House of Representatives. As a legislative assistant, I spent most of my time working on the Soviet Refusenik issue, putting pressure on President Mikhail Gorbachev's office to allow Russian Jews to emigrate out of the former Soviet Union. On any given day, I responded to constituent mail, and when given the opportunity, I poured myself into drafting "Dear Colleague" letters and op-eds, giving speeches, and traveling to Israel to meet with leaders about the housing loan guarantees that Congress had authorized for Israel—all this by the age of 24. I had a deep passion for basic, fundamental human rights. Working on Capitol Hill, I quickly acquired knowledge about power, and how power leads to access. I obviously didn't care about money on my $17,000 salary, but I wanted direct access to decision makers, and I wanted my phone calls promptly returned.

I worked on Capitol Hill by day and attended graduate school at Georgetown University at night, specializing in international affairs and economics. I worked incredibly hard to try to get a Ph.D. in Economics, but I just couldn't afford to go to school full-time, which Georgetown required for doctoral students. After three years on Capitol Hill, I was asked by the White House to serve as a political appointee in the administration of President George H.W. Bush. By the time my security clearance came through, however, I had spent only nine months at the Department of State before President Bush lost his re-election. On

January 20, 1993, the day of President Bill Clinton's inauguration, I received my pink slip.

I took off to Brazil on an extended hiatus, and it was there I was able to put aside my type-A personality and immerse myself in the Brazilian culture. The colors, the freedom, and the food were memorable, but more notably, I learned about incredibly joyous people who often had nothing—or the countless people I came across in cities of the state of Minas Gerais who often didn't know where their next meal was coming from. I saw them carry themselves with incredible grace and richness. I traveled to the Amazon, among my top three places I had always wanted to visit. On my first night, after trying to quell my own disbelief that I was actually sleeping outside in the Amazon, I was attacked by a troop of flying cockroaches. Later in the evening, an anaconda snake decided to pass through our open-air boat right next to me while I was sleeping. On my second night, a furious crocodile chased me, my traveling companion, and the Amazonian Indian we had hired to take us out there. This was an exhilarating experience, and I began to learn that I could be remarkably calm in adverse situations. I took my watch off in the Amazon and never put one on again. Brazil had taught me the meaning of life, and helped me to answer the question of what I wanted to do with the rest of mine.

In June of 1993, I inevitably returned to Washington. I looked for meaningful work, but in a down economy I reluctantly had to accept a job lobbying for many issues that I really didn't care about, such as financial derivatives.

A few years later during the Clinton administration, as the Monica Lewinsky scandal was starting to percolate, I was asked by the Republican National Committee to serve as a commentator on television, and days later I made my first appearance on MSNBC. Within weeks, I was espousing my opinions and debating some of the country's most brilliant minds, including Harvard professor Alan Dershowitz, O. J. Simpson prosecutor Marcia Clark, and former Labor Secretary Robert Reich. I later provided political and foreign policy commentary for Wolf Blitzer on CNN, an opportunity that I enjoyed immensely. On Wolf's show you had to deeply understand the substance of the debate, and not concern yourself about what your hair looked like or the type of collared shirt you would wear on air. I co-wrote a bestselling book with Dr. Julianne

Malveaux, *Unfinished Business: A Democrat and a Republican Take on the 10 Most Important Issues Women Face*. I swept into the media world, and for nearly a decade, I worked with producers, agents, managers, speaking coaches, and style consultants to mold myself into "great television." At one point, Henry Champ, a television personality, described me as "fit to be a war correspondent" after we co-anchored the inauguration of President George W. Bush for the Canadian Broadcasting Corporation and stood in freezing rain that relentlessly blew horizontally for hours. There was no heater at our media booth (although there was supposed to be), yet I never complained. I was grateful for the historic opportunity, so there was no reason to complain. Little did he know that I considered his comment to reflect the thick skin I had grown from all the televised shouting matches I endured, and eventually I came to realize that ratings were driven less by substance than by the decibel of the screaming matches. Although I was being groomed for my own television show, I no longer found this type of discourse productive, so I walked away from it.

To survive in the competitive worlds of national politics and the media, where the driving mantra is "Be careful on your way up, because you never know who you'll meet on the way down," you need to be schooled in the art of war. You are trained to go for the jugular when your opponent is most vulnerable. I made my living fighting my political enemy. I knew no other way—until I moved to the innovation capital of the world.

WELCOME TO SILICON VALLEY

My husband and I, along with our twin toddler boys, arrived in Silicon Valley on June 10, 2006, and were captivated by the rich sunshine and the sweetness of nectar flowers wafting throughout Los Altos, the town in which we initially settled in Northern California. While it all sounds like paradise, there was the sting of transitioning from a 4,000 sq. ft. home in McLean, Virginia, to our new, tiny 1,334 sq. ft. house in Silicon Valley, a house we paid in the low seven figures for. The home would have been big enough if it had been just my husband and me, but the twins had just discovered their 16-month-old sea legs, and every pounding of their little feet rippled through our diminutive house. There were virtually no insects or humidity in Silicon Valley, but there was also no central air-conditioning, which we could have used during the heat wave that hit for a week that July.

I didn't know anything about Silicon Valley. I had never been there before, although I had always hoped to one day live in San Francisco, as it seemed to offer the optimum balance of culture, elegance, and nature. A friend of mine who grew up in the area, Ed Hearst, with whom I had worked in the Bush White House, gave me a geography lesson on the Bay Area. "If you think of the area as a peninsula with the San Francisco Bay in between, Silicon Valley is mostly on the west," Ed said. Another political friend, Lisa Gable, whose husband, Jim, had made a name for himself at Apple and later as a co-creator of the precursor to satellite radio, reached out to friends in Silicon Valley to let them know I was coming. I was amazed at how many people responded, and all seemed to ask in some way, "Welcome . . . How can I help you?"

To get a better sense of the Bay Area's economy, I researched "Silicon Valley" and discovered that it is the world's headquarters of innovation. And here I still thought Washington, DC, was the center of the world. Within an approximate ten-mile radius from where we were living, are headquartered some of the most recognizable companies in technology, digital media, and social media including Apple, Facebook, Google, YouTube, Twitter, Yahoo!, Hewlett-Packard, Intel, eBay, Applied Materials, Juniper Networks, Adobe, Cisco, Oracle, and Symantec. The first time I drove around the area and looked at the various campuses, I wondered where the stuffy, high-rise corporate buildings were. Instead, most were sprawled in relaxed patterns across the landscape. And the Google campus looked so colorful and playful that it was almost impossible to take seriously.

When you come to Silicon Valley from anywhere else, you not only adapt quickly to the abundant sunshine, but you also have to quickly adapt to the culture, the lifestyle, and the openness of the people and the landscape. There is a shared set of attitudes, values, goals, and practices that characterizes Silicon Valley that is different from any place in which I have lived or spent considerable time, including Miami, London, Washington, or New York. With so much professional success and fulfillment, not to mention the sheer magnitude of consolidated wealth, you would expect an intense business atmosphere, but in many ways it is just the opposite. Elements of competitiveness certainly emerge, but you can easily disengage yourself from that sort of tension, unlike in the business climates of Washington or New York. Silicon Valley is filled with people who embrace a laid-back lifestyle, manifested in casual office dress and a disdain for hierarchical communication models. They take themselves and their jobs seriously, but they are able to maintain a refreshing sense of individuality and purpose.

It took a while to acclimate to these affable people who actually *talk* to one another, and even seem to *look out* for each another. Back east, you could live in the same building for years with the same people and never say a word to them. In Silicon Valley, people everywhere would talk to me: at the grocery store, in the bank, at the dry cleaner. One day our car broke down, and when we called Ladera Auto Works, panicked because my husband and I were both running late for meetings, John Franceschi, an employee there, not only offered to wait for the tow truck, but to pay for it until we could later get into his repair shop. During flu season, I ordered pizza for my hungry family from Pizza My Heart in Mountain View, and the woman on the receiving end detected my congested voice, and offered to pick up cold medicine at the drugstore before delivering my pizza. We lived next door to a guy who was confined to a wheelchair but who insisted on taking out our trash, whether we were home or not.

It was hard to trust—people would randomly talk to us and seem to be genuinely interested in what we had to say. People would ask me, "Who would you like to meet?" (And they were referring to leading venture capitalists and high-profile executives.) Individuals would stop their cars just because they anticipated that you might walk across the street, and working professionals—seemingly in the prime of their careers—would bike, run, and walk the hills in the middle of the workday. For months, my husband and I asked each other, "What in the hell do they do for a living?" We were very naïve about what this lifestyle prioritized.

I'd be in disbelief over the daily police report in the *Los Altos Towne Crier*: "On the 400 block of University Avenue, a dog was seen unleashed . . . . On El Monte, someone was reported playing music too loud . . . . In the 300 block of Pine, someone left a bicycle in the road." Where were the drug raids, drive-by shootings, and white-collar corruption that I had become accustomed to in Washington, DC?

Upon moving here, we were told that it was easy to meet people, but it was hard to get to know them. I agree. If I had to describe the archetypal personality here, I'd say that most people came with an idea and a dream of commercializing that idea. And often people with that kind of passion become absorbed—even borderline obsessed—with that passion. Yet despite that inner drive, they also smile for no reason, say "hello" on the streets to one another, and evoke a shared "help thy neighbor" virtue.

My uncle, an ex–Wall Street transplant himself, once said to me that when you come to Silicon Valley, you pay for entry into a very expensive country club. While he was referring to the exorbitant cost of living, he was also referring to the priceless amenities that come along with perfect weather and genial people. More than six years after our exodus, I see what he meant—it's a geographic club of visionaries, innovators, venture capitalists, academics, lawyers, and accountants; the tight, dense, but open ecosystem that makes Silicon Valley so unrivaled.

Silicon Valley has a distinct vernacular, and newcomers best learn it quickly. I had never even heard the phrase "venture capital," much less "term sheet," "pre/post money," "cap table," "open source," "b2b," "b2c," "HTML," etc., until we moved west. You essentially need an instruction manual on the distinctive language and culture just to engage in conversation with the parents of your children's classmates. There is a social *de rigueur* for all things technological, and I've been quickly reminded on multiple occasions just how behind the times I was. While jogging in our neighborhood for the first time, I ran past an elderly woman who had her iPod connected to her walker while I labored along with my Walkman from the early 1990s.

Few who have come here from anywhere else in the world can ever imagine going back to the way of life they once lived and worked—that is, if they can afford to stay. Stand among the hills in Silicon Valley, bearing witness to some of Northern California's most stunning panoramas, and for a moment you can actually understand why people here have become accustomed to thinking that it's reasonable to pay seven figures for a home that would be classified as *dated, dilapidated, a tear down* in any other part of the country. In 2006, the median home price In Los Altos was $2.5 million, and with limited inventory, there remained a fierce bidding war to get your foot into certain neighborhoods.[1] There was once actually an effort to democratize the area by providing affordable housing. From 1950 to 1974, homebuilder Joseph Eichler built over 11,000 modern track homes in the peninsula that the middle class could afford. His designs became known as "Eichlers," but unfortunately they too even sell in the low seven figures today.[2]

Top Silicon Valley real estate agents were managing multiple contracts per listing, and Kathy Bridgman, an agent at Alain Pinel, sold enough volume that in 2009 she was ranked #21 as a *Wall Street Journal* top real estate performer—she sold over $82 million worth of properties that year.[3] Kathy even has to occasionally sign a non-disclosure agreement to conceal the identity of a very wealthy buyer or seller. Yuri Milner, an investor in Facebook, Groupon, and Zynga, paid $100 million for his Los Altos Hills mansion, "Palo Alto Loir Chateau."[4] Other leading real estate agents, such as Ken DeLeon of DeLeon Real Estate (who had $275 million in sales in 2011), specialize in premiere Silicon Valley neighborhoods like Los Altos, Los Altos Hills, Palo Alto, Menlo Park, Atherton, and Woodside, and compete with partners at blue-chip law firms in earnings.

Even at these prices, it was possible to live next door to a guy who fixes cars on his front lawn, which we did. He also happened to work as a maintenance manager at Google during its initial public offering (IPO). When we were in the market for a new nanny, we were stunned to learn that they earned an average of $20 an hour. During the dot-com boom in the mid- to late-1990s, it was rumored that the Silicon Valley nanny was often presented with a new car as a signing or Christmas bonus so that the next newly minted millionaire didn't steal her away at $25 an hour.

The irony is that Silicon Valley, in many ways, is not a place that emphasizes opulence or materialistic flash. In fact, ostentatious consumption is frowned upon. Irrespective of Yuri Milner's estate, which is hidden from the road, there was an emotionally charged debate in 2005 whether Los Altos Hills should place a square footage restriction on homes in order to prevent them from blocking views or to make it mandatory for them to blend into the natural landscape. Nobody wants to look at manmade sprawl instead of the pastoral milieu they pay a fortune to live near. Surrounding neighborhoods such as Los Gatos and Saratoga have restrictions of 6,000 and 8,000 square feet respectively.[5]

People in Silicon Valley also assume that large homes aren't necessary as most people want to spend their time outdoors. My husband and I couldn't figure out why a majority of 1950s rambler homes in our area remain unrenovated with lawns that remain unmanicured. We realized, later, that these types of things are either unimportant or cost prohibitive to their owners, or that such maintenance distracted the owners from their passions.

I have seen cars here that I have never seen before, such as the Bugatti Veyron, with a base retail price around $2.25 million. It's not unusual that those with stratospheric earnings occasionally want to reward themselves with a fun toy, and as such Porsches, Maseratis, and Ferraris dot the roadways. But even Google co-founders Larry Page and Sergey Brin are fans of the more moderately priced Toyota Prius and Tesla Roadster. At Google, it's considered unacceptable to have a parking lot full of extravagant cars, no matter how much money those who work there make. Instead, environmentally friendly electric, hybrid, and other fuel-efficient vehicles are the preferred modes of transportation.

At neighborhood barbecues and children's birthday parties when we first moved here, Page and Brin always came up in conversation. They were the golden boys in 2006, and all you had to do was mention "Lair" or "Serge" and there was an immediate understanding of who was being talked about. Facebook co-founder Mark Zuckerberg was starting to gain notoriety, but he was too young at the time to be spoken of with any level of seriousness. There was a lot of chatter about Elon Musk, whose company PayPal had been acquired by eBay in 2002 for $1.5 billion in stock, and less than a year later, Musk was building out SpaceX, Tesla Motors, and taking a hefty stake in SolarCity and Halcyon Molecular—all simultaneously. What was so remarkable about these entrepreneurs is that not only were they hardly unique, but also that they ranged in age from 22 through 35.

Some of the most-talked-about leading stars at Google were women in their twenties and thirties, reaching the peaks of their careers, such as Sheryl Sandberg, Melissa Mayer, Susan Wojcicki, and Sukhinder Singh Cassidy. I was introduced to one woman after another who had made her own money either by working at the right company or by creating her own company, in sectors ranging from technology, biotech, and digital media companies to venture capital firms, hedge funds, and land development corporations. Weeks after our move in 2006, I met a woman whose husband was one of the leading venture capitalists in Silicon Valley. With my East Coast mentality, I foolishly believed her to be a trophy wife until years later, when she divulged that she had put up $1 million for her husband to start his own venture capital firm, money that she had earned by opting to take greater equity in the companies she worked for instead of negotiating a higher salary.

After a few months, I started to appreciate how much people are in the driver's seat here. This culture of mavericks is more interested in moving the needle forward than following the path of tradition. They look in their own backyards rather than shifting their focus east to New York or Washington for inspiration. Famed venture capitalist Marc Andreessen said it best in an appearance on *Charlie Rose* when he referred to Silicon Valley as an innovation town:

> [T]he core theory we have, is that the fundamental output of a technology company is innovation and that's very different than a lot of businesses, right? The fundamental output of a car company is cars. Or the fundamental output of a bank is loans. . . . So the challenge tech companies have is they can never rest on their laurels with today's product, they always have to be thinking in terms of the next five years of what comes next and if they're good at running internally and are indeed a machine that produces innovation, they tend to do quite well over time.[6]

FINDING OPPORTUNITY

After I settled in, I started to panic about how I was going to transcend my background in politics and media in the land of Intel and Google. With a far-reaching network of friends and colleagues in high-level circles of influence, I mistakenly anticipated that Silicon Valley would pay deference to my background in politics and traditional media, but people here don't care much about such things. They care about issues, not politics. In fact, the only place my background carried any weight was in areas that didn't pay any money, such as on-air commentary. When I was asked to provide political perspective on the death of President Richard Nixon at the local NBC station, I figured I'd have a lively discussion about his merits and the demise of the divisive man, and I inquired with whom I'd be debating. "We don't do that here," replied the assistant news director, the answer surprising me.

A few weeks after our move, I got a call from Google's People Operations shop, as their human resources department is known, a perplexing development because I hadn't applied for a job there. I merely had a DC connection put me in touch with the head of Google's government relations office to pick his brain on how someone like me could transition into the Silicon Valley landscape. But the call was about joining their government relations office, so I thought, "Why not?" The first "Googlers" I encountered were unquestionably bright and articulate, yet held a complete disregard for the value I could bring to the table, particularly relating to the impending privacy issues Google was facing in China. Apparently they didn't understand that I had worked for the then-ranking member on the House Foreign Affairs Committee. More astonishingly, I learned that Google ranked schools to determine if you make it to the next stage, and my educational pedigree in addition to my other bona fides of being a bestselling author and on-air television commentator did not pass muster. Had I succeeded at this stage, they would have next vetted my GPA and possibly SAT scores. I could see that I needed to look elsewhere for guidance and a job.

A few weeks later, I landed a government relations position at a small mobile startup company—not because I had a burning desire to work in government relations, but because I needed to make a living. I figured that, living in Silicon Valley, I should experience life at a startup. The company's business was held at the investor's home every Monday on Coleridge Avenue in Palo Alto, the street known as VC (Venture Capital) Row. Over a lavish lunch of halibut dijonnaise and roasted asparagus, we discussed marketing plans and public relation strategies. I traveled to Barcelona for a mobile conference where I utilized car services, flew business class, and ate at five-star restaurants for most meals. Money flowed, and with a spendthrift CEO at the helm, the startup fell apart as he blew through a small fortune in less than six months. Through his failed experience, I learned a lot about startups—mostly what *not* to do. I also met my future co-founder, Shaun Marsh, and our investor to be, Francine Gani, and collectively we started a company.

Shaun is a really bright guy. He graduated high school at 15 and has a Ph.D. in computer science. When I met him, he had already had a patent and a successful exit under his belt, a domain company that he single-handedly ran as a side project. When his company sold in 2004, Shaun cleared what he likes to say is his "FU money," but not enough money for him to retire on. Raised mostly in Beverly Hills and Silicon Valley, Shaun is confident and calm. He opted out of the workforce for three years to care for his young daughter while his wife managed multimillion-dollar trials for Roche Pharmaceuticals. I respected him, and we quickly joined forces to build Desha Productions, Inc., a media company that owns and operates content, e-commerce, and community websites. We started out by mapping the vision for our first business unit, BettyConfidential, an online magazine that targets the coveted women's market.

Just prior to settling on developing BettyConfidential, our angel investor, Francine Gani, approached Shaun and me and said, "I like you guys . . . figure out something to do, and I'll fund you." Just like that. No detailed business plan. No projected revenues. Just a belief in our talent.

We received an initial angel investment of $250,000 in July 2007, but knew that we'd soon have to raise millions more in order to successfully build our company. With this in mind, I set up my first-ever meeting with a venture capitalist, Emily Melton at Draper Fisher Jurvetson. I was an hour from informally pitching her for a Series-A investment, and I suddenly discovered that I couldn't button the pants on my pantsuit. Later that day, I found out that I was very unexpectedly pregnant, which concerned me enormously for a variety of reasons. How was I supposed to prove that I could work 24/7 and make a return on someone's investment as a pregnant CEO?

Weeks later we were in business development discussions with Yahoo!, and I had to time my vomiting just right so I could do it on the way there and back, but not during the meeting. This was six years before Marissa Mayer got hired as CEO of Yahoo!, at 37 years old, while pregnant, and at a salary of $117 million over five years. But I was new in town and terrified of pregnancy discrimination because it was so routine back east.

It wasn't acceptable to talk about your kids or bring them around with you in DC because it would give the appearance of being distracted, not solely focused on the task at hand. Several high-profile friends of mine in DC and New York came close to filing lawsuits when networks tried to force them off air or Fortune 500 executives asked inappropriate questions like, "How do you expect to get work done while you're pregnant?" It was even common practice not to offer a seat to a pregnant woman on the Metro. I once attended a closed-door meeting in a small conference room on Capitol Hill in preparation for a press conference, and Rep. John Boehner, years before he became Speaker of the House, actually lit up a cigarette with a very pregnant congressional staffer in the room.

Yet no one in Silicon Valley seemed to care that I was pregnant and was going to be the CEO of a company—in fact, the prevailing attitude was quite to the contrary. Many of the investors to whom I was pitching actually believed that the fact that I was pregnant made me closer to the company we were creating. The many men with whom I was dealing even seemed to enjoy reminiscing and sharing their stories about the births of their own children.

A CULTURE SHOCK FULL CIRCLE

In Washington, I was indoctrinated into the philosophy of "destroy your enemy, eat your young." While I am grateful for the "how to win" skills that serve me well today, I was sold a bill of goods. I didn't really "do" anything, because most people in Washington, DC, *don't* do much except opine and deliberate over the latest, often inconsequential, political and/or policy spin. Most people are observers, vacillating over which group to join, which side to align with, who to work for next, because working for the winning candidate and jockeying to the winning side of the issue is paramount in DC. It is the only thing that matters. I spent a lot of time espousing my "hot air" opinions, and made a good living at it, but only upon moving west did I begin to understand just how detrimental that conformist attitude was to my own professional development.

My transition to Silicon Valley was smooth. I had no job, few connections, and little guidance, but something just felt right. It felt like home, and now I know why. Silicon Valley is a meritocratic culture that rewards innovative ideas, independent thinking, and hubris. It is a culture that also embraces youth, failure, and transparency. I knew I had found my tribe. Regardless, I share this story as an outsider. My story is not typical of someone who comes to Silicon Valley with a dream or a specific passion; rather, it's the story of someone with no business experience who accidentally fell into entrepreneurship and thrived at it, all within a completely alien culture.

Since our arrival in Silicon Valley, I have co-founded and successfully built three companies: BettyConfidential; Alley to the Valley, a platform for female entrepreneurs, angel investors, venture capitalists, and corporate executives; and Chump Genius, an educational gaming company that provides science, technology, engineering, and math (STEM) learning for kids. I've been fortunate in that someone offered to take a chance on me, more than once. I am confident that this would have never happened had I remained on the East Coast. On September 19, 2011, my story was documented in a Stanford University Graduate School of Business case study about how an outsider can find opportunity in Silicon Valley.

All things being equal, business is just business in Silicon Valley. Operating plans, profit and loss statements, and cash flow all look the same no matter where you are. What makes Silicon Valley such an inherently different place in which to live and work? Why do people come here, and why don't they leave? Is it the weather, the lifestyle, the innovation, the commitment to meritocracy, the investors' trickle-down wealth and knowledge, the risk tolerance, and/or the appreciation of failure?

There is something in the air here—between Stanford University in Palo Alto, Google in Mountain View, and Apple in Cupertino—that has significantly empowered people here more than any other place on earth. It has taken me over six years to put my finger on it.

1 WHY YOU SHOULD CARE ABOUT SILICON VALLEY

Singularity University, NASA Research Park, Moffett Field

Singularity University (SU) occupies a few former military barracks on the campus of NASA-Ames Research Center at Moffett Field, half-way between the cities of Mountain View and Sunnyvale, California. When entering Moffett Field past the guarded gate, you feel as if you have left Silicon Valley far behind, with the only exception being the ubiquitous Spanish-tiled roofs that adorn the main buildings. The old, musty smell of a prewar establishment greets you as you walk through the front doors of Singularity's main office. But beyond the aroma, there is nothing stagnant or backward about this place. The concepts being taught here are futuristic, evolving, and accelerating technologies: robotics, artificial intelligence, nanotechnology, biotech, design theory, space exploration, and other *Jetsons*-like ideas that are headed our way. Singularity University's overarching purpose is to forecast, analyze, and create the science and technology that will define our world five to ten years into the future. Some of the world's most brilliant scientific minds have gathered to collaborate on a single mission: to solve the world's biggest challenges, impacting one billion people at a time.

Why did the founders of this unique program use the term "singularity"? In its simplest definition, singularity is "the hypothetical future emergence of greater-than-human superintelligence through technological means."[1] It stems from the idea of a possible future emergence of a greater-than-human intellect through means such as biological enhancement of our bodies and minds, the meshing of humans and computers, and even artificial intelligence—events that would thrust humanity into a new world of technological change. If this concept sounds far-fetched, consider this quote from SU co-founder, famed inventor, and futurist Ray Kurzweil:

> The whole twentieth century was actually not one hundred years of progress at today's rate of progress. It was twenty years of progress at today's rate of progress. And we'll make another twenty years of progress at today's rate of progress, equivalent to the whole twentieth century, which was no slouch for change, in another fourteen years. And then we'll do it again in seven years. That pace will continue to accelerate, and because of the explosive nature of exponential growth, the twenty-first century will be equivalent to twenty thousand years of progress at today's rate of progress; about one thousand times greater than the twentieth century.[2]

In our age of ever-increasing complexity, previously unimagined possibilities are becoming reality with greater rapidity. And it is this rate of change that keeps Dr. Peter Diamandis, the co-founder, chairman, and the driving force behind Singularity University, up at night. The dynamic and optimistic Diamandis unapologetically dares to dream big. In 1987–88, he founded the International Space University in Strasbourg, France, with the idea of finding the smartest people on the planet and putting them in a room together to work on big, audacious goals. "It was a ton of fun," says Diamandis.[3] Holding degrees in molecular biology and aerospace engineering from MIT as well as a medical degree from Harvard, and founding and acting as CEO of the X Prize, an educational nonprofit that offers incentivized prize competitions to solve radical breakthroughs for the benefit of humanity, Diamandis is someone who has the fortitude to predict the emergence of and intersection amid science and technology.

Diamandis was inspired to start Singularity University while trekking through Patagonia with his wife, Kristen. He couldn't stop thinking about Ray Kurzweil's book, *The Singularity is Near,* which he had lugged along on the trip. "The book was the heaviest thing in my backpack," says Diamandis. "I had followed Ray's work, but purposely put off reading his book for a few months. I knew once I read it, I was going to jump in hook and sinker." The book not only defined the characteristics and impact of the coming singularity, but also described the landscape wherein our "intelligence will become increasingly non-biological and trillions of times more powerful than it is today—the dawning of a new civilization that will enable us to transcend our biological limitations and amplify our creativity."[4]

After returning from his travels in South America, Diamandis couldn't wait to connect with Kurzweil and immediately set up a strategic dinner engagement to meet him for the first time. The two men met in Orange County, California, and Diamandis pitched Kurzweil on how the two could collaborate on his vision. Kurzweil was intrigued. These are two of the world's great futuristic thinkers who act on their passions, but it was Diamandis who insisted that there should be a place where the greatest scientific and technological minds from various domains should converge to tackle the world's most pressing problems—those brilliant minds who have the potential to alter the human experience and life on Earth as we know it. During an early planning meeting for Singularity University, an executive education program rather than a traditional four-year degree, they identified dozens of people who shared their fervor and invited them to convene at Moffett Field. The "who's who" of guests included Google co-founder and CEO Larry Page, who was so convinced of the need for Singularity University that Google became the first sponsor, and in February 2009 Diamandis and Kurzweil held a press conference at the annual TED (Technology, Entertainment, and Design) conference and announced the birth of Singularity University.

While Diamandis strives to keep his finger on the pulse of accelerating technologies, Kurzweil likes to promote the potential of taking exponential steps, rather than viewing life as linear. He notes that if you take 30 linear steps forward, you will get exactly 30 steps as your outcome. However, if you take 30 exponential steps forward, your outcome will be a billion steps.[5] They feel humanity will need to embody this exponential growth to overcome life's grand challenges in eight critical areas, which Singularity University has adopted as its chosen disciplines: education, energy, environment, food, global health, poverty, security, and water. They ask one simple question of anyone who attends their executive or graduate studies programs: "What will you do to affect one billion people at a time?"

EXPONENTIAL CHANGES

Only in Silicon Valley is the culture of science and innovation given such free reign that people can study and experiment with these ideas despite the fact that the payoff may be years or decades down the road, financially or otherwise. But what makes this epoch even more significant than any prior era of change in human history is how enormously Silicon Valley technologies impact the world's most basic ideas about work, learning, and lifestyles. These technologies will allow anyone—at any age, anytime, and anywhere in the world—to enter the entrepreneurial marketplace, create a personal brand or platform, and build things that were only recently considered very capital intensive. Take, for example, then-15-year-old Jack Andraka, a high-school freshman from Maryland who invented a viable early prevention test for pancreatic cancer.[6]

Andraka, who was inspired to find a cure after his uncle died of pancreatic cancer, was mostly rebuffed by the medical establishment, likely due to his young age, but he remained undeterred. Using carbon nanotubes, he ran a series of experiments to test the electrical conductivity between them at various distances. Andraka then wanted to share his findings with the medical establishment, but received 197 rejection letters from notable doctors. However, Dr. Anirban Maitra, professor of Pathology, Oncology, and Chemical and Biomolecular Engineering at Johns Hopkins School of Medicine, wanted to see what this young pioneer had discovered, and invited Andraka to spend time in his lab.[7] There the teen scientist found that when the antibodies on the surface of the nanotubes came into contact with a target protein, the protein bound to the tubes and spread them apart. Andraka's testing determined obvious changes in the electrical conductivity of the nanotubes when the distances between the charges changed. That shift in the spaces between tubes can be detected by an electrical meter. Andraka used a $50 meter from the Home Depot to do the trick. Now, Andraka believes that this same dipstick sensor could be used to detect ovarian and lung cancers as well. According to Andraka, his diagnostic test is 28 times faster, 28 times less expensive (costing around three cents), and over 100 times more sensitive than the current methods.[8] In 2012, Jack Andraka won the Intel International Science and Engineering Fair grand prize of $75,000 and, after winning, patented his sensor.

Entrepreneurship is the future of the world, as anyone can partake. We're just beginning a global startup revolution in talent development and idea creation, a movement so widespread that it could redefine the foundational concept of business and work in the twenty-first century. Don't believe it? Consider the culmination of these three factors, which will greatly enhance the probability of instantaneously commercializing any idea:

1. Technology is faster, available to everyone, and accelerating toward microscopic and free;
2. Outsourcing, crowd-sourcing, and P2P (person-to-person) collaboration make us more efficient at little to no cost; and
3. Social media is completely redefining how we communicate with one another, work across domains and boundaries, and market our ideas.

Gordon Moore, an Intel co-founder, popularized the phrase "Moore's Law," a concept that soon became the foundation for the exponential revolution, in a 1965 paper. Simply, Moore's Law characterized the "history of computing hardware whereby the number of transistors that can be placed inexpensively on an integrated circuit doubles approximately every two years."[9] Since then, Moore's Law has been uncannily accurate in predicting the growth of technology and its declining costs. While the specifics of Moore's Law have shifted slightly over the decades, it has been universally recognized in nearly every segment of the global technology marketplace as affecting processing speed, memory capability, sensors, semiconductors, and even the number and size of pixels in a digital camera. Over time, technology indeed becomes exponentially better, stronger, faster, and more financially accessible to the masses.

In his book *Abundance,* Dr. Peter Diamandis observes: "Folks with no education and little to eat have gained access to cellular connectivity unheard of just thirty years ago."[10] This technological emergence has staggering implications, as Diamandis illustrates in relation to the common man: "If he is on a smart phone with access to Google, then he has better access to information than the president of the United States did 25 years ago."[11] As a matter of fact, physicist Michio Kaku has noted that today's average cell phone has more computing power than all of NASA did when it sent two astronauts to the moon.[12] With that level of technology available to every citizen in every country, what sort of new markets, new economies, and new innovations can we expect? In 2000, only 2 percent of Africans had access to a cell phone. In 2009, that number grew to 28 percent, and is expected to swell to 70 percent in 2013.[13] This rapid expansion of mobile technology in the sub-Saharan region is already giving birth to an economic revolution that will be exported to the rest of the world—a prime example of what might be called "reverse innovation," where the innovation is first seen in the developing world before spreading to the industrialized world.[14] Carol Realini, the executive chairman of California-based mobile-banking innovator Obopay puts it this way: "Africa is the Silicon Valley of banking. The future of banking is being defined here. The new models for what will be mainstream throughout the world are being incubated here. It's going to change the world."[15]

David Rose, an entrepreneur and investor who is credited with bringing "Silicon Alley" to New York, gave a talk at SU on how the rapid "acceleration to free" will change the financial implication of the way business is conducted and who can enter today's marketplace.[16] Now anyone can create a sustainable small business practically for free, and grow it into a dynamic and potentially game-changing enterprise in very little time. Peter Diamandis once told me that individuals with a small cadre of experts who are connected via shared passions and the internet can now do what only large corporations and governments were able to do in the past.[17] They can advertise for no cost via social media; offer "freemiums" (services and experiences that the consumer gets for free, but will subsequently be charged for once the consumer is hooked); cross-subsidize; do a labor exchange; or offer virtual goods, all at zero marginal cost.

Web 2.0, the mid-2000s evolution of web capabilities like information sharing, collaboration, and user-generated design, brings us real-time information, allowing us to not only find and sample whatever we want whenever we want it, but also to outsource and crowd-source. Outsourcing means that we can allocate specific tasks at which we are less proficient to outside experts or "freelancers," making us more efficient in our areas of expertise. Today, we can also leverage the knowledge and power of the "crowd" through the internet, harvesting the best talent available to design business cards, create logos, develop marketing plans, mock up websites, or code apps. Crowd-sourcing offers a plethora of choices, allowing us to pay what we want to access an unprecedented range of expertise in design, services, ideas, business development, or technology.

Social media, which dominates much of our time on the internet, couples real-time information with the acceleration-to-free concept. This tool has made us simultaneously more connected to our past, present, and future than at any time in human history, and gives us access to others with whom we may have wanted to associate but lacked the real-world connection to meet under normal circumstances. Sites such as Facebook, Twitter, and LinkedIn have forever changed the way we interact, both personally and professionally. We can reach anyone at any time, allowing us to work in collaboration with others who can help build on our ideas, contribute their own opinions, or popularize a concept virally without any formal agreement or campaign. Through social media, individuals develop a social graph that can be leveraged to create more overall well-being than ever before.

The Power of Social Media

A musician by the name of Dave Carroll got frustrated after nine months of unsuccessfully trying to get United Airlines to reimburse him for his treasured Taylor guitar after it was damaged by baggage handlers.

Carroll wrote and produced a catchy tune about the whole experience and posted it on YouTube. As of the writing of this book, the video has received over 12 million views.[18] While United still refused to take responsibility, Taylor Guitars sent Carroll two new instruments as gratitude for all the free publicity they received.[19] As a side note, Carroll was also able to launch a speaking tour based solely on his song, "United Breaks Guitars."

You could argue that Al Jazeera, the Qatar-based news network, may have been the trigger of the "Arab Spring," the revolutionary wave of protests in the Arab world that began on December 18, 2010, but it was Facebook and Twitter that galvanized people to the streets.[20] The grassroots demonstrations that began in Tunisia and Egypt and consequently rippled through much of the Middle East enabled civilians to launch coups against authoritarian governments. No longer must disenfranchised or oppressed citizens go underground or flee to the jungle in order to create a revolutionary movement. Could it be that social media has enabled more democracy movements over the course of a year than our entire foreign aid program has since being signed into law by President Gerald Ford in 1974?

The Arab Spring leaves little doubt that social media can have a groundbreaking effect on arenas as large as geopolitics, and ranking politicians are rethinking and revamping our current foreign aid program.

Frank Spencer is a professional futurist—one of a handful of scientists who attempt to systematically predict the future. He's also cofounder of the innovation firm Kedge. In a series of conversations with him, I saw how convincingly he believes that social media is bringing people together based on common protests or passions, and is even causing us to move away from traditional models of generational segmenting, allowing individuals and groups to coalesce around cohorts based on similar interests, projects, and democracy movements. Spencer has often shared the idea that social media, as a tool, allows us to share knowledge and create communities that are conducive to large-scale inspiration, innovation, and invention.[21] All of this will impact the way we live and work, transfer more power to more people, and provide accessibility to information like we have never seen before. But what makes this shift even more unprecedented is that we are experiencing a simultaneous cultural values shift.

The financial crisis of 2008 caused everyone to pause. Even as people were losing their homes, their life savings, or their morale, the most central question on most people's minds was, What gives me meaning? Even though we remain a consumer spending economy with a personal savings rate averaging about 2 percent, the financial crisis had us questioning American cupidity and the accumulation, and often duplication, of material goods.[22] With the use of technology, we can now buy things one day, experience buyer's remorse, and sell those same items on eBay or Craigslist the following day. And we are able to do this in the privacy of our own homes, with a few clicks on the web. The shift away from hyper-consumption toward a more conscientious consumption has sparked a movement to share goods with our neighbors and fellow city dwellers rather than to exclusively own them—from forms of transportation such as bikes and cars to more personal products such as dresses and handbags.[23] This new trend of "collaborative consumption" not only points to big changes ahead for economic models and cultural dynamics, but also suggests completely new pathways in technology and business development for the unpredictable decades ahead.

We are now dependent on innovations and technologies that didn't even exist five to ten years ago. As with any new technology, we go through the steps of an innovation continuum: We first cannot fathom the technology being a part of our lives, and then we go through a process of resisting it. We transition into being annoyed by it, until finally we give in to it, and ultimately cannot live without it. Jon Pittman, vice president of Corporate Strategy at Autodesk, a 3D design software company, lays out this chronological sequence of technological innovation as follows: impossible, impractical, possible, expected, and required.[24] This adoption of technological innovation not only changes how we interact with people, but also radically shifts the way we work.

THE RISE OF THE "SOLOPRENEUR"

A September 2011 report by MBO Partners, a support firm that helps people become independent consultants, predicts that by the year 2020 more than 40 to 45 percent of the workforce will be "contingent work-ers," meaning they will be self-employed, freelancers, or accidental en-trepreneurs laid off from full-time positions. MBO Partners states that the "contingent worker" will be the majority of the workforce by 2030.[25] Frank Spencer likes to refer to this rising segment as "solopreneurs," and he believes that they are becoming the talent of choice for some of the world's largest companies.[26] The reason may surprise you: It is not the cost savings that the companies are after, but rather the specialized talent and potential that these individuals offer—individuals who are more en-gaged in producing breakthrough results than fulfilling traditional roles. By becoming talent-centric, the balance of power within companies is shifting toward the individual, meaning that companies who approach human capital more holistically will thrive.

One of the best examples of the convergence of accelerating tech-nology, disruptive innovation (when innovation changes the course of an earlier technology that then becomes obsolete), and the cultural shift toward solopreneurship is "generative cities." It is estimated that by the year 2050, over 70 percent of the world's population will live in cit-ies,[27] meaning that these hubs of business, government, and economic distribution will either be the source of humanity's greatest problems or the fountain from which springs our greatest solutions—perhaps both. As such, a great deal of entrepreneurial brainpower has been aimed at making our cities "smart" through the development of ubiquitous infor-mation technology. But is this smart technology enough? In an article en-titled "Generative Cities: The Future of Urban Intelligence," co-founder of the Hybrid Reality Institute and faculty advisor at Singularity Univer-sity Ayesha Khanna stated that:

> The globally mobile entrepreneur will decide where to invest capital
> and where to live depending on a city's ability to be generative, i.e., cre-
> ate a productive, participatory, and personalized urban experience . . .
> the key to unlocking a city's greatness lies not in technology but the
> principle of generativity. Generativity is the ability to use technologies
> to create an enabling infrastructure for connectivity and creativity. The
> internet is our best example of a generative structure: it was designed to
> have a seemingly infinite capacity for people to connect to each other;
> to create content, disruptive business models, and successful compa-
> nies; and to store, consume, and share vast amounts of information.[28]

Through exponential technology that is also generative in nature, cities could become the ultimate laboratories for solving our grand challenges.

Which brings us back to our original question: Why should you care about Silicon Valley?

First, simply put, Silicon Valley is responsible for creating almost every technological innovation that has and will continue to change the global world in the way we live, work, and socialize. It continues to prove that the region hasn't lost its edge to create innovative new products that appeal to the world at large.

Second, Silicon Valley boasts an incredibly muscular regional economic advantage within our global economy, despite the rest of America largely struggling. As such, Silicon Valley is emblematic of why this century will not be defined by the classic nation state, but rather by the regionalization of cities as the hubs of economic development.

Third, Silicon Valley is constantly evolving. It's like an active volcano that erupts every few years, with creativity bringing forth new ideas, technologies, business models, and commercialization. "We are a bubble-based economy that continues to reinvent itself," says Doug Henton, chairman and CEO of Collaborative Economics.[29] Henton believes that Silicon Valley's economy is a series of natural growth curves, which is not dependent on one product or technology. Rather, it is a place where ideas bubble up, boil for a while, and then once the market is saturated, these ideas transform into new and innovative ideas.

With companies like Google and Apple that continue to evolve and define the global technological markets, the regional economy grows large enough to have an impact beyond its location. And where countries, states, and localities will be forced to diversify their economies in order to relieve the burden of their bankrupt budgets and limited options for increasing tax revenues, regionalization will take on even greater importance. (The same argument can be applied to entire countries, such as Greece and Spain.)

Unfortunately, governments and big business still tend to think of the future in a straight line. It's understandable, since human development before the last half century *was* largely local and linear, as our ancestors would only encounter a handful of close neighbors on any given day. But technology has now accelerated our connection to disparate cultures and civilizations all over the world. This has changed our perspective, offering new ways to frame our most pressing problems and draw upon our collective knowledge to make our own lives better. It has required our brains to move beyond linear thinking, instead operating from a much more complex and exponential framework.

This change in framework will decimate those companies wedded to traditional management structures or outdated products. Fortune 500 businesses such as Eastman Kodak will continue to experience disruptive stress if they choose to ignore where Silicon Valley technologies are heading. The fact is that Silicon Valley does not have much in the way of big business. Of the Fortune 100, only six companies are based in Silicon Valley (although there are several in San Francisco and other parts of the Bay Area). Yet within this handful are the very companies— Hewlett Packard, Apple, Intel, Cisco, Google, and Oracle—that continue to think and act entrepreneurially. They have learned that they can both collaborate with their competitors and compete against them in the global marketplace.

Technology is both heating up our world and vaporizing it. Because of the pace of exponential technologies in today's market, you will be out of business by the time you go to market—that is, unless you can literally create and commercialize something overnight. Most of the world lets Silicon Valley take the lead, and then replicates its ideas, saturates the market, and fizzles until the next wave of innovation appears. This is why today's disruptive entrepreneurs and visionaries need to be thinking about technology five to ten years out.

Though Silicon Valley is comprised mainly of small- to medium-size businesses, Peter Diamandis believes that its companies will continue to see billion-dollar valuations overnight, while traditional multinational corporations go out of business in the next two to ten years. In my opinion, it is now more important for every company with global interest to have an office in Silicon Valley rather than in Washington or New York.

At the micro level, the region is not only responsible for creating the disruptive and innovative technologies that we can't seem to live without, but also for inspiring innovative, less-capital-intensive business models. The secret to this type of economy is the right mix of people, those who are risk tolerant, constantly adapting, and don't enjoy being sedentary. A collaborative culture where people trust one another to cross-pollinate and strengthen an idea's commercial viability is crucial.

And most importantly, an acceptance of failure must be in place. It is easy to attract the brightest talent to Silicon Valley because they know they will not be stigmatized for being part of a venture that doesn't pan out. "It is a hell of a trampoline for those serial entrepreneurs who are ingratiated into the ecosystem," says Doug Henton. If you fail at one thing, Henton believes you can just jump to the next big idea.

This is what makes Silicon Valley so tough to compete with. It is not just a tech park next to a university, but an ecosystem. Dr. Bill Miller, the former provost of Stanford, likes to call it a "habitat" because it is not just about invention, but also about the people who can help commercialize an idea.[30] The habitat contains not just the seeds, but the soil as well. The first computer was created at the University of Pennsylvania, and the first semiconductor was invented at Bell Labs in New Jersey, yet neither one was commercialized there. It all happened in Silicon Valley.

At the core of Silicon Valley's success is that people rarely ask, "Who do you work for?" but rather, "What's your passion?"

In researching this book, I was fortunate enough to spend considerable time with some of the world's leading scientists and technologists at Singularity University. A friend of mine forewarned me before visiting SU's executive program, "Deborah, it is going to change your thinking." After a week of hanging out at SU, my response to him was, "It didn't just change my thinking; it changed my life." Like the rest of Silicon Valley, Singularity University is a place that oozes with passion.

2 WHY SILICON VALLEY EXISTS

Hay Fields, Rancho Los Robles, circa June 1936

SILICON VALLEY (NOUN)

1971: A region of land that is south of San Francisco. "Silicon" refers to the silicon chip manufacturers that dominated the region in the 1970s, and "Valley" referred to Santa Clara Valley, the southern part of the San Francisco Bay.

For most people—even those living in the Bay Area—it is difficult to pinpoint how Silicon Valley came into being. Some of the history is transparent, but some is a bit more obscure. An executive from Samsung who learned that I was there doing research for this book asked, "Do you go back 50 years to when the culture began?" I replied, "Technically, you could go back to the years 1884–1885, when Leland Stanford thought about what a university in his son's honor could look like."[1] It was Stanford who envisioned a school that could offer tighter coordination and greater connectivity with the business community, teaching real life experiences.

I also said, "You could argue that had it not been for someone such as Mary Whipple, Moffett Field may have been located somewhere else on the West Coast." Then you can thank people such as Frederick Terman, who was appointed as Stanford's Dean of Engineering in 1944 and later provost from 1955 to 1965,[2] or the Traitorous Eight out of Shockley Labs who abhorred hierarchical management structures and thought companies should treat people like families. There are so many to thank for what we know as the Silicon Valley culture, but there are a handful of people whose monumental decisions laid the foundation for the Silicon Valley we know today. With that in mind, here are the top seven reasons why Silicon Valley exists today.

REASON 1: STANFORD UNIVERSITY

Leland Stanford Jr. University, otherwise known as Stanford, received its founding grant of endowment in November 1885, from Leland and Jane Stanford in honor of the passing of their only child in 1884. The Stanfords chose Palo Alto Stock Farm, their country estate, as the site of the university, and to this day it is often referred to as "The Farm."[3]

When Leland thought about what a world-class education for a nineteenth-century world would look like, he reflected back to his earlier business dealings. He had met with graduates from the East Coast whose education, he felt, had not properly prepared them for the real world. One of the directives of a Stanford education was for each student to be offered "personal success and direct usefulness in life."[4] Through a tradition that included intensive fieldwork, classroom lectures, laboratory experiments, and book study, all integrated with the surrounding industry, Leland's vision was fully executed by David Starr Jordan, Stanford's founding president. Professors were strongly encouraged to form lasting relationships with leaders in business and government so that their students would understand the relevance and practicality of their education through those who experience it firsthand. Leland insisted that science provides that "direct usefulness in life" and would be the vanguard of the university mission, since most other universities ignored its relevance.[5]

Stanford's charter also included maintaining the Palo Alto estate as a farm for instruction in agriculture, teaching the advantages of cooperation, and equality of the sexes in education at a time when few universities offered higher education for women.

When President Theodore Roosevelt came to visit Stanford in 1903, he was not prepared for the physical beauty of the campus and its surroundings. President Roosevelt remarked that "we have here a great institution of learning absolutely unique, even in its outward aspect, situated in this beautiful valley with the hills in the background, under this sky, with these buildings, and if this university does not turn out the right kind of citizenship and the right kind of scholarship, I shall be more than disappointed."[6]

The university officially opened on October 1, 1891, with 555 students, with Herbert Hoover being the university's first official student.[7]

REASON 2: THE VACUUM TUBE

One of the most significant inventions of the twentieth century was the vacuum tube. In simple terms, vacuum tubes control electric currents through a vacuum in a sealed container, and are either used for rectification, amplification, or switching electrical signals. The effects of the vacuum tubes greatly advanced electronic technology and drove the development and commercialization of radio broadcasting, television, radar, sound recording, reproduction, and reinforcement, and later, large telephone networks, analog and digital computers, and industrial process controls.

The tubes are roughly cylindrical and made of thin transparent glass, like an incandescent light bulb with an extra electrode inside. When the bulb's filament is heated, electrons are burned off its surface and into the vacuum inside the bulb, giving the extra electrode a positive charge. When the extra electrode is made more positive than the hot filament, a direct current flows through the vacuum to the anode, and since the current only flows in one direction, it makes it possible to convert from alternating current (AC) to direct current (DC).

Many famous inventors experimented with the earlier evacuated tubes, among them Thomas Edison, Eugen Goldstein, and Nikola Tesla. With the exception of their use in the original light bulbs, these evacuated tubes were only used in scientific research or as novelties, but the groundwork laid by these scientists was instrumental in the development of the vacuum tube. In 1880, Thomas Edison was working with Frederick Guthrie's earlier discovery in thermionic emission, in which a

heat-induced flow of charge, such as electrons or ions, overcomes its bind-
ing potential. Edison was trying to explain the reason for the breakage
of lamp filaments and uneven blackening of the bulbs in his incandescent
lamps, so he built several experimental bulbs, some with an extra wire
separate from the filament, which accidentally created a one-way current.

Later known as the "Edison effect," the classic example of thermionic emission is discharge of electrons from a hot cathode into a vacuum
tube. Edison didn't realize the potential of his discovery in part because
he did not understand the underlying physics, but it laid the groundwork
for another inventor, Lee De Forest, who came to the Bay Area in 1910.

Prior to his move, De Forest invented the audion, an electronic am-
plifying vacuum tube, in 1906, which later became known as the triode
vacuum tube. This single invention led to great advancements in tele-
phony and enabled the engineering of the first coast-to-coast telephone
line, as well as revolutionizing the technology used in radio transmitters
and receivers. By placing additional electrodes between the filament, De
Forest was able to amplify signals of all frequencies.

> As the voltage applied to the so-called control grid was lowered from
> the cathode's voltage to somewhat more negative voltages, the amount
> of current from the filament to the plate was reduced. The negative
> electrostatic field created by the grid in the vicinity of the cathode
> would inhibit thermionic emission and reduce the current to the plate.
> Thus, a few volts difference at the grid would make a large change in
> the plate current and could lead to a much larger voltage change at the
> plate; the result was voltage and power amplification.[8]

A bronze plaque at the corner of Channing Street and Emerson Avenue
in Palo Alto marks where De Forest invented the three-element radio
vacuum tube at the Electronics Research Laboratory. This discovery sig-
nified the beginning of the electronics revolution of the twentieth century, and solidified the area's reputation for innovation in electronics.[9]

REASON 3: MOFFETT FIELD

Laura Thane Whipple had an uncanny sense for economic development.
In the 1920s, she obtained her real estate license and began brokering

deals for prominent landowners. Among her listings was a large parcel of farmland between Sunnyvale and Mountain View. Whipple believed that if she could attract a U.S. Navy air base to "Rancho Ynigo," which was nothing more than thousands of acres of hay and broccoli farms at the time, it would bring jobs, commerce, and research and development prospects to the area. She felt that a military base would help bolster real estate values in the agricultural area, known at the time as the Valley of Heart's Delight.[10]

Through a friend, Whipple had learned that U.S. Navy Rear Admiral William A. Moffett was lobbying the federal government to develop a fleet of two airships, the *Akron,* to be stationed at Lakehurst, New Jersey, and the *Macon,* to be stationed somewhere on the West Coast. She also learned from friends stationed at the Presidio in San Francisco that the army was searching for a West Coast base to solidify its line of defense. Sensing an opportunity, Whipple and leaders at the Mountain View and Sunnyvale Chambers of Commerce produced a short, silent film in 1929 to convince the navy brass of the area's benefits. The film was also used to convince locals that establishing an air base in the community's midst would be good business, and encouraged everyone to financially support a sum in excess of $476,000 that would be required to purchase the land.[11] Residents actually flocked to the theaters all over the Bay Area to see the film, and proceeds contributed to the fundraising effort. The San Francisco Chamber of Commerce pledged to raise a half million dollars, and Laura Whipple convinced each landowner to accept a sales price of $450 per acre.

In under ten minutes, the film identified three key assets of the Mountain View/Sunnyvale region that were used to entice the Navy:[12]

1. The position of the San Francisco Bay, bordered by the Santa Cruz mountains on one side and the Sierra Nevadas on the other;
2. The favorable weather conditions; and
3. The resources of the local universities.

There were already airports at San Francisco, Oakland, and Palo Alto, and an air base in Alameda. A Mountain View/Sunnyvale air base would consolidate the necessary line to protect the West Coast, along with Puget Sound to the north and San Diego to the south. The reliability of the great weather, wind conditions, and the bowl-like valley made the area an exceptional testing ground for the Navy's innovative air technologies. Stanford University, just seven miles away, offered a top-notch aeronautical program, and both Santa Clara University and San Jose State offered substantial research libraries. Although not explicitly stated in the film, the region also presented an immediate gateway to Asia.

After a brief debate in Congress, the bill to authorize the land and appropriate $5 million to construct the essential structures and development passed and was signed into law by President Herbert Hoover on February 20, 1931.[13] The land was transferred to the U.S. Navy on July 31 for $1. Whipple and the members of the surrounding Chambers of Commerce agreed to this nominal amount of money because they were convinced that the presence of a military base was going to provide great economic benefits and growth opportunities to the area.

On October 16, 1933, the *Macon* arrived at its new home at Sunnyvale Naval Air Station (later named Moffett Field), less than four years before the *Hindenburg* exploded in New Jersey, killing 36 people.[14] The 785-foot airship was approximately 10 feet longer than the German *Graf Zeppelin,* which made its first intercontinental trip in 1928 and its first round-the-world flight in 1929. There was so much excitement and anticipation over the *Macon* that upon its arrival people took off from work, schools closed, and the community came out and lined the streets with incredible fanfare. One bleak spot for the locals, however, was the airship's name, as *Macon* had no connection with the Bay Area, but rather was christened after the largest city in the Georgia district of Rep. Carl Vinson, Chairman of the House Committee on Naval Affairs.

The military and civilians in the area held high expectations for the airship, and it was soon sent out on maneuvers in the Pacific. But during a mock battle, it was shot down twice in the first eight hours, and less than two years after its arrival, it crashed near Point Sur, California, on its fifty-fourth voyage. A radioman was killed when he jumped into the ocean and another died trying to retrieve his belongings, but in all, 81 out of the 83 passengers survived.[15]

With the loss of the *Macon,* the Navy no longer had a need for the Sunnyvale Air Station, so it was turned over to the War Department and then handed over to the U.S. Army in exchange for the army's North Island field in San Diego. Two years later, the renamed Moffett Field became the Army Air Corps' (the predecessor for the Air Force) central training center for the West Coast.[16] Actor James Stewart even did a stint as a cadet at Moffett Field in 1941, and eventually rose to the rank of brigadier general in the Air Force Reserves.

After the attack on Pearl Harbor on December 7, 1941, U.S. military leaders wanted to strengthen their forces on the West Coast and developed aircraft that could patrol for submarines and mines. The Navy came back to Moffett Field, rounded up some of the key personnel behind the airships, and commissioned the LTA (lighter-than-air) squadron, ZP–32, to patrol the Pacific Coast during WWII. "The Santa Clara Valley is ideal for our lighter-than-air ships," said Rear Admiral John Greenslade, who was in charge of the program.[17] He was referring to the atmospheric conditions, terrain, and proximity to other bases for patrol.

The pilots of the airships learned valuable skills beyond serving as search patrols. They became knowledgeable about how to spot and identify schools of fish in the Pacific, and then report their locations to fishing fleets in San Francisco and Monterey. This practice became so popular that Moffett Field began offering official classes for pilots and crew on how to properly identify various schools of fish. As a result, the local fishermen saved enormous amounts of time and money.

Moffett Field later became a place where airships were assembled, and where vertical and horizontal fins, elevators, and rudders were manufactured. In mid-1942, the Navy designated the base as a joint LTA and HTA (heavier-than-air) facility, and in the following two years the HTA came into significance just as the LTA program began to decline. In August 1947, the last airship went down off the Cape of Mendocino, and the LTA program shut down for good. By 1940, the National Advisory Committee for Aeronautics (NACA) needed a West Coast site due to the magnitude of aircraft manufacturing on the West Coast, so Ames Research Center found a permanent home with NASA at Moffett Field in 1958, and engaged in research on wind tunnels and the aerodynamics of propeller-driven aircraft. Today, NASA Ames Research Center at Moffett Field provides broad leadership from astrobiology and the search for habitable planets to supercomputing and intelligent/adaptive systems.[18]

REASON 4: FREDERICK TERMAN

Frederick Terman is often referred to as the father of Silicon Valley. He received his undergraduate degree in chemistry and master's degree in electrical engineering from Stanford before finishing his Ph.D. at MIT in 1924.[19] He moved back to Stanford to teach electrical engineering, but was called up during World War II to run the Radio Research Lab at Harvard, the country's standard of excellence for research and development at the time.[20]

The military had been the primary driver of technological innovation, more so than research laboratories or private industry. Yet after World War I, Dr. Vannevar Bush—the famed inventor, author of the formative report on how the U.S. government could innovate in science and engineering following World War II, and head of the National Defense Research Committee (NDRC), as well as Frederick Terman's advisor at MIT—pushed for greater coordination between the military and academic research labs in order to advance military technologies. The military agreed, and allocated a total of $450 million (in 1945 dollars) in weapons R&D spending. Unfortunately, Stanford University wasn't considered a credible research lab in the eyes of military decision makers, according to Steve Blank, a serial entrepreneur and expert on the Silicon Valley's military history.[21] Stanford only received $50,000 whereas Harvard and Columbia each received $30 million, Cal Tech $83 million, and MIT $117 million.[22]

Terman, who was then Stanford's Chair of Engineering, was so infuriated that Stanford wasn't recognized as a respected research laboratory that he vowed it would never happen again, and traveled to the East Coast to recruit the best talent to Stanford. He hired 11 members of the Harvard Radio Research Lab, where Terman had worked during World War II. By 1950 he had set up his own lab in the Engineering Department, and in the words of Steve Blank, "effectively turning Stanford into the MIT of the West." By the early 1950s, the Korean War changed everything. The military asked Terman to bolster Stanford's Applied Electronics Lab and assist them in performing covert operations. Stanford thus became a full partner with the military, and cultivated an R&D standard of excellence for the CIA and NSA as the Cold War escalated.[23]

Stanford had greatly advanced R&D for the military, and at that point, Terman found that he was doing something great for his country. Instead of steering his best engineering students to get PhDs, he encouraged them to leave Stanford and start companies so that the United States could lead in innovation. This one shift in focus—to seek growth in electronics rather than increased defense contractors—made the difference in diversifying the region's economy. Rather than imitating San Diego or Seattle, where much of the focus was on the defense contracting industry, Frederick Terman laid the groundwork for the future innovation capital. Silicon Valley blossomed economically in the 1950s and 1960s, not as a result of a drive for profit but for national survival.

Frederick Terman's time at Stanford stretched into four decades as he moved from professor to dean of engineering to provost to acting president. Before his passing in 1982, Terman reflected, "When we set out to create a community of technical scholars in Silicon Valley, there wasn't much here and the rest of the world looked awfully big. Now a lot of the rest of the world is here."[24]

REASON 4: THE GROWTH OF THE ELECTRONICS INDUSTRY

Prior to the 1940s, the peninsula was mostly agricultural, but there were a handful of radio enterprises that operated under the auspices of the Radio Corporation of America and other East Coast firms. At the time, it is estimated that the collective workforce was a few hundred machinists and engineers. Three decades later, the story was dramatically different, as the area's electronics workforce swelled to 58,000 in the 1970s, more than half of which worked at electronics component firms that manufactured power grid tubes, microwave tubes, and semiconductors. These firms accounted for about half of the microwave tubes and more than a third of the silicon transistors and integrated circuits produced in the country. Because these components were used in a majority of industrial goods and military weapon systems, the area developed into the backbone for manufacturing and military procurement. Two of the more enduring firms that helped to grow the electronics industry were Hewlett Packard and Varian Associates.[25]

Hewlett-Packard (HP)

Bill Hewlett and Dave Packard were electrical engineering students at Stanford when they took one of Frederick Terman's classes. Irrespective of it being the height of the Depression, Terman sensed brilliance in Hewlett and Packard and strongly encouraged them to start a company.

On January 1, 1939, with a $538 capital investment, the two joined forces in Packard's garage.[26] One of their first orders of business turned out to be the most widely recognized: a coin toss to determine whose name would go first in the company name, and, of course, Hewlett won.[27]

In the 1940s and for the decades that followed, HP concentrated on making electronic test equipment such as signal generators, voltmeters, oscilloscopes, frequency counters, thermometers, time standards, wave analyzers, and other electronic components. Where HP excelled is that many of its measurement range instruments were far more sensitive, accurate, and precise compared to those of competitors. Yet it still took time for the company to launch a financially successful product. The first was a precision audio oscillator called the Model HP 200A. The innovation of the HP 200A was a "low-distortion audio oscillator used for testing sound equipment," the subject of Bill Hewlett's master's thesis. The HP 200A simply used a small incandescent light bulb as a temperature-dependent thermistor in a critical portion of the circuit, where previously there had not been a device for temperature regulation.[28] One of the company's first customers was Walt Disney Productions, which used the HP 200B, a second-generation oscillator, for the surround-sound systems installed in movie theaters for the movie *Fantasia*. Disney had bought eight Model 200B oscillators for $71.50 each.[29]

Varian Associates

The Varian brothers, Russell and Sigurd, grew up in Palo Alto and on the central coast of California. Russell, the elder brother, had dyslexia, a misunderstood affliction at the time, causing people to write him off as slow or ignorant. Russell was a hard worker, however, and managed to graduate from Stanford with bachelor's and master's degrees in physics. Sigurd was the opposite of his brother in many ways: outgoing, adventurous, and impatient in the classroom. He dropped out of California Polytechnic to experiment with cars and airplanes and never graduated from college. Despite the brothers' personality differences, they were very close.

Russell worked for Philo Farnsworth and helped to lay the critical groundwork for the invention of television. Russell's electron tube provided the instigation for Farnsworth's method of electromagnetically focusing and deflecting electron beams. Sigurd went on to become an airline pilot for Pan Am and facilitated inaugural flying routes into Mexico and South America.

The Varian brothers later collaborated, and the two of them worked rent free in a Stanford lab on their klystron tube, "a specialized linear-beam vacuum tube used as an amplifier at microwave and radio frequencies. Klystron amplifiers hold an advantage over the magnetron because the former amplifies a reference signal so its output may be concisely controlled in amplitude, frequency, and phase."[30]

Their epic discovery encouraged them to commercialize the klystron, so in 1948, along with William Webster Hansen and Edward Ginzton, the brothers launched Varian Associates. Once word got out about the klystron, both U.S. and U.K. researchers working on radar equipment were greatly influenced. The seven-pound radar equipment Varian Associates invented was used on Royal Air Force planes during the Battle of Britain, which allowed the Royal Air Force to effectively locate and intercept German bombers.[31] Not only was Varian Associates one of the first leading companies on the Peninsula, it "pioneered profit-sharing, stock-ownership, insurance, and retirement plans for employees long before these benefits became mandatory."[32] Among their first employees was Steve Jobs' mother, Clara, whom they hired as a bookkeeper.

REASON 5: SHOCKLEY SEMICONDUCTOR

Another person often credited with being the father of Silicon Valley is William Shockley, the man whose work gave Silicon Valley its name.

Shockley had worked with two other lab engineers at Bell Telephone Laboratories, John Bardeen and Walter Brattain, and successfully amplified an electrical current using solid semiconducting materials. This proved that it was possible to selectively control the flow of electricity through the use of silicon, an element that has favorable electronic properties. The process involved designating some areas of pure monocrystalline silicon as current conductors and others as insulators, resulting in the device that would come to be known as a semiconductor.[33]

With this discovery in mind, the men set out to find an alternative to the defective and unpredictable vacuum tube, which often broke when being transported or exposed to increased vibration or heat. They needed a mechanism that would mimic the tube's voice amplification and electromechanical circuit switching, and they developed the solid-state transistor, a semiconductor device used to amplify and switch electronic signals and electrical power. The transistor became the fundamental building block of modern electronic devices, and is ubiquitous in modern electronic systems. It was one of the most influential discoveries of the high-tech revolution. Shockley, Bardeen, and Brattain received the Nobel Prize for physics in 1956 for their research on semiconductors and their discovery of the transistor effect.[34]

Shockley was going through a painful divorce in addition to growing increasingly concerned for his mother's ailing health, so he returned to Palo Alto to be close to her. He set up Shockley Semiconductor Laboratory in a small warehouse on San Antonio Avenue in Mountain View. Shockley easily attracted some of the brightest young scientific and engineering minds, including Julius Blank, Victor Grinich, Jean Hoerni, Eugene Kleiner, Jay Last, Gordon Moore, Robert Noyce, and Sheldon Roberts, a group that later became known as the "Traitorous Eight."[35]

Five of these men had Ph.D.'s in physical sciences, and three others were engineers, but it was Noyce, a solid-state physicist from MIT, who had a strong background in semiconductors and piqued everyone's interest. Shockley's team took much of what had already been learned at Bell Laboratories and built on that knowledge to develop silicon transistors, which later became the key ingredient of all modern electronics as we know it. Yet, at the time, there was very little understanding of the processing or the physics behind silicon, and its commercial viability was years off.

Working for Shockley, a moody, heavy-handed micromanager who treated staff poorly and constantly changed directions, proved to be incredibly difficult. Less than a year into the job, seven out of the eight original recruits, with the exception of Noyce, rebelled and went to Shockley's financial backer, Arnold Beckman, of Beckman Laboratories, to try to remove Shockley as CEO. Beckman refused, and the group had to quickly figure out what their next move was going to be.

The rebels contacted Hayden, Stone, & Company, a small investment bank in New York where Eugene Kleiner's father had an account, to see if any corporation wanted to develop a new semiconductor division that they could set up on the peninsula about 30 miles south of San Francisco. In their letter to the investment bank, they suggested offering themselves as collective employees with "the initial product [being] a line of silicon diffused transistors of unusual design applicable to the production of both high frequency and high power devices." The group requested "an expenditure in the neighborhood of $750,000."[36]

The letter attracted the attention of a young security analyst by the name of Arthur Rock, and a managing partner, Alfred Coyle, who were both interested in scientific industries. Rock and Coyle were curious about the growth of electronics, and wanted to diversify their own firm's involvement in financial services. They flew to California to meet with the seven men, and were impressed by the brainpower of the group. Rock and Coyle were confident that these bold men could commercialize the semiconductor, and made them an unusual proposition—to start their own corporation.[37]

Arthur Rock set out to raise the capital from various corporations, but encountered enormous resistance. Some of the corporations to whom he pitched the idea were already starting a division in silicon, and most were perplexed at the proposal to start an outside corporation, so they couldn't figure out how to structure the deal. Many of the corporate executives also worried about the appearance of supporting outside research and the effect it might have on the morale of their current employees. Only Fairchild Camera and Instruments, a medium-size military contractor based in Long Island, expressed an interest.

Sherman Fairchild started Fairchild Camera in the early 1920s, but by the mid-1950s, its sales had declined from $42 million in 1954 to $36 million two years later, and its earnings dwindled from $1.6 million to $260,000 in the same period.[38] To stop the bleeding, Sherman Fairchild made a swift move into the electronics industry, with a particular focus in data gathering, transmission, and storage technologies. He was also IBM's largest shareholder and looked for opportunities in the transistor business, but was surprised by the lack of qualified talent.

Thus Arthur Rock negotiated, on behalf of the rebels, one of the first venture capital agreements on the West Coast. Fairchild Camera financed the newly formed Fairchild Semiconductor Corporation to the tune of $3 million for the first eighteen months of operation.[39] The new firm was jointly owned by Hayden Stone, the seven rebels, and Robert Noyce, who they inevitably recruited as the technical leader. While Hayden Stone owned about 20 percent, the remainder was split among the Traitorous Eight. The contract also allowed for Fairchild Camera to have the opportunity to acquire Fairchild Semiconductor after two or eight years for $3 million or $5 million, respectively, provided it met requirements of strong profitability.[40]

The Traitorous Eight set up shop in Palo Alto in October 1957.[41] They made their first product delivery to IBM in early summer 1958.[42] That fall, Fairchild went from revenues of $65,000 to $440,000, and reached $2.8 million in the first eight months of 1959.[43] By 1960, its sales had grown to $21 million.[44] And while the commercial viability of its products waxed and waned depending on the demand from private industry and the federal government, as well as on the occasional challenge with the technology itself, Fairchild Semiconductor Corporation revolutionized the silicon manufacturing industry. It became one of the largest electronics component manufacturers on the San Francisco peninsula, and the second largest manufacturer of silicon components after Texas Instruments. Robert Noyce is often credited with being the strategic brain behind Fairchild's success and the primary driver of the silicon technology, although the Defense Department can also lay claim to shaping the innovation and technical changes of the semiconductor. More recent material suggests that the development of the silicon technology was a collective effort.[45]

REASON 6: SPIN-OFF CULTURE

A Fairchild ad in the late 1960s showed a collage of logos of the regional companies with the slogan, "We Started it All." The Traitorous Eight later became known as the "Fairchildren" because many of the original founders left to spin off new companies. Robert Noyce and Gordon Moore founded Intel, which by 1971 had developed a process of miniaturization that culminated in the creation of what was until then the young industry's Holy Grail—a computer on a chip. These microprocessors proved capable of performing the millions, then billions, of humble on-off switches that are at the very heart of a computer's operation.[46] This marked the definitive turning point in processing power.

Jerry Sanders and John Carey started Advanced Micro Devices. Charles Spork went on to renew the operations of National Semiconductor, and moved its headquarters from Danbury, Connecticut, to Silicon Valley. The knowledge of the transistor moved outside the walls of Bell

Labs and ended up on the San Francisco peninsula in a series of companies that began with Shockley Semiconductor, then Fairchild Semiconductor, and beyond to over 130 companies credited to the Fairchildren.

Robert Noyce encouraged anyone who left Fairchild to take the "Noyce culture" with them. It was not enough to start a company; each new founder had a moral obligation to start a culture where not only no hierarchy existed, but also no social distinction. At the end of the 1960s, the San Francisco peninsula, and even more specifically Santa Clara County, was a hub of successful companies. This spinning-off culture, wherein parent organizations spawn new "generations" of companies, solidified the area's reputation as the innovation capital of the world. High value-added work and revered successes attracted ideas, talent, money, and firms from around the globe to come to what would soon be known as Silicon Valley.

The Traitorous Eight created a culture wherein spin-offs were acceptable and encouraged, and venture capital soon followed.

REASON 7: THE GROWTH OF VENTURE CAPITAL

The early successes of the electronics and semiconductor industries started to pique the interest of wealthy East Coast investors. But three monumental events occurred that catalyzed the swell of venture capital in Silicon Valley. First, the initial public offerings (IPOs) of the first three Silicon Valley companies to go public were fruitful: Varian in 1956, Hewlett-Packard in 1957, and AMPEX, a company that made the first tape recorder devices, in 1958.

The second event was the passage of the Small Business Investment Act of 1958, which enabled the Small Business Administration (SBA) to license private Small Business Investment Companies (SBICs) to help finance the management of the small entrepreneurial business. This act was a critical incentive for would-be venture capitalists because it provided firms structured as SBICs to access federal funds that could be leveraged at a ratio of up to 4:1 against privately raised investment funds.

The third event was the development of the limited partnership in the 1970s, which offered a better way to structure an investment company rather than that provided through SBICs. The limited partnerships also solidified the venture capital model where general partners in a typical fund could charge the limited partners 1 to 2.5 percent of the total fund raised for management fees that would cover the firm's salaries, overhead, etc. In addition, the general partners would also charge around 20 percent for profits made off the fund, otherwise known as the "carry." This was monumental because for the first time, venture investors were granted a performance incentive for their investments.

A PLACE CALLED SILICON VALLEY

In 1970, Ralph Vaerst, a central California entrepreneur, branded the term "Silicon Valley," but it was Vaerst's friend, Don Hoefler, who branded the phrase in a series of articles in the weekly trade paper *Electronic News,* which was first published on January 11, 1971. At the time, "silicon" referred to the silicon chip manufacturers that dominated the region, and "valley" referred to the Santa Clara Valley, the southern part of San Francisco Bay. If Silicon Valley were renamed today, it may be called something like Innovation Alley.

The pioneers behind Moffett Field, Stanford University, and the development of the electronics and semiconductor industries laid the foundation for Silicon Valley's high-tech industry. The solid-state technology and development at Stanford University, from the 1950s on, led three waves of industrial innovation made possible by support from private industry such as Bell Telephone Laboratories, Shockley Semiconductor, Fairchild Semiconductor, and Xerox PARC. The spin-off culture and the introduction of venture capital began integral assets of the ecosystem.

Silicon Valley morphed into an environment where the brightest talent gathered and attracted a large pool of skilled engineers, scientists from leading universities, and people who thought in an entrepreneurial mindset.

Whether it was the high-value work, the sense of an atmosphere where you could actually make a living off your passion, the disdain for hierarchy, concern for social justice, or the healthy work culture, something kept people from returning to their hometowns. If you look at the cycle of innovation over the years, despite all the success, there have also been downward shifts, when sheer resilience led Silicon Valley to reinvent when most people had written it off. These original newcomers set the individualistic, iconoclastic, and innovative tone that epitomizes the Silicon Valley mindset to this day.

PART II
SILICON VALLEY
ECOSYSTEM AND CULTURE

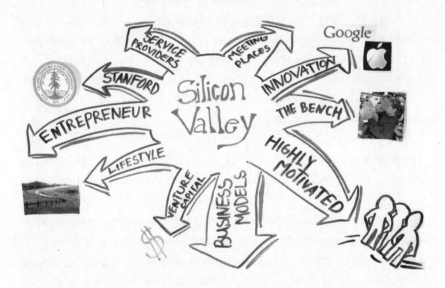

Characteristics of the Silicon Valley ecosystem and culture

SILICON VALLEY (NOUN)

2013: *A vibrant ecosystem of visionaries, innovators, investors, and destructive management (those not afraid to buck the status quo) whose culture and human capital is relationship-driven collaborative, and rewarded through meritocracy. Silicon Valley is the leading place to start an entrepreneurial venture due to its openness, nourishment, and tolerance for high-risk and failure.*

The innovation capital of the world is on the verge of exponential technologies, and the synergies between them will have a monumental shift on the world's economy. It is an ecosystem that provides a competitive advantage for those who embrace it.

On June 27, 2012, Tony Perkins, the dynamic founder and editor of *AlwaysOn,* a leading business media brand that runs conferences on "need-to-know" topics in Silicon Valley, hosted a kick-off breakfast at KPMG's Silicon Valley office for its forthcoming Innovation Summit.[1] Tony asked the group of a few hundred, "How many people grew up in Silicon Valley?" About three people raised their hands. He then proceeded to ask, "Okay, how about the rest of you . . . how many of you would ever return to your hometown?" Not a single hand went up. Just then, a venture capitalist from U.S. Venture Partners asked, "Why would we ever do that?" We all laughed, hard. The love for this place is astonishing when you consider that the cost of living in Silicon Valley is 178 percent compared to the national average.[2]

What makes Silicon Valley so irresistible? For one thing, it thrives on re-invention, as evidenced by its core innovation cycles—from radio, television, electronics, and semiconductors to software, personal computers, biotech, internet, disk storage, social media, clean tech, big data, and so on. Fittingly, its business models, capital requirements, company structures, management, and global connectedness have been equally nimble in adapting to new ideas and ways of doing things. And despite this nearly constant change, Silicon Valley has only solidified its stronghold as the global innovation capital.

Governments around the world, most notably China, Russia, India, Norway, Taiwan, South Korea, and Finland, continuously send delegations to Silicon Valley to try to discover its secrets. Just stand in the middle of the Arbuckle Dining Pavilion at the Graduate School of Business at Stanford and you'll hear a myriad of languages spoken among the foreign delegates, recognizable by their impeccably tailored business suits. Or hang out in Stanford's main quad on any Thursday evening, and you will witness busloads of Chinese tourists who actually consider Stanford a "not-to-be-missed" destination. Businesses and universities have also followed suit, spending billions of dollars to study what makes Silicon Valley work.

But can it be replicated elsewhere? What would Google have looked like had it been launched and based on the East Coast? Would Google's self-driving car or reality-altering goggles have been stifled in regions that once had great innovation potential, but failed to prosper, such as Route 128 in Boston, Research Triangle Park in North Carolina, or Dulles Corridor in Virginia? Would Facebook have scaled its heights had Mark Zuckerberg not moved from Cambridge, Massachusetts, to Palo Alto? Does being based in Silicon Valley create higher valuations? There are certainly examples of companies that have seen explosive growth and strong valuations outside of Silicon Valley—but are they the exceptions? And can even they compete with the pace of Silicon Valley?

John O'Farrell, a venture capital partner at the firm Andreessen Horowitz in Menlo Park, remarked on the potential for New York–based startups: "The concept of New York as a real rival to Silicon Valley can make some Californian eyes start rolling. You can definitely build great companies elsewhere, but I have not seen any place in the world that builds true global franchises—technology-based franchises—like this place does."[3] Though his venture capital firm has invested in several New York–based startups, O'Farrell also suggests that the bar is higher for them, largely because he believes they are less likely to succeed because they just don't have the network or the commercialization know-how of people in Silicon Valley.

It would take teams of anthropologists, sociologists, economists, technologists, and experts in innovation and business models to collectively spend concentrated time to figure out the cultural mechanics of this place. People such as Marguerite Gong Hancock, who is an expert on strategies for advancing the understanding and practice of innovation and entrepreneurship in regions such as in Silicon Valley and Asia, believe that Silicon Valley will continue to define what innovation hubs around the world will look like.[4] In 2000, Gong Hancock and her colleagues Chong-Moon Lee, William Miller, and Henry Rowen at the Stanford Program on Regions of Innovation and Entrepreneurship (SPRIE), co-edited *The Silicon Valley Edge: A Habitat for Innovation and Entrepreneurship,* a series of commentaries from Silicon Valley notables on topics ranging from knowledge dynamics to the guiding of innovators. The book lays out many of the characteristics of the Silicon Valley ecosystem, although I wanted to know the "whys" and "hows" of the culture's evolution, as well as the details of this unspoken set of guiding principles that everyone seems to follow.

Throughout the years, I've taken copious notes on how business is done here, and how people live their lives. I wanted to capture the best of Silicon Valley so that others might share in its success. To accomplish this, I pinpoint the ten characteristics that are intrinsically distinctive to Silicon Valley, the traits of the culture and ecosystem one would want to replicate within one's own culture. In doing so, admittedly, I am mostly reporting on the highly educated and/or the highly intelligent, and even then I focus on the very few among this subset who have risen to the top in Silicon Valley and around the world.

I spend less time on American advantages not specific to Silicon Valley, such as our country's more business-friendly laws and regulations compared to other industrialized countries. In fact, Silicon Valley thrives in one of the worst states to do business, a state whose government, at this book's writing, is broke and dysfunctional. However, I do confront the question of how the U.S. government is going to keep up with exponentially changing technologies, and how the regulatory barriers that exist will impact the effectiveness and speed of progress.

In settling on the ten characteristics of Silicon Valley's ecosystem and culture, I found these questions useful to consider:

- What role does Stanford play as a borderless partner to industry and the surrounding community?
- Why is the population of Silicon Valley so highly motivated? Does it thrive on type-A competitive personalities, or has much of its population come from places that lack opportunity?
- How has Silicon Valley adapted through its continuous cycles of innovation?
- What is the unique profile of the Silicon Valley entrepreneur, and how do they differ from entrepreneurs elsewhere?
- How does the Silicon Valley business model, including its generous employee benefits, contribute to a company's overall success?

- Why has venture capital swelled in Silicon Valley but not spread comparatively in other metropolitan cities?
- How does the web of support services, such as the law and accounting firms, banks, etc., play into the ecosystem?
- How does the quality of life in Silicon Valley attract the brightest people, contribute to the area's overall productivity, and keep them despite the high cost of living?
- How do the local hangouts and meeting places foster a culture of openness and nourishment?
- What are the competitive advantages of being raised in Silicon Valley?

Over the next chapters, I lay out what I see as the unique characteristics of the Silicon Valley ecosystem, with an eye to suggesting how other communities can achieve a similar alchemy.

3 THE UNIVERSITY: STANFORD

Stanford University, Main Quad

Over the course of his lifetime, Leland Stanford was a railroad baron, a governor, and a visionary. He changed the world in his day, and the world still reaps the benefits of his remarkable foresight. In 1852, at the height of the California Gold Rush, Leland left his wife, Jane, behind to migrate west to Eldorado County, where his five brothers had already founded a successful hardware business for gold miners, where they made large sums of money.[1] In 1855, after being apart from his wife for three years, Leland returned to Jane in Albany, New York, but found the pace much too slow in comparison to the exhilaration of being in the Golden State.[2] He convinced Jane to go to San Francisco with him in 1856, and it was then that he massively expanded his mercantile pursuits and became extremely wealthy. Leland then decided to focus his energy on the vital infrastructure that California's growing population so desperately needed, so he started investing in railroads.

Stanford, along with Collis Huntington, Mark Hopkins, and Charles Crocker became known as the "Big Four," and incorporated the Central Pacific Railroad on June 28, 1861.[3] In that same year, Leland was elected governor of California. During his two-year term (the normal length of term of a governor at that time), he fought for California to remain part of the Union and backed President Lincoln during the Civil War. Later, the Big Four completed the western portion of the First Transcontinental Railroad over the Sierra Nevada mountains in California, Nevada, and Utah, and Leland presided over the ceremonial driving of the "last spike" in Promontory, Utah, which connected the Central Pacific and Union Pacific Railroads.

When Leland was 44 years old and Jane was 39, they welcomed their only child into the world on May 14, 1868, Leland DeWitt Stanford Jr.[4] Leland Jr. became the center of their lives, and they poured their energy into his education and well-being. Over the years, Leland Jr. developed an insatiable interest in machines, history, and the natural world, and studied languages and mathematics with private tutors. On a family trip to Europe, he became fascinated with archaeology and started collecting Egyptian, Greek, and Roman artifacts.

EL PALO ALTO

In 1869, Leland started buying racehorses after his doctor recommended he ride them as a way to regain his strength after his body endured years of hardship during the building of the transcontinental railroad. He developed such a love for horses that within two decades, Leland owned more than 700.[5]

In 1876, the Stanfords searched for a country retreat that would allow them to raise Leland Jr. in the outdoors, and where Leland could develop his love for racehorses and trotters, horses that harness-race in a trot.[6]

The Stanfords initially purchased 650 acres at Rancho San Francisquito, and began development of their Palo Alto Stock Farm. Leland later purchased the adjoining property that amounted to a total of 8,000 acres near *el Palo Alto,* meaning "tall branch," so named in 1769 by the Spaniards in honor of the landmark redwoods.[7] Leland built the farm of his dreams, a complex of stables, paddocks, shops, racetracks, and employee housing that was ranked among the premier horse establishments in the country. He had his horse trainer Charles Marvin experiment with new breeding and training techniques, and while even the trainer thought the methods dubious, the payoff came.[8] In the years 1890–1895, the Stanfords' horses set 19 consecutive world records, and in 1891 held the trotting mile record for each age group.[9]

Leland and Jane Stanford lived such an opulent lifestyle that newspapers throughout the nation regularly reported on "the thickness of the carpets of the Stanford's San Francisco mansion . . . the fine pedigree of the trotting horses at their Palo Alto farm . . . the weight of the gems in Mrs. Stanford's celebrated jewel collection."[10] There was no doubt that the Stanfords were considered royalty in their time. Yet no money in the world could prevent the tragedy looming.

On a family trip to Europe in 1883–1884, Leland Jr. contracted typhoid fever in Athens, and his worried parents rushed him to Italy for help. There they spent weeks by his bedside as his condition fluctuated. Two months before his sixteenth birthday, on March 13, 1884, Leland Jr. died in Florence. Leland and Jane Stanford were heartbroken, and cabled a friend, "Our darling boy is taken from us . . . pray for us."[11] Through their devastation, as the Stanfords considered about how to best commemorate their son, they decided "the children of California shall be our children."[12] Leland Jr.'s death accelerated their long-held plan to use part of their wealth for philanthropic purposes. They considered several options, including founding a technical school, a hospital, a museum, or a university in Leland Jr.'s memory.

Legend has it that Leland dressed in a "suit of homespun cloth" and Jane "in a faded gingham dress" and approached Harvard University president Charles W. Eliot about dedicating a building in Leland Jr.'s memory, but that Eliot was so appalled by the Stanfords' appearance that he rebuffed their offer.[13] The truth is that when the Stanfords met with Eliot, they had yet to decide how they wanted to memorialize their son, and it was the Harvard president who recommended the conception of a university out West. The Stanfords thought they could comfortably manage a $5 million endowment to do so, but that didn't stop them from visiting Cornell, MIT, and Johns Hopkins as well to explore each university's unique offerings.[14]

Leland engaged Frederick Law Olmsted, the man who designed New York's Central Park, to build a campus devoid of walls—the better to take advantage of the spectacular vistas that surrounded the land—that would inspire students. Leland wanted every detail to be emblematic of California: Spanish mission buildings, gardens, palm trees, and open fields where students could enjoy solitude.[15] On October 1, 1891, the tuition-free Leland Stanford Jr. University opened its doors to 555 men and women with 15 original faculty members that expanded to 49 the second year.[16] The administration was able to attract world-class professors, which in turn enticed the world's best students. As mentioned earlier, Herbert C. Hoover is considered the university's first student, as he was the first person to sleep in the dormitory. He graduated in the inaugural class of 1895 with a degree in geology.[17]

From there on, Stanford was on the fast track to becoming a beacon of excellence in education as well as a borderless partner to the community and industry that surrounded it. Leland Stanford, Stanford's first president David Starr Jordan, and later Frederick Terman embraced any possible opportunity to make the relationship between academia and industry seamless and, in many respects, singular. From Palo Alto's incorporation in 1894, Stanford professors played key roles in its civic affairs.[18] Engineering professors Charles D. Marx and Charles B. Wing acquired ownership in all of the major utilities, providing a strong infrastructure when high tech came to town decades later. In 1909, Jordan became an angel investor for a Stanford graduate student, Lee de Forest, who started one of the first big waves of innovation in Silicon Valley: Federal Telegraph, a company that played a vital role in the development of radio communications.[19]

In 1925, Frederick Terman joined the Stanford faculty as the dean of the School of Engineering, and in 1955 became provost.[20] Less than a decade into his tenure, as mentioned earlier, Terman had the keen foresight to begin directing faculty and graduates to start their own companies rather than continue a path in academia, but he also started to lay the groundwork in 1946 for his vision of what became Stanford's greatest connectivity in the industry relationship: Stanford Industrial Park. A few years later, Stanford unveiled the first university-owned industrial park, a complex that played a key role in the advent of Silicon Valley.[21] No other university allotted, or held, this amount of land for industrial growth. It leased land to evolving firms like Hewlett-Packard, General Electric, and Lockheed, and today Stanford Research Park, as it is now known, is home to about 150 companies.

Likewise, in a move unheard of in its time, Terman encouraged Stanford faculty to serve as paid consultants to corporations, a shrewd directive that bridged the gap between academia and industry. He believed that it would not only be beneficial for professors to keep up-to-date on industry interests and future directions, but it would be an effective vehicle to provide research funding and fellowships for Stanford's most promising students. Terman's policy is so valued among faculty that, to this day, they credit it as the single most important contribution of the academic-entrepreneurial environment. Because of this, Stanford is well placed to foster partnerships when inventions and innovations occur.

The payoff is that Stanford is now a bastion of innovation, helping to spawn nearly 6,000 highly innovative companies.[22] Companies whose technology or business plan was developed during a student or researcher's time at Stanford include: Atheros Communications, Charles Schwab & Company, Cisco Systems, Cypress Semiconductor, Dolby Laboratories, eBay, E*Trade, Electronic Arts, Gap, Google, Hewlett-Packard, IDEO, Intuit, Intuitive Surgical, Kiva, LinkedIn, Logitech, MathWorks, MIPS Technologies, Nanosolar Inc., Netflix, Nike, NVIDIA, Odwalla, Orbitz, Rambus, Silicon Graphics, Sun Microsystems, SunPower, Taiwan Semiconductor, Tensilica, Tesla Motors, Varian, VMware, Yahoo!, Zillow, and Instagram.

John Swan, a partner at Business Development Accelerators, a Silicon Valley–based firm that specializes in private-public partnerships in emerging markets, likes to say that Stanford has this classic *Wizard of Oz*–type myth when it comes to growing companies and commercializing ideas. "When you look behind the curtain, what Stanford does is not magic, just very practical steps and strong encouragement, much like the Wizard," John insists.[23] Perhaps there is no greater example than the founding of Google.

THE BIRTH OF GOOGLE

Larry Page and Sergey Brin met in March 1995 during a spring orientation of new computer Ph.D. candidates. Page's advisor, Terry Winograd,
strongly encouraged his idea for a dissertation: the mathematical properties of the World Wide Web. It was the best advice Larry Page ever got.
In his dissertation, "BackRub," he was joined by his good friend and
polymath, Sergey Brin, and the two worked from the premise that if
there was a method to count and qualify each backlink on the web, the
internet would become a much more valuable commodity. "BackRub"
laid the groundwork for Google's PageRank algorithm.[24]

In December 1996, Page walked into the office of Stanford's Office
of Technology Licensing. Luis Mejia, a senior associate in the office, just
happened to be in the reception area. The two ended up discussing a
paper Page wanted to publish on the PageRank algorithm, but what he
really wanted was Mejia's help with the patent, as well as help licensing
it to search companies. In 1996, the internet was still in its infancy and
search engines weren't making any money, but Mejia and his colleagues
thought it was worth the time and investment for Stanford to file the
patent on Page's behalf. Thereafter, Mejia took Page around to the other
local search engine companies to see if they would be interested in licensing the technology, but no one at Infoseek, Excite, Yahoo!, or AltaVista
showed any enthusiasm. PageRank had only been tested on a small data
set, so the recommendation then—much as it is for many new technologies now—was to "test on a larger sample and get back to us."[25]

After six months of shopping the potential license, Page and Mejia
had only received mild interest from one company, which eventually took
a pass. Larry Page and Sergey Brin felt that these companies didn't get it,
and while Page was not originally interested in entrepreneurship, he and
Brin eventually took seed funding from some angel investors, including
a few Stanford professors and Andy Bechtolsheim, one of the founders
of Sun Microsystems. Thus Google was launched, but since Stanford
owned the intellectual property (IP), Page and Brin had to negotiate for
exclusive licensing from Stanford in exchange for royalty payments and
equity in the company. After Google went public in 2004, the net earnings for Stanford from its equity at cash-out were $336 million.[26]

Other than Google, Stanford's Office of Licensing and Technology has really only had two other huge hits over the last 40 years—out of 9,000 inventions.[27] The first came from licensing recombinant DNA, which are DNA sequences that result from the use of laboratory methods (molecular cloning) to bring together genetic material from multiple sources, creating sequences that would not otherwise be found in biological organisms. The second came from licensing a functional antibody technology. But many other smaller hits have created the long tail, and they have grossed over $1.3 billion in royalty income in the history of the office, with $66.8 million gross annual royalties in 2010–2011.[28]

According to Luis Mejia, the real key to entrepreneurial success at Stanford is its strong licensing department and the cooperation of the Stanford infrastructure, which includes:

1. A focus on education and research mission;
2. Openness in research;
3. Faculty consulting;
4. Clear and flexible conflict of interest policies;
5. Consistent tech transfer practice; and a
6. Malleable entrepreneurial curriculum.

Stanford also has a strong relationship with the U.S. government. The university receives about $1.2 billion annually for research funding, and 84.1 percent of that comes from the federal government.[29] Because of the Bayh-Dole Act of 1980, the legislation that gave universities, small businesses, and nonprofits control of intellectual property of federally funded research, Stanford gets to keep control of their inventions and other intellectual property that results from the funding. The Bayh-Dole Act transpired when the government amassed 28,000 patents, yet fewer than 5 percent were commercially licensed. Before Bayh-Dole, the government had no unified patent policy, and universities, private industry, and nonprofit organizations had to deal with 26 different agencies. In the 1970s, the University of Wisconsin-Madison led a coalition to retain title to their inventions, and laid the groundwork for Bayh-Dole less than 10 years later.[30]

There is also a collaborative relationship that is ingrained in the culture, a partnership between faculty, researchers, and students that overrides traditional vertical hierarchies. The partnerships build community, and no division of age or experience segments the population. While Stanford enjoys the perception of having a "secret" behind its entrepreneurial process, it largely boils down to how people treat one another. If a young student has an idea, there is an expectation that he or she will have direct access to professors or faculty advisors who can provide basic and strategic business advice or help strengthen a vision. Additionally, because of the network between academics and professionals, introductions could be made to corporate executives such as Eric Schmidt from Google or venture capitalists such as John Doerr from Kleiner Perkins Caufield & Byers, both of whom make regular stops to Stanford's campus to seek out new ideas and/or extremely bright students. It all goes back to Frederick Terman's vision: If you offer a pillar of excellence, then you can attract the best faculty and students, over whom the world's most powerful corporate executives and venture capitalists swarm around like bees to honey.

"Competition is really a foreign concept to me," says recent Stanford human biology graduate Ben Lauing. "In my years at Stanford, not once did someone not help me or work with me when I asked."[31] Perhaps that collaborative environment stems from the fact that 96 percent of Stanford undergrads live on campus—4 percent live off campus.[32] Or perhaps it is because 71 percent of Stanford classes have fewer than 20 students, creating an intimate environment. Collaboration is so built into the fabric of Stanford that teachers have to document it in their syllabi when students are required to work independently.

Because Stanford is on a quarterly system, the administration is extremely flexible if a student wants to take time out to do an internship, travel abroad, or start a company. Student research is so supported, even among incoming freshmen, that countless hands-on seminars are offered. If a student decides to pursue research over the summer, he or she can apply to the Office of Undergraduate Advising and Research and get paid $5,000 for their work.[33] Other university departments offer their own research grants. Drop-in tutoring, at any time, is available to every student, almost always for free, through Stanford's Center for Teaching and Learning.

IN LINE WITH THE QUAD

All you have to do to understand how Stanford will continue to maintain its competitive edge is spend a few minutes in one of its quads or
out-of-the-box disciplines and marvel. Whether it's the Science and Engineering Quad (SEQ), the Graduate School of Business at the Knight
Management Center (GSB), or the Design School, otherwise known as
the d.school, you'll get an instantaneous taste of how far ahead of the
curve Stanford is in the design of the future.

The concept behind the quad came from Stanford's original planner, Fredrick Law Olmsted. In the late 1800s, Olmsted's vision for
Stanford's growth included quads that expanded along an east-west
axis, according to David Lenox, Stanford's current architect.[34] In Olmsted's tidy handwriting, a rectangle designated "A"—now the main
quadrangle of academic department buildings and Memorial Church—
sits front and center. It is flanked on both sides by six more neat boxes.
Since arriving in 2005, Lenox has committed to restoring Olmsted's
vision though a contemporary architectural lens. "Instead of quads on
a horizontal axis, Lenox envisions a "spine" of aligned buildings" that
will encourage interaction between the multiple disciplines. "Today,
with people from the School of Medicine working closely with their
counterparts in biology and chemistry, it's really important that their
spaces connect, and that it is clear how to get from one to another,"
Lenox said in a Stanford press release.[35] Over 100 years later, the quads
for SEQ and GSB were approved and created according to Olmsted's
original vision.

The Apex of SEQ

In 1994, Dave Packard and William Hewlett donated $77.4 million dol-
lars to build upon Olmsted's vision, creating the Science & Engineering
Quad.[36] SEQ's buildings are in "close physical proximity to encourage
the collaboration and tangential thinking necessary to produce world-
changing innovation."[37] The buildings symbolize the interdisciplinary
and synergistic energy among earth sciences, engineering, humanities
and sciences, law, medicine, and research. SEQ offers open, luminous
common spaces as a way to invite people to engage informally, and

fosters a twenty-first-century approach to solving some of the most challenging scientific questions of our time.

At least 28 percent of Stanford students are doing at least one degree in engineering.[38] Stanford has struck a flawless balance between encouraging the acquisition of a valuable skill set and fostering intellectual discovery. The university pushes for an interdisciplinary education, whereas students can design their own major or any other interdisciplinary area of concentration. Ben Lauing was the only person in his graduating class, if not the first person ever at Stanford, with a concentration in health communications and health policy.

If you have even a passing interest in science or engineering, you're likely to be excited by the who's who of celebrities on SEQ buildings. The first building is the Jerry Yang and Akiko Yamazaki Environment and Energy Building (nicknamed Y2E2), named for the co-founder and former CEO of Yahoo! and his wife. The second building, the Jen-Hsun Huang Engineering Center, is titled for the co-founder of NVIDIA, a Silicon Valley technology company best known for graphic processing units (GPUs).

Encased in the basement of Huang is Google's first server, mostly made up of colorful LEGOs—it is these LEGOs to which Google's chromatic logo pays homage.[39] The Center for Nanoscale Science and Engineering is the third building of SEQ. The fourth and final building, to be completed in 2014, is the Bioengineering and Chemical Engineering building, and is almost identical in appearance to the Y2E2 building. Surrounding SEQ is the Gates Computer Science Building, Varian Physics, the Paul A. Allen Building, Moore Materials Research, and Gilbert Biological Sciences. There are two different buildings that now bear the Hewlett or Packard name, though neither Dave Packard nor Bill Hewlett wanted their names to be used on SEQ buildings. After the two men passed away, their families requested that their names be restored on the Hewlett Teaching Center and Packard Electrical Engineering Buildings at SEQ, as a tribute to the university that launched their success. In the basement of Jen-Hsun Huang Mechanical Engineering, the HP garage is replicated as a private study area. There is also Room 36, the machine shop that every little boy dreams of, where anyone can try out and play around with all sorts of machines, including a 3D printer.

When planners were thinking about all that SEQ could be, they solicited thousands of ideas from students, including innovations such as "installing dual flush toilets," some of which are now memorialized on the walls of Huang's stairwell. The buildings are connected underground, and are so environmentally friendly that they don't even need air conditioning. Instead, rooftop panels open at night to take in the cool Northern California breeze and maintain the coolness throughout the warmest of days. SEQ has been so meticulously planned that even the Center for Nanoscale Science and Engineering building, with three stories above ground and a basement and sub-basement below, is balanced like a skyscraper. The building is supported with a framework by which its walls are suspended as opposed to a typical building with load-bearing walls, so that the tiny nanoparticles being studied within won't be disturbed by the vibration of a passing dump truck.

Graduate School of Business (GSB)

The Knight Center of Management, where the Graduate School of Business is housed, has the same approachable feel of SEQ, but does so with an entrepreneurial bent. It is a quad of eight buildings with a central courtyard, and has won the U.S. Green Building Council's LEED Platinum certification, the highest sustainable building award. The Knight Center of Management is designed so that the maximum amount of natural light and open space is available for GSB students, creating an atmosphere that is conducive to the entrepreneurial mindset. Even the Arbuckle Dining Pavilion at the GSB retains the entrepreneurial spirit, as cafeteria-style foods are compartmentalized into business terms: Action Items (sauté foods), Free Market Grill (grilled foods), Foreign Exchange (ethnic foods), Social Networking (coffee station), Liquid Assets (beverages), Stock Exchange (soups), Hot Commodities (pizza and flatbreads).

Approximately 40 percent of GSB students pursue entrepreneurial endeavors. "GSB attracts the students who are interested in technology and innovation, so we're able to adapt our curriculum that flexes and adapts with the changing times and do so with an incredible amount of support from the administration," says Jonathan Levav, Associate Professor of Marketing at Stanford University. He continues, "When I joined

GSB, I created a new class on product launches and was told by my dean not to worry about course enrollment my first few years." The point is to do something of extreme value to the students, and do it well. For instance, the school paired Levav with a retired venture partner to team-teach the product launch course. "One of my colleagues is even creating a Market Research for New Enterprise Class, tapping in to those students who care about launching their own ventures," says Professor Levav.[40]

Through GSB's Global Innovation Programs such as Innovation and Entrepreneurship, Global Executive Summits, and Social Innovation, students receive exposure to the fundamentals of business by developing a plan for commercializing a new product or service for an existing organization or new venture, and address opportunities and challenges in scaling global companies. GSB pushes hard for its students to have hands-on entrepreneurial experience, as one of my companies, Alley to the Valley, witnessed firsthand. When we attempted to hire Stanford MBA student Lauren Westbrook in the summer of 2011, we needed to meet certain criteria and be vetted by GSB administrators to ensure that Lauren would truly get exposure to the entrepreneurial experience in her internship, and not just perform meaningless tasks. Once we passed that test, not only did the business school subsidize Lauren in a stipend above what we were paying, but after Lauren had worked for us a few weeks, I received an email from Lisa Sweeney, Associate Director for the Center for Entrepreneurial Studies at GSB, inviting me to lecture at an evening class on finding entrepreneurial opportunity in Silicon Valley.

The d.school

On the day that I toured the d.school, there were nearly 100 people from around the world just as intrigued by the school that offers so much mystique.[41] Stanford's Hasso Plattner Institute of Design, known as the "d.school," popularized the phrase "design thinking." While the term "design thinking" can be traced back to Herbert A. Simon's 1969 book, *The Sciences of the Artificial,* it was David Kelley who led the creation of the d.school, and re-purposed the phrase as a way of creative action that was adapted for business problem-solving. The d.school offers a non-degree program that draws students from all of Stanford's seven graduate schools, offers a method of looking at problem-solving in an almost anthropological way to gain basic human insight into solving simple challenges. The school teaches Stanford students to think of the design process by combining empathy for the context of a problem, creativity in its insights, and rationality in problem-solving in five steps: 1) empathy (feeling another's pain points); 2) definition (insights from your users to define the need); 3) ideate (generate solutions); 4) prototype (experiential); and 5) test (in hopes that your solutions are viable to execute). It is often that the "test" phase won't work, and students are sent back to an earlier stage of the design thinking process.

Design thinking, as opposed to the traditional research of focus groups, gives new meaning to the development of new products, processes, or services that are more specifically in line to a company's needs and a consumer's wants. The underlying mantra is "innovators before innovation," as the school's leadership is more interested in finding solutions to existing problems than concern for the future of innovation. For example, Kelley once gave a TED talk on "Creative Confidence," and cited how CT scan machines and the rooms that housed them could alleviate children's fears if they were painted with playful pirate ship murals so kids would think they were on a pirate adventure.[42] Another example is that of JetBlue, a long-term client of the d.school. The airline continuously aspires to be more in line with the consumer's desires. Instead of sitting around in some conference room, d.school designers headed over to San Francisco International Airport (SFO) to observe the frustrations of waiting passengers, and occasionally asked passengers questions that would elicit detailed responses, such as "What would make your experience waiting for your plane more pleasurable?" rather than questions that would render a "yes" or "no" response.[43]

The d.school was created in 2005 after Hasso Plattner was inspired by the work of IDEO, the Palo Alto–based design firm that David Kelley had started. Hasso Plattner, who co-founded SAP AG, the German multinational enterprise software company that has a vast presence in Silicon Valley, provided the initial $35 million donation to create what looks like a superfun playground for grown-ups.[44] Scott Witthoft and Scott Doorley, co-directors of the d.school's Environments Collaborative, strategically designed its unusual, interactive environment to encourage supreme innovators. Every feature of the school fosters ingenuity, from the intentionally discombobulated periodic table designed to keep students thinking about the way things could be rather than how we learned them to be to the glassy garage door–style entrance, symbolizing the humble beginnings of powerhouses such as HP and Apple. Then, there is the Prototype Room that is filled with open containers of supplies such as magic markers, colored paper, and scissors for projects surrounded by vertical workspaces with movable furniture and wheeled chairs so students can adapt their workspaces to their liking and comfort. The furniture is high and vertical because the d.school leadership has found that being in high, vertical chairs, when not standing, encourages the most collaborative posture. In one of the main class areas, different-colored magic markers cover whiteboard walls as students reconfigure the hallways with collaborative ideas. These collaborative ideas offer subtle cues to remind students that a project is never truly complete; each ending point provides a new starting point.

TO BE IN PARADISE

Walking around the stunning country club setting of Stanford, you'll see cyclists in every direction. Consummately "green," biking is the best way to get around campus, and there are an estimated 12,000 bike racks to accommodate the demand.[45] If you don't have a bike, no problem; Campus Bike Shop offers daily rentals. Euphoric Stanford students also bike past a milieu of world-class athletic facilities, a museum with a sculpture garden that boasts one of the world's largest collections of Rodins, and the Spanish-Mediterranean architecture that sits against a backdrop of tropical gardens and the breathtaking Palo Alto hills.

Today, Stanford is an unincorporated area in Santa Clara County that has its own post office and ZIP codes and is home to over 13,000 people, according to the 2010 census.[46] Within campus boundaries lies the "Faculty Ghetto," a quaint neighborhood of approximately 500 acres, with single-family homes and condos available only to Stanford faculty and administration, who purchase their own properties but reside on leased Stanford land. The idea of faculty housing began when the university was founded in the 1890s: The Stanfords had a vision of a residential campus with faculty and students close together, increasing the opportunities for interaction between them. Faculty housing is offered at a lower price than surrounding housing, and like other leading universities, Stanford offers its faculty a living stipend or discounted, often deferred, interest rates for financing.[47]

According to Stanford's admissions office, the university is constantly on the lookout for applicants who embody "PIE" qualities—Passion, Intellectual Vitality, and Engagement. Of over 34,000 applicants for Stanford's 2012 freshman class, only 2,400 were accepted, a mere 7 percent.[48] The campus is also quite multicultural: About 60 percent of Stanford's undergrads and more than half of its graduate students are of Asian, Indian, African American, Hispanic, Native American, or other descent.[49] Stanford also isn't just for the financially gifted: Half of Stanford's undergraduates receive financial aid, and if a family's household income is below $100,000, then tuition is free.[50] An amazing 17 percent of Stanford's undergraduates are the first members of their families to attend college.[51] The alumni's remarkable loyalty and enthusiasm is proven in their willingness to give back to the university that gave them their start. In the last 13 years, Stanford's endowment has grown to approximately $17 billion. To date, Stanford has raised more money than any other American university.[52]

Stanford's current president, Dr. John Hennessy, is a successful entrepreneur himself, having co-founded MIPS Computer Systems, a semiconductor design company that is known mostly for developing the MIPS architecture and a series of RISC CPU chips. MIPS technology provides processor architectures and cores for digital home, networking, and mobile applications. In 1992, Silicon Graphics acquired MIPS for $333 million.[53] President Hennessy is also a board member at Google, Cisco Systems, and Atheros Communications, all companies founded at Stanford. He believes that Stanford's entrepreneurial foundation comes from a great pioneering spirit.

4 A POPULATION OF HIGHLY MOTIVATED PEOPLE

California Gold Rush, circa 1916

U.S. President James Polk very much believed in westward expansion across the continent, and in Manifest Destiny,[1] a concept coined by journalist John L. O'Sullivan declaring that the United States had a "divine destiny" to promote its values of equality and "establish on earth the moral dignity and salvation of man."[2] President Polk also had an ulterior motive for adopting Manifest Destiny: The San Francisco Bay is a great natural harbor in the Pacific, and he wanted to thwart Britain or any other European country from gaining a port on the West Coast, even though at the time the surrounding area was a harsh landscape that was largely inaccessible to the rest of the world.[3]

After several futile attempts to buy the region from Mexico, the United States declared war on May 13, 1846. The war lasted until 1848, when the Treaty of Guadalupe Hidalgo was signed, confirming U.S. control of what had formerly been about half of Mexico's national territory, a parcel of land stretching from Texas to California. President Polk also signed a treaty with Britain, who ceded control to the United States of what is today the Pacific Northwest. Thus, through conquest and diplomacy, America achieved its "Manifest Destiny" to stretch from the Atlantic to the Pacific, from "sea to shining sea." California became the thirty-first state of the union on September 9, 1850.[4]

Northern California attracted the first risk-tolerant immigrants, known as "Argonauts" and "forty-niners," who ventured far and wide into the Wild West with a dream of striking it rich during the California Gold Rush in 1848–1850.[5] They exhumed gold worth tens of billions of dollars in today's value, leading to enormous prosperity, and the effects on the Bay Area were seismic. The Gold Rush sparked the development of San Francisco and the Sacramento Valley, and by 1852, the population of San Francisco had swelled to 36,000 residents, up from roughly 200 just six years earlier.[6] San Francisco Bay became one of the world's greatest seaports, dominating the shipping and transportation in the American West. In just a few years, towns with roads, schools, and churches were built all throughout Northern California.

By 1855, 300,000 gold seekers, merchants, and other immigrants of various cultures arrived in California.[7] In addition to Americans, tens of thousands of Mexicans, Chinese, Britons, French, Latin Americans, and Australians came to work as miners. As people from all around the world came to settle in Northern California, they brought their own ideas, beliefs, and value systems.[8] The migrants' motivations were very different from those of the *Mayflower* Pilgrims who came to the New World for religious freedom; instead, these migrants took overwhelming risks, choosing to go West and endure extremely harsh conditions. They had to adapt and be flexible and tolerant of racial discrimination, all in the pursuit of economic prosperity. Because no one could claim that they were *from* Northern California, the ideas they brought were not entrenched in one tradition, and as such they were able to cross-pollinate intellectually and culturally.

THE RACE FOR SPACE AND TALENT

In 1957, the Soviets launched the first satellite, *Sputnik,* into space. The unexpected launch triggered the space race. The Soviets' unknown intentions sparked fear in the American government and throughout the general populace. President Dwight Eisenhower responded by pushing the U.S. House Select Committee on Astronautics and Space Exploration of Congress to draft and pass The National Aeronautics and Space Act of 1958.[9] The Act was a direct response by a U.S. military infrastructure that seemed incapable of keeping up in the space race. Section 102 of the Act specifically authorized the creation of the National Aeronautics and Space Administration (NASA), and was given the objective to effectively utilize "the scientific and engineering resources of the United States for aeronautical and space activities for peaceful and scientific purposes."[10]

Government officials started to question whether the United States had the essential knowledge base for the space age or the ability to compete with the Soviets, so they aggressively promoted science education, engineering, and mathematics throughout primary and secondary schools. The military assembled advanced research groups for the development of weapons such as ICBMs and spy satellites. After several failed attempts, the United States finally launched its own satellite, *Explorer 1,* in 1958.[11]

Irrespective of the satellite success, debates continued in Congress over whether the U.S. workforce had the skills necessary for the next generation of war. Opinion was split on whether attracting immigrants who could potentially provide the skill was the right direction to go. "Congress was saying, 'We need to open the door for some more British doctors, some more German engineers,'" Stephen Klineberg, a sociologist at Rice University, said during a 2006 NPR interview. "It never occurred to anyone, literally, that there were going to be African doctors, Indian engineers, Chinese computer programmers who'd be able, for the first time in the twentieth century, to immigrate to America."[12] By a vote of 326 to 70 in the U.S. House of Representatives and 76 to 18 in the U.S. Senate, Congress passed the Immigration Act of 1965, otherwise known as the Hart-Cellar Act.[13] The legislation gave preference to immigrants' skills and family ties to citizens or permanent residents. Most of the American populace was against the act, so political surrogates such as Secretary of State Dean Rusk estimated that only a few thousand Indian immigrants over the next five years would emigrate, and U.S. Senator Edward Kennedy reassured the population that the demographic mix would not be affected.[14] Yet all these assertions would later prove to be completely inaccurate. Highly skilled professionals gradually flowed into the United States, many of whom were of Asian origin, and they disproportionately settled on the West Coast.

When the explosion of Silicon Valley in the 1970s and 1980s called for even more engineers, the Immigration and Nationality Act of 1990 encouraged highly skilled immigrants to move to urban centers such as the Bay Area and Los Angeles. By 1990, according to the U.S. Census, 25 percent of engineers and scientists in California were foreign born.[15] Countries such as China and India invested heavily in science and engineering education, yet many of their most talented citizens were leaving for Silicon Valley. This phenomenon became known as the "brain drain," which was originally coined by the Royal Society of London for Improving Natural Knowledge to describe the emigration of scientists and technologists to North America. For many countries, the brain drain had an enormous economic cost since emigrants often took with them the training or education that was offered and sponsored by their native government or organization that they worked for. The opportunities in higher education, work, and compensation were significantly better here.[16]

Silicon Valley became remarkable in its cultural diversity and startlingly educated population, with over a third of the adult population having a graduate degree, according to the 2010 U.S. Census.[17] Unlike earlier migrations to Northern California and other regions such as Miami, San Antonio, and Manhattan that concurrently took in high numbers of immigrants, Silicon Valley was inundated with highly educated and motivated professionals. They also brought with them their entrepreneurial spirit and passion to make a difference in humanity, often coming from places where they lacked opportunity.

The initial challenge for many of these Silicon Valley newcomers was that they were not always accepted into the existing, "white-male" world of entrepreneurship and venture capital. At times, they bumped against the glass ceiling despite the abundance of opportunity, as they didn't have the right skin color or the right look for senior management.

More and more launched their own businesses. Many felt so excluded that they didn't bother wasting energy trying to ingratiate themselves within established organizations, instead starting their own social networks, investment clubs, and alliances with strategic partners. Not only were these new immigrants entrepreneurial in technologically sophisticated industries, but also many of them helped to expand embryonic industries such as life sciences, biomedical science, biotechnology, and genomics. Their participation in Silicon Valley helped the economy diversify beyond electronics and semiconductors.

A ROAD TO PROSPERITY

Kanwal Rekhi left his native India to pursue a master's of science at Michigan Technological University in 1967.[18] After graduation, Rekhi was laid off from his first three jobs. "It wasn't a good time to be in my line of work, as the space program and the Vietnam War were winding down," he reminisces. So, in 1971, Rekhi and his wife packed up and headed to San Jose, which he heard was an extraordinary place for engineers who wanted to start their own businesses. Rekhi thought it would be in his best interest to work first for a defense contracting company so he could get a sense of Silicon Valley before starting his own venture. He found employment at Singer-Link, a subsidiary of the Singer sewing machine company that made flight simulators. He quickly grew bored, and joined Zilog, a company started by Federico Faggin, the engineer who co-invented the first popular microprocessor, a programmable device that incorporates a computer's central processing unit.

Yet Rekhi had a burning idea to connect computers into a local area network, so in 1982, at the age of 36, he started to seek out venture capital. Even though he had established a reputation as a really bright engineer, "I was seen as an outcast," Rekhi recalls. As an Indian, he found it incredibly difficult to raise venture capital. Rekhi decided that he and his two Indian co-founders, Inder Singh and Navindra Jain, would figure out a way to start what would become Excelan, so they self-funded and took in money from friends and family. Not long thereafter, the fledgling high-tech company pioneered ethernet networking technology, one of the basic building blocks of the internet, and later the internet protocol TCP/IP, which is the set of communication protocols that specifically addressed how data should be communicated, transmitted, and routed. Before the company went public in 1987, the investors he later attracted asked Rekhi to step down, but they insisted that the transition would preserve his investment. "I didn't look the part," says Rekhi, so he reluctantly supported the decision to hire retired Hewlett-Packard executive Richard Moore. Excelan was the first Indian company to go public, and it was acquired by Novell in 1989.

Eric Schmidt, who later became the CEO of Novell and is the current executive chairman of Google, said in 1998 that Rekhi became an important player in a very short period of time. *Forbes* magazine referred to Rekhi as the "dominant investor for the Indian community" and a "sage of Silicon Valley."[19] Still, that was not enough.

One day in 1992, Rekhi was waiting with friends to hear India's Secretary of Electronics speak in Silicon Valley. The secretary's flight was delayed, so Rekhi and his friends started talking about that taboo topic: what it was like to be an Indian businessman in Silicon Valley. Out of that conversation, Rekhi; Suhas Patil, former MIT professor and founder of Cirrus Logic; and Prabhu Goel, founder of Gateway Design Automation, co-founded the nonprofit The Indus Entrepreneur (TiE) as a way to help the next generation of South Asians hoping to start businesses. They called themselves Indus, rather than Indian, so that other South Asians such as Pakistanis, Bangladeshis, and Nepalese would feel welcome. TiE was designed as an organization that would provide an opportunity for South Asian entrepreneurs who could come to find widespread support in raising capital, opportunities for mentorship, strategic partners, and even exit strategies. By the early 1990s, the three men had come to know Silicon Valley as a meritocracy, but it was still limited by the perception that if one wasn't connected to the right company or to Stanford University, one had to work harder to bolster a reputation. The TiE leadership was now able to provide wealth, knowledge, mentorship, and connections to their South Asian counterparts that were previously unavailable.

Today, TiE has over 13,000 members in over 14 countries. While TiE's primary mission is to mentor, network, and posture their constituents for success, they are "dedicated to the virtuous cycle of wealth creation and giving back to the community."[20] They are responsible for helping to fund, launch, and create alliances and exit strategies for hundreds of companies. One of the more recent success stories is that of

Muddu Sudhakar who founded Cetas, a company that provided a data application that is designed to run on virtual resources such as Amazon Web Services and VMware's vSphere. Within 18 months of starting Cetas, the company was acquired by VMware in 2012.[21]

A SOUTH ASIAN BRIGADE OF LEADERS

Between 1990 and 2000, the population of Indian scientists and engineers in Silicon Valley grew by 646 percent in comparison to the region's total science and engineering population, which grew by 103 percent.[22] By the 1980s and 1990s, some of the most recognizable companies in technology and internet innovation were starting to show Indian and Asian co-founders at the helm: Vinod Khosla, co-founder of Sun Microsystems; Jen-Hsun Huang, co-founder of NVIDIA; Pehong Chen, founder of Broadvision; Jerry Yang, co-founder of Yahoo!; Keng Lim, co-founder of Kiva Software; Pradeep Sindhu, co-founder of Juniper Networks; Naveen Jain, co founder of InfoSpace and later a co-founder with Niraj Shah Chandan Chauhan of Intellius; Sabeer Bhatia, founder of Hotmail; and Steve Chen, co-founder of YouTube. These leaders supported each other and inspired the next generation of immigrant entrepreneurs.

Another Indian who came to the states and made a name for himself in Silicon Valley is Vivek Wadhwa. Once a successful entrepreneur, Wadhwa had co-founded a company called Relativity Technologies, which created and licensed conversion technology software. His broad interests carried him into academia, research, writing, and social commentary. Wadhwa dedicates his time to studying the intricacies of Silicon Valley innovation, and then delivers his outspoken message on television programs such as *60 Minutes* and *Bloomberg* and in his regular columns in the *Washington Post, TechCrunch,* and *Bloomberg Businessweek,* among others. He has become the lead advocate or iconoclast on the topics that few ever think about, and/or are too afraid to deliberate. Some of his column's titles suggest examples: "The Gangsters of Silicon Valley" (his reference to the patent trolls); "My Wasted Day on Capitol Hill"; and "Would the Facebook IPO Have Bombed if Mark Zuckerberg had an MBA?"

"Visit any Silicon Valley technology company, and you'll notice that it looks like the United Nations—with people from all over the world working together toward a common goal," says Wadhwa.[23] In his 2007 research, he found that the percentage of immigrant-founded startups in Silicon Valley had increased to 52.4 percent. Wadhwa says,

> Silicon Valley's entrepreneurship ecosystem included people from almost every nation in the world—from Australia to Zimbabwe. Indians were the most numerous of the immigrant tech-company founders. They had founded more startups than the next four groups (from Britain, China, Taiwan, and Japan) combined. The proportion of Indian-founded startups in Silicon Valley had increased from 7 percent to 15.5 percent, even though Indians make up just 6 percent of the Valley's working population. Indian immigrants were standing shoulder-to-shoulder with the world's most innovative tech workers, and were matching them in entrepreneurship.[24]

One of the competitive advantages that the Indian and Asian entrepreneurial community enjoys is something AnnaLee Saxenian, a professor at University of California, Berkeley, who has made a career of studying regional economics, calls "cross-cultural connections." In her book, *The New Argonauts: Regional Advantage in a Global Economy*, Saxenian states that strategic business relationships in their homelands gives the immigrant population an instant competitive advantage when expanding to global markets, a lead that would be nearly impossible for anyone other than a multinational company to have in a particular market.[25] Indians and Asians created cross-Pacific networks with friends and family in home countries. Chinese engineers established technical ties between Silicon Valley and Taiwan, and their Indian counterparts began the foundation for outsourcing work to low-cost, but highly skilled, technical workers. "This bridge was far more important to their success than just the relationships; it enabled them to have an advantage of language skills, cultural norms, and other 'know-how' that the Silicon Valley white male community had virtually no experience or exposure to," Saxenian states.[26] Raj Desal, the current Executive Director of TiE Silicon Valley, actually started a subsidiary company in Gurgaon, India, called Rhythm Mobile Media in 2007. "Rhythm Mobile Media was a U.S. company that was VC-backed, and therefore considered a foreign-funded company that was able to get around the barriers of India's mountain of government regulations, but could benefit from my family connections and know-how of India's high demand and fast growth for video streaming," says Desal.[27]

Silicon Valley is not a perfect meritocracy, but it is open to all who are highly motivated. For example, there is a dearth of women, Hispanics, and African Americans in Silicon Valley. Many of the highly educated women in Silicon Valley have opted out of the workforce, been caught in the numbers game, or made a different lifestyle choice. But it's difficult to account for the staggeringly low populations of African Americans and Hispanics in high tech—according to the *San Jose Mercury News*, as of 2008 African Americans account for 1.5 percent and Hispanics 4.7 percent,[28] which is below the national averages of 7.1 percent of African Americans and 5.3 percent of Hispanics in high tech. Despite the billions of dollars poured into encouraging women and minorities into STEM (Science, Technology, Engineering, and Mathematics) education, the interest level has actually declined, except in the Indian and Asian population.

By all accounts, the Indian entrepreneurs have done well in Silicon Valley in the relatively short time they have been there. According to Vivek Wadhwa, they have done so for the following reasons:

The first few who cracked the glass ceiling had open discussions about the hurdles they had faced. They agreed that the key to uplifting their community, and fostering more entrepreneurship in general, was to teach and mentor the next generation of entrepreneurs. They formed networking organizations to teach others about starting businesses, and to bring people together. These organizations helped to mobilize the information, know how, skill, and capital needed to start technology companies. Even the newer associations had several hundred members each, and the more established associations had more than a thousand members. The first generation of successful entrepreneurs—people like Sun Microsystems co-founder Vinod Khosla—served as visible, vocal role models and mentors. They also provided seed funding to members of their community.[29]

The Indian community is the primary focus of this chapter because it has proven a strong case study of how well outsiders can do in Silicon

Valley in a short period of time, although the bar of expectation was initially set much higher for them than for their white counterparts. The mindset of the Indian population is not only conducive with the Silicon Valley economy but also helps to spread the cultural values of hard work and morality in the workplace and within the community, and places high expectations on their children's education. These esteemed virtues set a powerful example, and this undercurrent can be felt throughout the rest of Silicon Valley. This is not to suggest that the existing white culture in Silicon Valley did not also emulate this extraordinary foundation of beliefs and practices, but the Indian community not only embraced it, it also proselytized it.

In the time that I prepared to write this book, I conducted many interviews, and asked one common question: "What keeps you motivated?" The answers varied and included fear, passion, and belief that anything is possible. If we just propagated a culture of self-reliance, then perhaps we'd be able to give people the tools to be self-reliant. We need to recognize and understand the situation of the Indians in Silicon Valley, many of whom came with no English language skills, no family or friends, varying degrees of education, but a common drive to seek out better opportunities. If you are motivated in Silicon Valley, than you can make it, period.

Kanwal Rekhi, once the son of a poor merchant, is now at the center of the affluent Indian-born entrepreneurial community. "Kanwal's got a good nose," Yogen Dalal, an Indian-born venture capitalist once said. "When someone tells me Kanwal's in on a deal, I take a look."[30]

5 THE CYCLE OF INNOVATION

Elon Musk, co-founder of Tesla Motors and founder of SpaceX

Every five to ten years, someone in Silicon Valley creates something that inspires everyone else to follow. The Silicon Valley innovators not only believe that anything is possible, but they also attain the seemingly impossible, often with Herculean effort. Throughout the 2000s, no one has embodied the role of the Silicon Valley innovator more than Elon Musk. Before the age of 40, Musk had founded and co-founded four companies, and sold two of them for substantial sums of money: Zip2 and PayPal. He currently serves as CEO of the other two—SpaceX and Tesla Motors—simultaneously. He is also the chairman of another company, SolarCity.[1]

Born on June 28, 1971, in Pretoria, South Africa, Musk was ten years old when he first bought a computer and taught himself how to program it. Two years later he created, programmed, and sold his first software—a computer game called *Blaster*—for $500.[2] At the age of 17, he moved to Ontario, Canada, where he attended Queen's University. At the age of 18, Musk would have had to serve a mandatory stint in the South African military, but he felt that "suppressing black people just didn't seem like a really good way to spend time." His real desire was to move to the United States, "where great things are possible."[3] He matriculated to the University of Pennsylvania on an academic scholarship, and earned a degree in economics. He then stayed on another year to finish a degree in physics.

In 1995 he moved to California to begin a graduate degree at Stanford, but only stayed for two days, because he was eager to start a company. Inspired by inventors such as Thomas Edison and Nikola Tesla, Musk, the entrepreneur, zeroed in on the three areas he thought were "important problems that would most affect the future of humanity . . . one was the internet, one was clean energy, and one was space."[4] With the help of his brother Kimbal, Musk started a publishing software business called Zip2. Four years later, Compaq bought Zip2 for $307 million dollars cash, which at the time was the largest sum ever paid for an internet company. In March 1999, Musk used some of his newfound wealth to co-found a new startup company, X.com, which let people make payments over the internet via email. X.com later acquired the name PayPal, and in October 2002 eBay acquired it for $1.5 billion in stock.[5]

That same year, Musk fed his passion for space and launched SpaceX, a company that develops and manufactures space launch vehicles with the larger goal of "extending life beyond earth." The company focuses on advancing the state of rocket technology and spacecraft that orbit Earth and beyond. On May 25, 2012, SpaceX made history when its craft *Dragon* became the first commercial vehicle to successfully dock at the International Space Station.[6] Part of Musk's vision for SpaceX is to eventually colonize Mars, ensuring the ongoing existence of humanity there in case Earth eventually becomes uninhabitable. Musk thinks of this as "insurance on a grand scale."[7]

If perpetuating the dawn of commercial space travel is not enough, then consider Musk's other company, Tesla Motors, which is renowned for its sexy Roadster, an electric plug-in sports car. According to the company website, the Roadster is the first electric car to use lithium-ion battery cells and the first battery electric vehicle (BEV) to travel more than 200 miles per charge. At a base price of $109,000, the electric sports car can reach a speed of 125 mph.[8] The next generation is the Tesla Motor S, a more family-friendly vehicle with a base price around $59,900. Don't let the "family-friendly" designation fool you into thinking the Motor S is just another minivan—it's been described by one Silicon Valley executive as "the closest thing you have to a spaceship that travels on land—it is smooth, slick, lighting fast, elegant, hi-tech, amazing!"[9] The S-model also allows customers to choose from three battery packs which determine the cars range—160, 230, or 300 miles—before it must be recharged.[10]

In addition to serving as the CEO at SpaceX and Tesla Motors, Musk is the chairman of SolarCity, which designs solar power systems, performs energy efficiency audits, and builds charging stations for electric vehicles. Musk claims that he got the idea for SolarCity after attending the Burning Man festival in 2004, and encouraged his cousins, brothers Peter and Lyndon Rive, to launch the company. According to Greentech Media Research, SolarCity is the leading provider of residential solar power in California after only one year of operation, as well as the leading residential solar installer in the United States since 2011.[11]

Elon Musk strives to create companies that will significantly "impact in the future of the world." His philosophy is simple: Start an internet company that has little to no barrier of entry and can quickly grow to generate capital. Then do the seemingly impossible: Build a company that specifically supports your passions. For a man who believes "engineering is the closest thing to magic that exists in the world," it was fitting, then, that he received the Innovator of the Year Award from *R&D* magazine in 2007.[12] In 2008, *Esquire* listed him as one of 75 most influential people of the twenty-first century.[13] With a net worth of $2 billion as of 2012, he stands at number 634 on *Forbes'* list of the richest people in the world.[14] Not bad for a guy who is barely over 40 years old at the writing of this book.

THE CONTINUUM OF INNOVATION

Among the steady cycle of inventors and innovators in Silicon Valley, some have made encompassing discoveries and others have cultivated long cycles of innovation that spawn countless new companies, business models, and supplementary innovations. The conventional wisdom is that these innovators have greatly moved the needle forward. The list includes men and women of great passion and vision: Cyril Frank Elwell, Philo Farnsworth, William Hewlett, Dave Packard, Russell and Sigurd Varian, William Shockley, Eugene Kleiner, Robert Noyce, Gordon Moore, Sandra Kurtzig, Steve Jobs, Steve Wozniack, Larry Ellison, Roger Melen, Harry Garland, Robert Swanson, Dr. Herbert Boyer, Robert Metcalfe, Howard Charney, Bruce Borden, Greg Shaw, Leonard Bosack, Sandy Lerner, Erich Drafahl, Herry Yang, David Filo, Al Shugart, Tom Mitchell, Doug Mahon, Finis Conner, Syed Iftikar, James McCoy, Jack Swartz, Raymond Niedzwiecki, Larry Page, Sergey Brin, Mark Zuckerberg, Jack Dorsey, and, of course, Elon Musk.

SILICON VALLEY CYCLES OF INVENTIONS / INNOVATIONS

Year	Industry Created	Companies/Spinoffs (in later years)
1909	Radio	Federal Telegraph
1927	TV (signals)	Farnsworth
1939	Electronics	HP / Varian (1948)
1956	Semiconductors	Shockley Labs / Fairchild (1957) Intel (1968)
1972	Software	ASK / Oracle (1977)
1976	PCs	Cromemco, Apple
1976	Biotech	Genetech
1979	Internet	3Com / CISCO (1984), Yahoo! (1994), Google (1998)
1979	Disk Storage	Seagate / Maxtor (1982)
2003	Social Media	Facebook / Twitter (2006)
2007	Smartphones	iPhone (Apple)
2010	Cloud, Big Data, Clean Tech	*

*Which companies will define this innovation cycle are still to be determined.

THE GREAT DEBATE

Innovation has always been defined quite differently from invention. It used to be that innovation was "the introduction of something new; a new idea, method or device; a novelty."[15] In a more modern and revised definition, innovation is "the creation of better or more effective products, processes, services, technologies, or ideas that are readily available to markets, governments, and society."[16] The definition of innovation has now changed to reflect its differentiation from *improvement,* in that innovation refers to the notion of doing something differently rather than doing the same thing better.

The question of whether innovation is still happening is hotly debated in Silicon Valley circles. There are those, such as mega venture capitalist Peter Thiel and serial entrepreneur Max Levchin, who argue that the United States, which holds itself up as a beacon of innovation, is somewhere between "dire straits and dead."[17] There are also those such as Peter Diamandis and Ray Kurzweil who believe that the Singularity is near, and our modern definition of innovation has only just begun. Others ask a broader question still: How much innovation do we really need?

Technically, nothing Elon Musk has done is inherently inventive. Electric cars were manufactured in 1996 when General Motors (GM) prepared to sell the EV1.[18] This electric vehicle's second generation could travel between 80 and 140 miles before recharging. (It is largely believed, although there is speculation over what really happened, that GM self-sabotaged the electric car to avoid potential losses in spare parts sales, and caved in to pressure from the oil industry.[19]) Musk realized there was an underserved market in electric cars, with consumers who were environmentally conscious, but who wouldn't be caught driving the un-sexy Toyota Prius. So, the question remains: Did Musk really *invent* something new or did he simply *innovate* upon what already existed?

I think few on the street would disagree if it was suggested that Steve Jobs and Bill Gates are the paramount innovators of our time. But if you wanted to split hairs, neither man really *invented* the products that initially marked them as entrepreneurial icons. Steve Jobs's and Steve Wozniack's fourth-generation computer—the Apple Lisa—was very much influenced by a three-day visit to Xerox PARC in Palo Alto.[20]

Jobs was convinced that the future of the computer was going to be its graphical user interface (GUI), and wanted to see what Xerox PARC engineers had done with GUI technology, although the GUI had been earlier invented by Doug Engelbart, who was at the time an employee of Stanford Research Institute.[21] Xerox granted Jobs, Jef Raskin (the man best known for starting the Macintosh computer), and Apple engineers access to its GUI in exchange for an opportunity to purchase 100,000 shares of Apple at the pre-IPO price of $10 per share.[22] The result was that Jobs and his staff were able to replicate, enhance, and, in 1984, successfully mass produce and commercially market what Engelbart had invented and Xerox PARC engineers had innovated.[23]

Bill Gates and Paul Allen first licensed Unix, a multitasking computer operating system, but gave it the original name Xenix, which Microsoft licensed from AT&T in 1979. They didn't commercially market Xenix to consumers, but rather licensed it to other software companies such as Intel, Tandy, and Santa Cruz Operation (SCO).[24]

In 1981, Microsoft acquired the CP/M (Control Program/ Monitor) clone called 86-DOS from Seattle Computer Products (SCP) for $50,000. Microsoft branded it as MS-DOS, and worked with IBM to get it up to the CP/M standards that IBM was in the market for. Microsoft then licensed 86-DOS to IBM, and it became PC DOS 1.0, but the license also allowed Microsoft to license it to other companies in the process. The acquisition turned out to be a windfall, so much so that SCP took Microsoft to court and claimed that "Microsoft had concealed its relationship with IBM in order to purchase the operating system cheaply." SCP received a $1 million settlement for its pain. These early shrewd business decisions are what helped solidify Microsoft's early dominance in the marketplace. Regardless, it is irrefutable that what these men did remarkably altered the course of the world through the technological innovations that they were able to commercially market for both industry and home use.[25]

INSIDE THE INNOVATOR'S MIND

In 2011, Clay Christensen, an authority on disruptive innovation, and his co-authors, Jeff Dyer and Hal Gregersen, who are professors, of strategy at BYU and of leadership at INSEAD, respectively, attempted to qualify the characteristics that the world's leading innovators had in common. In their book *The Innovator's DNA*, they assert that innovative people have "creative intelligence, which enables discovery from other types of intelligence." The co-authors studied how innovators go about their business, how their methods differ from traditional business-people, and what other leaders can learn from their habits. They found that these people possess five discovery skills: innovators are associating, questioning, observing, networking, and experimenting. Innovators are also curious, observant, and ask a lot of questions. Such individuals are chronic experimenters who are not afraid to play around with their products and business models. It would be rare for an innovator to see an object and not question how it could be improved upon in his or her mind experiment and visualize an improved creation. Innovators are more likely to create new ideas if they have lived or spent considerable time in another country.

The authors believe that the companies that have the highest innovation premiums display the same habits as individual innovators. In addition, these companies work hard to attract the most creative people and develop the types of environments that will keep them around to help the company to innovate. One way to stimulate innovation is through the practice of job swapping, something that Google executives have found to be an advantageous way to provoke questions and stimulate greater efficiency. Job swapping—which can take place within the context of different divisions inside of one company or between different companies—provides the means for businesses to create an environment of surprise that is needed to free employees from traditional biases and assumptions. This "outsider's perspective" is also a way for individuals and companies to recognize the trends and ideas that are emerging from the larger global environment.

It is this very environment of increasing complexity that is changing the rules of innovation. IDEO designers believe that the inventive design thinking process is best thought of as a system of overlapping sequences of, rather than a series of, orderly steps: inspiration, ideation, and implementation. Inspiration comes from recognizing a problem or opportunity that motivates the search for solutions. Ideation is the process of generating, developing, and testing ideas. Implementation, of course, is effectively executing the idea.[26]

IDEO designers talk about how "design thinking is a deeply human process that taps into abilities we all have but get overlooked by more conventional problem-solving practices. It relies on our ability to be intuitive, to recognize patterns, to construct ideas that are emotionally meaningful as well as functional, and to express ourselves through means beyond words or symbols. Nobody wants to run an organization on feeling, intuition, and inspiration, but an over-reliance on the rational and the analytical can be just as risky. Design thinking provides an integrated third way."[27] IDEO's CEO, Tim Brown, believes that the best innovators are T-shaped—they need to have deep expertise in one area and a broad interest in many others.[28]

INNOVATION BENCHMARKS IN SILICON VALLEY

The Joint Venture Silicon Valley Network is a collaboration of experts who annually produce the "Index of Silicon Valley," a report on the state of Silicon Valley which monitors the rate of innovation through three lenses: venture capital investment in the near- and longer-term direction of development; the generation of new ideas; and the value added across the economy overall. According to the 2011 Index of Silicon Valley, venture capital experienced its first increase since 2007, rising 5 percent over the previous year, reaching a staggering $5.9 billion. Silicon Valley venture capital accounted for 27 percent of the nation's total VC investment and 53 percent in the state of California. While software still dominates venture capital investment, there has been a resurgence of invested capital in biotech and medical devices and robust investment in industry and energy. Information technology (IT) services and telecommunications saw an increase of 55 percent and 196 percent respectively from 2009 to 2010. Clean tech investment increased 11 percent from the prior year, exceeding $1.5 billion in 2010, although down from its peak of $2.2 billion in 2008. Along with innovation, there has been an increase in patents registered in Silicon Valley, having jumped by 9 percent in 2009 compared to an increase of 6 percent of U.S. patents during the same time period.

Silicon Valley will always be a leader in innovation when you have companies like Apple and Google leading the way. Steve Jobs once said, "Innovation distinguishes between a leader and a follower."[29] To no one's surprise, Apple is the world's leading innovator, and there is quantifiable proof. Consider Apple's innovation premium, which is the "proportion of a company's market value that cannot be accounted for from the net present value of cash flows of its current products."[30] It was 52 percent during Jobs's second tenure at Apple in comparison to –30 percent from 1985 to 1997 when he left the company. Call it Steve Jobs's vision or his marketing genius for being in touch with what consumers wanted—the company thrived when he took it over again.

Today, while Apple may have slipped to an innovation premium of 35.7 percent according to *Forbes*'s "The World's Most Innovative Companies," it does remain a leading tech innovator in the world due to the iPhone and its spinoff innovations, companies, business models, and processes. The smartphone has singlehandedly altered the course of the way people live their lives. By 2013 the number of downloaded apps is estimated to hit 49 billion. And there truly is an app for everything: health, transportation, entertainment, social networking, business, organization, design, and philanthropy.

Just wait until your smartphone offers you personalized healthcare. A company called Alivecor is testing how to turn your phone into an EKG monitor that will automatically transmit data to a cardiologist, a product that is expected to cost $100 or less. Withings has also created a smartphone-enabled blood pressure cuff that automatically inflates, deflates, and then records the pulse rate and the blood pressure of the patient. Its app will graph the pressure over time to make trends more apparent, and then will share the information with a doctor via your iPhone or iPad. The cuff retails for $129. SkyHealth has an app that monitors blood glucose levels.

If this all sounds like the full-body diagnostic "tricorder" from *Star Trek,* it's not far off. A day is coming soon when your smartphone will be able to provide full-body personalized healthcare. There is currently a $10 million prize offered by the X-Prize Foundation for anyone who can invent it.

THE NEAR FUTURE

It is the current switch-on era of smartphones, tablets, social and digital media, mobile commerce, nanotech, and the cloud that is going to dictate the next few years of innovation. In 2012 KPMG survey entitled

"Mobilizing Innovation: The Changing Landscape of Disruptive Technologies," 56 percent of the global respondents identify cloud computing as the next cycle of innovation that will change consumer technology and shake up business the most. The survey, which reflects the viewpoints of 668 global technology leaders, was designed to take the pulse on the scope of change over the next three to four years. "Everyone is looking to get more leverage from cloud technology, whether for computer systems or storage. It is about business agility. If you can minimize time to bring up a product, it allows you to be more efficient and productive," says respondent Jeanette Horan, Vice President and Chief Information Officer of IBM.[31]

Another major innovation cycle in the coming years will be how to solve big data, a collection of data so large and complex that it can't be processed using on-hand database management tools. It may not be at the top of most people's minds, but it will soon be considered a transformational technology as the cloud, mobile, social, and data models expand and converge. "These days we are so completely overwhelmed with information from the internet that we need ways to sort through this information, such as navigation, tagging, search technologies, and visualization to help people narrow in on something much more quickly. There is a need to marry how the human brain works with PC systems and technologies," says Horan.[32]

THE 3D PRINTER

On February 12, 2011, the front cover of *The Economist* read, "Print me a Stradivarius," referring to that most esteemed violin. The magazine was referring to the new age of 3D printing, which is the process of making three-dimensional solid objects from a materials printer, where instead of printing with ink you use materials such as plastic. Around since 2003, 3D printing is the next form of a function that started with woodblocks and movable type almost 2,000 years ago. If you think about traditional manufacturing as a "subtractive" form of manufacturing in that it breaks down materials to create objects, 3D printing is an additive manufacturing technique that joins materials layer by layer in horizontal sequences, resulting in a three-dimensional object. Instead of having an ink cartridge in a digital printer, you may have a cartridge of plastic or steel in a material printer to output anything from jewelry to shoes to clocks to DNA sequences and beyond.

As 3D printers become available for home use in the next decade or so, we will have the capability to print whatever we desire. AutoDesk, a Bay Area company that focuses on 3D software for architecture, engineering, construction, manufacturing, and media and entertainment industries, unveiled the world's first full-scale custom motorcycle in 2008, all printed on a 3D printer.

The proliferation of 3D printing is also going to revolutionize the healthcare industry. Already, 3D printers are being used for prosthetic limbs for wounded soldiers, and being able to construct human organs and tissue is underway. Such advancements signal that the sky is the limit on what we will be able to imagine and produce over the coming years, which opens up a world of questions about the ethical direction of 3D printing and disruptive technologies in general. On the one hand, when you think about what 3D printing can do in terms of human organs, it can be seen as life-changing. On the other hand, how do you regulate the proper use of this technology, and who gets to decide the rights and wrongs of 3D printing into the social consciousness? We already know what a hot-button issue stem cell research became, but this was at a time when stem cell research was left solely to scientists and medical professionals. What happens when this machine becomes sophisticated enough for home use? Will these 3D printers give us the power to make "God-like" decisions? These are very complex questions that will have to be addressed both scientifically and philosophically.

BIOTECHNOLOGY

Andrew Hessel, a leading biotech thinker, has interests that lie squarely in genetic engineering and the falling barriers to accessing this technology. He believes that coming innovations will mirror those of personal computing in the 1980s, and he boldly suggests that biotech will be bigger than the internet. "The only thing we all have in common, not just humans but all creatures, is life, which is the basis of biotech," Hessel says. "When you stop and take a look the living things that touch our lives, plant compounds in medicines, food of all types, the microorganisms that make soil fertile and clean our water, wood for our homes, and the like, it's significant. You get a sense of how biotechnology is going to reach into each of those areas, of how important it will be."[33]

What's changed in the last ten years is the appearance of digital biotechnology, which builds on the foundation of the Human Genome Project, the international science research project that determined the sequence of the chemical base pairs which make up DNA. "Now, we can write genetic code using software, and we have specialized printers for DNA—it's like a 3D printer for molecules," says Hessel.[34] This makes genetic engineering easier, plus it opens up new fields of design and engineering, such as DNA origami. Just a few years old, experts in this field have successfully folded DNA into 2D shapes such as happy faces and the letters of the alphabet, and 3D shapes as well, forming molecule-sized bottles and boxes. This is not just experimentation for its own sake. Researchers are exploring how to make theses shapes functional—for example, turning them into miniature robots for hunting down cancer cells. All this is built on the foundation of the internet.

Hessel can't emphasize enough how powerful a shift this is. "It used to take a Ph.D. to do genetic engineering. It's moving toward something that anyone can do if they want to learn." These advancements in technology will eventually be applied more and more to meet the needs of humanity. This makes matter programmable," continues Hessel. "Learning how to program life is exciting and important. After all, one of the most powerful computers is the living thing."

One thing is certain: Companies and startups are going to have to come up with innovative ways to ignite innovation itself. Futurist Frank Spencer says that in our age of rapid change and exponential growth, transformative innovation depends on developing the critical skill of "futures thinking":

We see innovation applied to new computing technology, our energy consumption, the clothes we wear, the food we eat, the cars we drive, and just about every area of life you can possibly imagine. So, is it such a stretch of the imagination to believe that foresight and futures thinking—developing anticipatory and alternative perspectives in organizational and global settings—would not only amplify, but be an imperative element in successful innovation processes? Honestly, the

bigger question might be why the marriage of futures thinking and innovation is not already a given?[35]

Why, indeed? At places such as the Center for Foresight and Innovation at Stanford University, educators and researchers are already
recognizing that innovation must be coupled with foresight in order to
create a sustainable model for today's volatile landscape. It is through
programs such as this that new business models are being designed that
will help us re-frame and redefine innovation beyond incremental ad-
vancement into "something completely different."[36] As Spencer notes:

> Without acquiring the skills and culture that foster long-term thinking—
> anticipation, multiple perspectives, alternative outcomes, adaptive and
> resilient thinking, and aspirational outcomes—innovation processes
> will lack the creative capacity needed to keep pace with the acceler-
> ating change and complexity in today's world of business and global
> development. If we are going to solve the big world problems of the
> twenty-first century, we will need to reframe innovation in the context
> of futures thinking and foresight, igniting a whole new way of seeing
> "that which does not yet exist" and fanning the flames of exploration
> beyond the tried and true. Organizations must adopt future-fit land-
> scapes and foresight practices if innovation is going to continue to truly
> be, well . . . innovative.[37]

THE CASE FOR INTELLECTUAL PROPERTY REFORM

In February 2008, two well-known players in the patent world, patent
enforcement executive John Amster and plaintiff's attorney Eran Zur, visited Mallun Yen, who was then-vice president of Worldwide Intellectual
Property at Cisco, to float a unique proposition. They wanted to leave
behind the lucrative business they were in of enforcing patents against
companies like Cisco and start a business that actually helped companies avoid risky patents in the first place. To be successful, their business
would require building a relationship of trust with a large number of operating companies and creating a network, including arch competitors,
who would collaborate to achieve efficiencies unattainable if pursued

alone. Two minutes into the pitch, Yen stopped the two men: "It's a great idea, you have to do it, and Cisco will be your first customer."[38]

Having been raised in Silicon Valley, she was accustomed to listening to new ideas and helping to incubate those that showed promise. This was one of those, and she proceeded to spend the next several months helping Amster and Zur refine the business model of what is now San Francisco–based RPX Corporation. Cisco did indeed become one of its first customers, and three years later, Mallun Yen joined RPX.

In less than four years of existence, RPX grew to over 120 members, including such innovative and patent-savvy companies like Google, IBM, Verizon, Microsoft, eBay, and Oracle, who pay millions of dollars each in annual subscription fees. This allows RPX to deploy nearly $500 million in capital to secure rights to nearly 3,000 patents that it will never enforce, but would have otherwise been enforced against its members. Backed by such notable VCs as Kleiner Perkins's John Doerr, RPX's revenue in the first three years grew extraordinarily fast, possibly more than any other startup in history, and by May 2011, it had gone public at a valuation of nearly $1 billion. RPX recognized early on the changing nature of patents, their growing impact on operating companies, and the need for a nontraditional, market-based solution.

No conversation on innovation is complete without a discussion about patents, which, depending on who you talk to, can be considered synonymous with innovation. The original intent of the U.S. patent system was to reward inventors by granting them temporary monopoly on their inventions to give them a clear head start in bringing their products to market. This right was granted with the intention that others would then improve upon these inventions and develop further innovations, which in turn would benefit society and as a whole. In other words, patents can be considered a legal embodiment of innovation, intended to both spur the creation of new products and provide legal protection of those products in the marketplace.

One reason for the confusing nature of patents has been the complete lack of transparency in the patent marketplace. Most transactions are guarded with strict confidentiality provisions, and so the market lacks its basic tools: readily available comparables, visibility into other licenses entered, commonly accepted valuation practices, etc. It is no surprise that technology companies are demanding reform and change from the status quo.

Perhaps equally important, a company's patent portfolio serves to preserve a kind of intellectual property balance of power. Companies have traditionally stockpiled patents on other companies not because they sue very often, but because they sought a détente in the face of "mutually assured destruction" if legal action was ever taken.[39] IBM, HP, and Microsoft have portfolios that consist of approximately 70,000, 30,000, and 26,000 patents respectively, with relative newcomers like Google, whose patents increased from approximately 701 to over 25,000 with the acquisition of Motorola Mobility, making big acquisitions to catch up. That being said, operating companies do assert patents against each other, sometimes for competitive reasons and other times purely for revenue generation, often but not always as the company's core operating business begins to decline or growth starts to slow.

But these kinds of disputes, especially in recent years, have happened relatively infrequently (such as in the case of Apple, Samsung, and Android's litigation) because there has always been a tacit understanding that any lawsuit will be met with a countersuit, and most companies prefer to work out their differences behind the scenes: "You don't want to sue me over those patents because I've almost certainly got some in my portfolio that you appear to be infringing yourself," says Yen. Defensive patent aggregation, a relatively recent phenomenon, is the pooling together of resources to proactively buy up risky patents before they can be asserted by patent enforcement entities.

Patents have little to do with innovation in the traditional sense. Because of the way the patent and litigation system has evolved, as well as how technology has converged, patents represent an unpredictable risk and a costly expense for the vast majority of technology companies rather than a means for, or an indicator of, innovation. Think about how much technology is embodied in a WiFi-enabled smartphone— RPX estimates there are over 250,000 patents related to smartphone technology.[40]

Further innovation is not stimulated by others reading existing patents. Most companies do not permit their engineers to read patents because of the very real fear they would be subjected to treble damages for having willfully infringed a patent. This is a legal standard that has nothing to do with actually intentionally copying a patented invention but stems from having been put "on notice" of the asserted patent even if years after the accused product was developed and first brought to market. Willfulness is alleged in nearly every case where the patent holder has an inkling that the company had come across the patent before the lawsuit is filed, and in most cases, the notice comes from a letter sent by the patent holder itself prior to the lawsuit and after the product has been on the market for years.

The majority of patent infringement lawsuits these days are not brought by innovative companies looking to protect their market share of products that embody their patented inventions. They are brought by what are called nonpracticing entities (NPEs)—often referred to as patent trolls—that do not develop, make, or sell products but exist for the sole purpose of enforcing patents against operating companies. NPEs have destroyed the aforementioned balance of power. Because they aren't operating companies, they have no products or services against which the operating company can countersue, and so they have no reason not to litigate. NPE suits account for roughly 80 percent of the patent infringement suits against technology companies and roughly 90 percent of defendants.

In fact, NPEs have made litigation their primary tool to generate revenue, and as such have changed the nature of patents entirely. Now, instead of regarding the patents they hold in their own portfolio as contributors to operating growth and legal stability, companies are being forced to consider more starkly than ever patents they *don't* own as a source of large and unpredictable risk and expense. What changed the game here was NPEs recognizing that patents are more than just invisible catalysts of new product development. They realized that patents are assets—properties protected by the U.S. legal system and a patent system that has shifted in favor of patent holders in recent years.

The use of the term "patent troll" to refer to NPEs is attributed to Peter Detkin, formerly an Intel patent attorney who derided NPEs but then became one of four principals with Intellectual Ventures, the largest NPE. Intellectual Ventures has launched numerous patent lawsuits against dozens of operating companies and threatened hundreds more. Patent trolls are viewed as such because they decline to notify the innovator of the NPE's patent at the time of product development, only to give the innovator the opportunity to design around the patent. Instead, they wait, like trolls under a bridge, until product development is complete, manufacturing processes are set, and the product has been widely adopted in the market before they file a lawsuit, logistically cornering the innovator and increasing the amount the NPE can demand to resolve the matter. This practice is the heart of the NPE business model, as the mechanism of transferring value from the user of the damaged asset to its owner becomes a *legal* transaction. And legal transactions are, almost by definition, inefficient, slow, and costly.

In the majority of cases, NPEs did not innovate or create the patents they own, but rather acquired them in the marketplace from failed or failing companies, though they are more often acquiring them from healthy companies who are under increasing pressure to recoup some dollars resulting from the rising number of NPE patent infringement lawsuits they are facing. NPEs have historically acquired their patents from small companies about half the time, from individual inventors about a quarter of the time, and from large companies about 10 percent of the time, with the remainder sourced from others including universities and bankrupt companies.[41] It is not uncommon for a patent plaintiff to acquire a patent days before filing the lawsuits, buying the patents solely for the purpose of suing operating companies. NPEs also take advantage of an unclear set of rules and guidelines that is currently within a part of our patent and litigation system.

The U.S. Patent and Trademark Office (USPTO), which is the agency responsible for issuing patents, is tasked with the enormously challenging job of reviewing over 500,000 utility patent applications filed each year, a number up from 175,000 in 1990. The office relies on its corps of examiners, many of whom are recent college graduates, to determine whether complicated, high-tech inventions are "novel, nonobvious, and useful"[42] enough to be worthy of being granted a patent. This includes reviewing the patent application, communicating back and forth with the inventors, reviewing all of the "prior art," which is the methodology to determine something new and novel, that exists relating to the claimed invention, and determining what patent claims they should ultimately issue.

For many years, the USPTO has been woefully understaffed, and therefore patent office fees are diverted to other agencies, and as a result of this, many patents that have been issued are of questionable quality. Improvements to the USPTO are underway, including a renewed focus on patent quality as well as on the process for re-examining questionable patents already in existence. With the average patent pendency being approximately five years from the filing of the application to issuance, it will still be many years before the effects are truly felt. Not only that, there are nearly 3 million patents in existence and the USPTO is still faced with an increasing number of applications filed each year.

Once a patent is issued, it is presumed valid, and companies against whom a patent is asserted have the burden of proving that it should not have been issued, a task requiring a high legal standard. On top of this, patents are not written in plain language, and cannot be relied upon to be interpreted according to strict dictionary meaning. There have been many court hours spent on determining, for instance, whether "a circuit" means "one circuit," "at least one circuit," or "more than one circuit." And once claim interpretation has occurred, jury trials of laypeople must determine whether highly complicated technologies are deemed to infringe highly technical patents. As a result, it is difficult without going through court proceedings to know what a patent will actually be deemed to cover and then whether a product will be found to infringe.

As a result of all this legal uncertainty, it is no wonder that the majority of all NPE cases settle, with the bulk of settlement terms held confidential. The settlement of these cases isn't necessarily troubling, because patents do and should have value as assets; rather, it is the mechanism by which patent negotiations and resolutions happen that is incredibly inefficient and distracting. More often than not, a lawsuit represents the innovator's first knowledge of the patent they're supposedly infringing. Attorneys' fees compose an average of 50 percent or more of the amount spent defending and resolving patent assertions. No other market has such high transaction costs, and in no other market is the first phone call you make to your attorney to determine how much and whether to pay for an asset. In doing so, you rack up costly legal expenses.

So the entire premise of granting an inventor time to bring a product to market is turned on its head when patent-holding NPEs sue to enforce their patents against operating companies, requiring those companies to pay amounts far greater than the patents are worth in the process.

And because a patent is infinitely divisible, meaning it can be infringed upon in infinite ways, it can be asserted against an unlimited number of companies. NPEs take advantage of this attribute and sue many parties on the same patent. Because subsequent defendants are often bound by earlier decisions, such as prior claim interpretation, each set of lawyers needs to coordinate with other sets, complicating the defense and adding to expense. In some cases, over 20 sets of lawyers could be participating on weekly status update and coordination calls, with the average hourly rate being several hundred dollars per attorney.

It is rare to find technology companies today that have not been sued by NPEs, and unfortunately even startups are not immune. RPX provided data to professors Jim Bessen, of the Berkman Institute of Harvard and Mike Meurer, of Boston University who then published a study estimating that the direct costs of NPEs on operating companies is $29 billion a year in the United States. While a large company like Apple can take upward of 70 lawsuits by NPEs at any given time,[43] smaller companies, those with less than $100 million in revenue, are greatly impacted as well.[44] The cost of legal defense for a large company ranges from $2 million to more than $10 million per case; with costs of a single lawsuit for a small company potentially costing over a million dollars in defense costs alone, the typical startup can hardly weather the expense and distraction of a patent infringement lawsuit. While the intent of patents was to stimulate innovation, most innovative companies, including startups, would agree that the patent system has stifled innovation due to the risks they present.

The NPE business model has proven very profitable, and success breeds imitation. Billions of dollars in capital have flowed in to both existing and newly formed NPEs, with private equity, hedge funds, and investment bankers getting into the game. They are expanding their patent assertion activities and casting their nets wider and wider to include more and more companies in their monetization campaigns. While technology companies were hoping for legislative fixes in the American Invents Act (AIA) in 2011, the legislation has not provided the type of relief those companies were hoping for. Due in large part to the strength of the pharmaceutical companies and other powerful contingents, who face a very different patent landscape, the AIA includes very little of what the technology companies were seeking, including changes to damages, willfulness, and venue law. With the passing of the AIA, it is commonly recognized that any future widespread legislative reform is unlikely, considering that the last major legislative overhaul was in 1952. So technology companies are turning to other means—more directed and targeted technical fixes with the AIA and USPTO procedures as well as working to evolve the law slowly through cases.

Beyond these purely legal fixes, however, what Yen was already realizing at Cisco when John Amster and Eran Zur walked into the room, and what other companies have subsequently come to realize, is that it takes an industry working together to shift the uneven playing field, with market-based solutions being the primary effective tool given the slow pace of other types of reform. On November 25, 2008, RPX launched its core business of defensive patent aggregation—the pooling of resources from a number of companies to proactively buy patents before they can end up in the hands of NPEs and asserted against its member companies; and if their patents do end up in litigation, RPX can work across companies to more efficiently resolve the costly litigation on behalf of its members. Recognizing that patents have value as assets, RPX was founded on the premise that it makes far more economic sense to transfer value for a patent through an open, multi-party market rather than a closed, unilateral lawsuit. As RPX describes in a blog post on its first anniversary:

> The company is the first participant in the secondary market to buy patents for purely defensive purposes, and by doing so RPX has established two important new realities about the IP market.
>
> First, patent owners are clearly willing and ready to sell their assets for a current fair-market valuation rather than go through a time-consuming and costly legal process with an uncertain financial outcome. Defensive aggregation has proven a very viable option in the secondary market.
>
> Second—and most important—the rapid scaling of the Defensive Patent Aggregation service has demonstrated that a neutral central clearinghouse, acting on behalf of multiple beneficiaries can provide both broadly effective protection and compelling economies of scale. By supporting the defensive model with subscription fees (which are far lower than the typical annual cost of dealing with assertions), the pooled resources of RPX members are making a highly capital-intensive

market possible while simultaneously reducing their own operating costs. They are also fundamentally changing how other companies facing NPE threats now view the problem—it has become a market solution rather than a legal solution.[45]

That RPX succeeded, despite being launched two months after Lehman Brothers collapsed and during one of the worst economic downturns, demonstrates that innovative companies who want to succeed are the ones that are no longer approaching patents in the traditional sense, but rather looking to adapt their business strategies to the changing IP landscape. Companies have realized that if they don't adapt, then Silicon Valley's unique attributes and its model of global innovation is in danger of being quashed by a problem that for the most part currently exists primarily in the United States.

6 THE UNIQUE PROFILE OF THE SILICON VALLEY ENTREPRENEUR

Alley to the Valley Summit, Rosewood Hotel, Menlo Park, November 10, 2010

When Richard Swanson was an electrical engineering student at Stanford University in the 1970s, the oil crisis (when a shortage of oil threatened to derail the industry) got him thinking about the potential of solar power. President Jimmy Carter had installed solar panels on the White House, and it seemed like the technology should have taken the world by storm considering its timeliness. It just so happened that Stanford was the only university research lab that had any real capability of making silicon chips, the main components in solar cells, and Swanson was able to spend most of his time researching them. Solar cells were already being used in satellites, but they were not cost-effective enough for commercial use.

Upon graduation, Swanson stayed at Stanford as a professor of electrical engineering, and continued to pursue his passion for solar power. He compiled a business plan, which he called "SunPower," and shopped it to more than 40 venture capital firms in 1978 and 1979. Not a single one offered him a term sheet for investment. One venture capitalist remarked that he had never seen a business plan with the year 2000 in it, meaning it would be over 20 years before SunPower would be profitable. He asked Richard, "Do you know how old I'll be in the year 2000?"[1]

Believing that solar cells would one day be commonplace, Richard Swanson continued his research at Stanford. In 1985, he was awarded a grant from the Electric Power Research Institute at the U.S. Department of Energy (USDOE) to support his solar power explorations, but even the USDOE required SunPower to find matching funds, because typically, when an investor wants to mitigate risk, even though it was the feds in this case, they will often require another investor to come on board simultaneously. Swanson was fortunate to find two venture capital firms who would back him, and SunPower was officially incorporated in 1985.

But any moment of glory didn't come until nearly eight years later. (Even today, we are far from having solar panels on every American household as Swanson envisioned.) In 1993, Honda executives asked SunPower to develop solar cells for a car race across Australia, and the SunPower-ed Honda beat the second-place winner by a full day. Four years later, in 1997, SunPower was commissioned to provide high-efficiency solar cells to power NASA's *Pathfinder*, an unmanned, high-altitude aircraft. Even after these successes, SunPower was not getting the government contracts or business traction it needed to remain sustainable, so in 2002, Swanson forged a strategic partnership with Cypress Semiconductor that fortuitously included an $8 million investment in SunPower. "If it hadn't been for that investment from Cypress Semiconductor, SunPower would not exist today," Swanson admitted. He also realized that he needed to hire a CEO with greater business expertise to take the company to the next level. In 2003, the company recruited Tom Werner, a former executive at a subsidiary of Cypress Semiconductors.

Nineteen years after its founding, SunPower opened up its first manufacturing facility in the Philippines and its first utility-scale power plant in Bavaria. By its twentieth year in business, SunPower was well positioned to go public, and its successful IPO yielded a market capitalization of over $2 billion and raised over $1 billion to fuel new growth in the solar power market. In 2007, SunPower acquired PowerLight, one of the largest solar integrators and installers in the world, resulting in a vertically structured company serving the residential, commercial, and utility power plant market. In 2008, SunPower announced a world record with the monocrystalline polysilicon solar cell prototype, a material containing small silicon crystals, with a conversion efficiency of 23.4 percent (up to 24.2 percent efficiency in 2009), and in 2011, SunPower launched their new AC Solar Panel, which they describe as "a cutting-edge solution for homes that maximizes energy output for each panel."[2]

Asked what kept him going all those years, Swanson responded, "I just believed that the world really needed PV [solar photovoltaic technology], and would eventually embrace it. That and the wonderful team we assembled at SunPower who were equally dedicated. Of course, the startup culture of Silicon Valley certainly made it more acceptable for our team to feel confident in persevering through the struggle. In most other places, the team would likely have abandoned ship in search of more secure employment."[3]

THE OVERNIGHT MYTH

Entrepreneurship is so embedded in the Silicon Valley culture that everyone else is an outsider. It's like living in Washington, DC, and not being a part of politics, or living in lower Manhattan with an MBA and not working on Wall Street. Entrepreneurship is Silicon Valley's sport, its religion, and there is no greater place in the world to be an entrepreneur. But some myths surrounding the Silicon Valley entrepreneur story still persist. First, Dr. Swanson's is the more typical Silicon Valley story—overnight successes that we've all come to glamorize are much rarer. It's true that an unrealistic expectation exists in Silicon Valley that if you haven't reached substantial revenues, gone public, or have exited with a merger or acquisition within four to five years, investors and the entrepreneurial community at large can tend to take you less seriously. "Overnight success" headline fodder obscures a much more common truth: The average Silicon Valley entrepreneurial venture can take much longer to reach its full potential.

Second, few people actually hit the proverbial home run and experience the lifetime financial payoff. "When you ask someone what they do, they show off about the number of companies they've screwed up, the number of failures they've had. In Silicon Valley, it's a badge of honor," says Vivek Wadhwa. For every success story, there are countless companies that fail.

Third, the number of older entrepreneurs is much greater than the amount of young ones. The Kauffman Foundation found that the average age of U.S. entrepreneurs is actually rising, with the highest rate of entrepreneurial activity in the range of 55 to 64 years old. Some of the reasons behind these statistics include:[4]

1. Many older members of the work force are fed up with the pressure-cooker work environment because of an unreliable job market in an unstable global economy;
2. They actually have real-life experience that can be applied to entrepreneurial ventures that are not capital intensive;
3. They like being their own bosses;
4. They want to take greater risk for wealth before they retire; and
5. They can't fathom retiring, sitting around, and doing nothing.

There is no doubt that a bias toward younger entrepreneurs exists among Silicon Valley VCs, but perhaps there is a correlation between younger entrepreneurs and poor returns on venture capital investment. There is a perception that young entrepreneurs, especially those who have grown up in the "techie" revolution and have all things "geeky" as part of their DNA, are accustomed to work 24/7 in an integrated lifestyle, and young enough to be devoid of personal distractions. This stereotype of funding younger entrepreneurs, particularly young white men, was perpetuated when venture capitalist John Doerr made a not-so-subtle offhand remark in 2007—publicly—about the types of entrepreneurs he prefers to fund: "white, male, nerds who've dropped out of Harvard or Stanford."[5] But the truth is that most entrepreneurs are married and have children.[6] The fact is that entrepreneurs might be on the far side of 40 years old before hitting their home run.

THE CHARACTERISTICS OF THE SILICON VALLEY ENTREPRENEUR

Silicon Valley entrepreneurs have a distinct profile. The mindset they embody is markedly different from that of a small business owner, a Fortune 500 CEO, or even entrepreneurs elsewhere.

After the 1929 stock market crash, Wall Street executives jumped to their deaths from the high floors of their office buildings. There is a running witticism in Silicon Valley that because there are no tall buildings, if an entrepreneur fails, he or she could jump from their second-story office if they really wanted to, mend a sprained ankle, and begin a new venture the following day. Perhaps the single most notable distinction of the Silicon Valley entrepreneur is the tolerance of failure, and the contentment of knowing that no one in Silicon Valley is immune to it—not even the late Steve Jobs. Futurist and Stanford engineering professor Paul Saffo once stated that in Silicon Valley, "the spires of success are built on the rubble of failure."[7] When one fails here, there is no ego involved, no shame—in fact, failure is more like a badge of honor and an invitation to become part of the club. Within the framework of failure, not only can you learn valuable lessons, but you may also find that innovations can often be an outcome of the botches, so failure is embraced as part of the entrepreneurial journey. While many Silicon Valley entrepreneurs are gifted individuals who process information rapidly, many of them are also inherently curious people. They look at things through another lens, see how things can be changed and improved upon, and often have the clarity for greater efficiency in products and processes. This runs counter to the sectional nature of most businesses, and is a key characteristic for the success of unique business models.

There is a sense of sweat equity that exists among Silicon Valley entrepreneurs, where they will pour their hearts and souls into their ventures, often working for free. They might work on a project while in school or while holding a full-time job, and for months, possibly even years, they may continue to work on that project before seeking out capital. So clearly there is a mental toughness one must exhibit, a mindset that encompasses a sense of hubris, that doesn't cut corners, and doesn't expect anything from anyone. The Silicon Valley entrepreneur is willing to do everything, from changing the ink cartridge in the printer to preparing profit and loss (P&L) statements, and everything in between.

For years, I observed Silicon Valley entrepreneurs and attempted to capture the unique characteristics they hold. I came to the conclusion that many of them are passionate, authentic, driven by ideas, fearless in risk-taking, trustworthy, and resilient.

Passion

(from the Ancient Greek verb πάσχω [paskho] meaning to suffer) is a term applied to a very strong feeling about a person or thing. Passion is an intense emotion, compelling feeling, enthusiasm, or desire for something.[8]

While greed and power drive much of the underlying culture in other spheres of influence, such as on Wall Street and Capitol Hill, the deep desire to change the world—and the full expectation that this will be achieved—is what drives the Silicon Valley entrepreneur. Passion is what adheres the unique relationships among entrepreneurs, their co-founders and employees, and the community of service providers who become part of their ecosystem. It is passion that venture capitalists often look for in an entrepreneur, because it usually comes with the mental strength and resilience needed to face the many peaks and valleys ahead. You need to be passionate about your idea and you need to feel so strongly about it that you're willing to risk everything. Starting a company is so hard that if you're not passionate about it—and don't sleep, breathe, and eat your passion—you might as well give it up.

Authenticity

Refers to the truthfulness of origins, attributions, commitments, sincerity, devotion, and intentions.[9]

In Silicon Valley, there is a stigma attached to the entrepreneur who wants to get rich quick, as they are perceived to be inauthentic in their convictions, more of a poseur rather than a true transformational personality. Authenticity is such a fundamental prescriptive for entrepreneurs in Silicon Valley that many venture capitalists will pass on an entrepreneur who walks into their doors with the goal of merely being acquired. Investors seek individuals who are so authentic that they don't conform to societal standards; these are often loners who would not win any popularity contests. But when the nonconformist authentics are right, we think of them in hindsight as geniuses. As Stanford professor Andrew Rachleff likes to say, "nothing pays off so well as a nonconformist strategy that wins."[10]

Idea-Driven

> *Being idea-driven is being immersed and surrounded in an environment where an idea can be exchanged, validated, or strengthened. An idea is a concept or mental impression.*[11]

Ideas in Silicon Valley are the commodity, produced and consumed in the way traditional goods are produced and consumed elsewhere. The Silicon Valley culture gives its entrepreneurs a special edge in ideation, because no idea is considered crazy. For example, who would have thought a social media tool like Twitter—that lets people know what you're doing at any moment of the day, from eating toast to pondering a nap—would become so popular? The high-functioning marketplace where ideas can emerge out of competition in free, transparent, public discourse acts as a vast petri dish where the world's brightest and most experienced humans can help strengthen and execute the ideas. Almost all the necessary talent is available locally, from software engineers to molecular biologists to sequencing scientists. The social network—both face-to-face and virtual—elevates these nascent ideas to a higher level of relevance and interest.

Risk-taking

> *The potential that a chosen action or activity (including the choice of inaction) will lead to a loss (an undesirable outcome).*[12]

In contrast to the rest of the world, Silicon Valley entrepreneurs embrace risk-taking. They take risks to create disruptive innovations or take on the competition, actions that are central to receiving the ecosystem's respect and encouragement. Be bold, and you will be told "Go for it" no matter how crazy an idea or value proposition may be. A unique culture of risk-taking entrepreneurship has been created, in which like-minded individuals take on a higher collective level of risk for the greater good and the lure of a substantial financial payoff. For every Google and Facebook there are countless startups that never make it. It is generally believed that with risk comes failure, but it is the knowledge that is gained from failure that will better prepare entrepreneurs for subsequent ventures. This is counterintuitive to big-business thinking where risk is mitigated at all costs, and also to traditional small-business owners, primarily because most self-employed people must mitigate risk to remain employed. Silicon Valley's rapid pace and "invent the future" orientation demands an opposite approach, one that thrives on risk. Sometimes you fail. But as mentioned earlier, failure is a rite of passage in Silicon Valley.

Trustworthiness

The degree to which one party trusts another is a measure of belief in the honesty, fairness, or benevolence of another party.[13]

In Washington, DC, I was schooled in the art of withholding information, keeping valuable data as close to the vest as possible. To the contrary, Silicon Valley entrepreneurs operate in an open and collaborative environment, rarely shying away from sharing what they're truly working on. Often, these entrepreneurs are willing to trust almost anyone with their latest products and platforms, even among their greatest competitors, because in this open ecosystem they can solicit and find help to improve expeditiously upon their innovations, and without the capital cost it may require to go to market. All of this may seem counterintuitive, but entrepreneurship flourishes in an environment where information is shared and exchanged. This type of sharing drives the entrepreneurs to keep evolving, since even the smallest bit of relevant information can allow one to keep pace with changing technologies or protect one from a fatal flaw in a business strategy or product. This is the dynamic, the reciprocal level of deep trust that entices firms. Even the great and powerful Seattle-based Microsoft moved part of its research arm to the valley in 1998 to take advantage of the network of information.

Resilience

Able to recoil or spring back into shape after bending, stretching, or being compressed. Able to withstand or recover quickly from difficult conditions.[14]

In an ever-changing landscape of business climate, Silicon Valley entrepreneurs must constantly shift and adapt. It is often that a strategic plan may be set for one course and then has to be dramatically altered due to new demands; evolving and obsolete technologies; and overall trends in the marketplace. This means that Silicon Valley entrepreneurs have to continue to build expertise and develop knowledge that might have nothing to do with their current specialty or proficiency, requiring from them a great deal of flexibility. It also requires them to undergo a tremendous amount of trials and tribulations or ups and downs—the reality is that 11 ideas will have to be thrown out before the twelfth one works.

FOUR SHADES OF ENTREPRENEURSHIP

Characteristically, an entrepreneur is someone who sees a need in the market and sets out to fulfill it with a product or service. This prototypical entrepreneur may have a particular technical skill or talent, and find out how to best approach the market or have a passion and find the person or people with the skills or talents to best fill that need.

In Silicon Valley, there are four distinct types of entrepreneurs:

1. Serial Entrepreneur

Serial entrepreneurs love to start companies, and can't imagine staying at any one company for too long. They find a formula that works and apply it over and over, often running several ventures concurrently. This highest-profile entrepreneur continuously comes up with new ideas and starts new businesses; a common trait that many of them share is their insane energy and shared passion for the chase and thrill of starting anew. They are often notorious for getting companies up and running, and then bringing in specialized talent to take over operations. There is no defining number on how many companies one must start to be classified as a serial entrepreneur, but the classic example thrives on risk, innovation, and achievement. Arguably, there is no greater collection of serial entrepreneurs in Silicon Valley than the top 10 below (in alphabetical order, along with their notable ventures):

1. Marc Andreessen—Mosaic, Netscape Communications, Opsware, Ning
2. Steve Blank—Zilog, MIPS Computers, Convergent Technologies, Ardent, SuperMac, ESL, Rocket Science Games, E.piphany
3. Jim Clark—Silicon Graphics Inc., Netscape Communications, Healtheon, myCFO
4. Angus Davis—Tellme, Mozilla, Swipely
5. Jack Dorsey—Twitter, Square
6. Max Levchin—PayPal, Slide, Yelp, Field Link, Quid
7. Elon Musk—Zip2, PayPal, SpaceX, Tesla Motors, SolarCity
8. Sean Parker—Napster, Plaxo, Facebook, Spotify, Airtime
9. Mark Pincus—Freeloader, Support.com, Tribe.net, Zynga
10. Evan Williams—Prya Labs, Odeo, Obvious Corp., Twitter

Serial entrepreneurs are revered in the venture capital world, especially those who have achieved past success and are highly effective at packaging strong ideas with solid teams and engineering talent. Serial entrepreneurs often have many ideas, and are good at crafting the initial strategy of a company. They can build a strong foundation and base of revenue, close a deal, and are great at getting people to buy into their vision. But they recognize that there is probably someone better suited to take the company to the next level—which frees them to move on to the next venture.

2. Transformational Entrepreneur

Transformational entrepreneurs, such as Dr. Richard Swanson in this chapter's opening anecdote, tend to drive the Silicon Valley culture. They are perceived as focused, committed, and revolutionary in their thinking. They would generally have a tough time working at any other place or in any other sphere of influence. These transformers see themselves as agents of evolutionary change; they have a proposed solution to any question about the world's problems. Even still, speed to market and expeditious returns on investor capital are also important to them. However, they are driven to follow their vision to the end, at all costs. Many of Silicon Valley's transformational entrepreneurs have known what they wanted to do since childhood, and they're able to turn their hobby or passion into a viable venture. Once these entrepreneurs are associated with particular issues, they will become entrenched in those issues for the majority of their working lives, whether they remain entrepreneurs or later become venture capitalists, academics, or mentors to others.

3. Acquisition Entrepreneur

Leonard Bosack and Sandy Lerner, a husband and wife who worked as computer operations staff members at Stanford University in the early 1980s, wanted to communicate with each other from their computers in their respective offices located in different buildings but were unable to do so. As a result, they created a multiple-protocol router, a router that supports two or more protocols, to resolve the challenges of disparate local area protocols. In December 1984, they founded Cisco Systems and they commercialized the router software, but were sure to pay homage to William Yaeger, another Stanford employee who originally wrote the code years earlier.

There is no doubt that Cisco played an enormous role in helping to shape the future of how people would connect via the internet, and although it was not the first company to develop and sell dedicated network nodes, it was the first to massively sell supporting multiple network protocols. Cisco also adopted a unique strategy, in that they don't engage in substantial R&D, but rather acquire companies to keep relevant in the marketplace. This is why Cisco is the best example of acquisition entrepreneurs. "We don't do R&D; we do A&D, acquire and develop," Don Listwin once said years ago when he was executive vice president of Cisco Systems. However, today, Cisco commits over $5 billion annually to its R&D budget in areas such as core routing and switching products, Telepresence, and Cisco's Unified Computing System.[15]

Since September 1993 to March 2012, Cisco has acquired 152 companies.[16] As a company built on a heavy acquisition strategy, Cisco has to generate a high return on its investments. But they don't always get the acquisition strategy right. In 2009, Cisco attempted to position itself as a household brand, and through its "Human Network" campaign,[17] acquired the Flip video camera for $590 million, a quick and easy video recorder that quickly became obsolete.[18] With the release of the iPhone 3GS in June 2009, video recording became a standard feature of the iPhone. Then, in 2011, Cisco issued a release stating that the company would "exit parts of its consumer businesses and realign the remaining consumer business to support four of its five key company priorities: core routing, switching, and services; collaboration; architectures; and video."[19]

4. Visionary Entrepreneur

Success is not necessarily defined by the money you have in your bank account, but by an ability to solve a problem or to have a vision and be able to effectively execute that vision. This is the definition of the visionary entrepreneur, and one of the great visionary stories is that of YouTube.

It may be hard to believe, but YouTube was once a side project for PayPal engineers Chad Hurley, Steve Chen, and Jawed Karim. Chen and Karim had both been computer science undergrads at the University of Illinois at Urbana-Champaign, and they became friends with Hurley while working at PayPal. Another friend from school who had moved out to the Bay Area was Christina Brodbeck, who later became an integral part of YouTube. While at the University of Illinois, Brodbeck developed a passion for design and technology, which would alter the course of her life dramatically.[20]

Before college, she hadn't been especially interested in science or technology, but in 1996, her freshman year of college, she returned to her dorm room after class to find her roommate, Sandy, creating a personal website. Brodbeck was intrigued. She picked up a copy of the book *HTML by Example* as well as a book about Photoshop, and taught herself both applications simultaneously. Brodbeck was captivated by the creative challenge of designing something out of nothing, and creating websites quickly became her hobby and passion. She begged her family and friends to let her create websites for them for free. She didn't care whether she was setting up corporate homepages, wedding sites, or personal pages, just as long as she got the chance to spend as much time as possible on her newfound passion.

In 2001 she moved to the Bay Area with the intention of turning her hobby into a career. Without a job, and staying at Steve Chen's apartment along with some other college friends, she often found herself hanging out with them at PayPal. Brodbeck didn't work there, but the people she met would become her mentors and friends, and she found that she thrived in a startup environment. Regardless, she took a job at NASA Ames Research so she could start paying some bills.

In spring 2005, at night and on weekends, she began to help out Chen and her other friends from PayPal on YouTube, which actually began as a video dating site. The team worked at each other's houses, at coffee shops, and wherever they could find space. Brodbeck began by working on designing and implementing the rating stars platform as well as the functionality that enables users to subscribe to others' videos.

Her family was deeply concerned when she officially quit a paying job in August 2005 to work for YouTube full time, with no pay or benefits, despite still having $40,000 in graduate school loans. She also only had very informal conversations with the founders about stock and equity shares; hers was largely a handshake deal. But that handshake came into play when in November 2005 Sequoia Capital offered the founding team of YouTube $11.5 million in capital to pay market rates for salary, benefits, and office space.

Just a year after the Sequoia Capital funding, in November 2006, Brodbeck got a phone call from Steve Chen very late at night. He had some news to share: Google was acquiring them for $1.65 billion in Google stock. Brodbeck was stunned.

Asked, years later, how it felt to be acquired by Google, Brodbeck responds, "I just wanted to work on something cool, and in my wildest dreams, I couldn't imagine something like this would have happened . . . needless to say, it far exceeded my expectations."

Now, Brodbeck has co-founded her own entrepreneurial venture called Theicebreak, a digital media site that keeps you connected to the people you love. In her spare time, Brodbeck gives back to other entrepreneurs. "On average, I'd say I give about 20 hours per month helping out other entrepreneurs," she says. She's a resident mentor at 500 Startups, an early-stage seed fund and incubator program, as well as an angel mentor with The Designer Fund, a community of technology entrepreneurs who invest in designer founders through mentorship and funding. In addition, Christina serves as an official advisor to other companies, some of which she holds stock in. "I also meet with various entrepreneurs who have been sent my way or introduced to me, and speak to entrepreneurs at various events," she adds.

Christina Brodbeck reflects on how she was inspired by her dad to always try new things: "I remember exactly what he said to me before I boarded a flight to San Francisco when I was moving out here: 'Good luck, little pioneer.'" A few years after that flight, as a founding member of Google's newly acquired YouTube, Brodbeck bought her parents a condo in Coronado, San Diego. "It is a place that my dad always dreamed of retiring."

7 WHAT MAKES SILICON VALLEY BUSINESS MODELS DIFFERENT

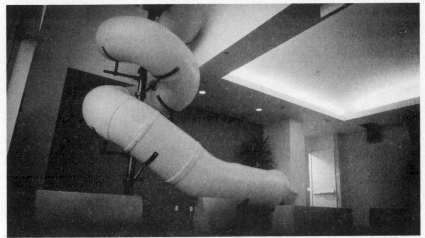

Main Lobby, Box, a file sharing software startup, Los Altos, California

Traditional business models ask one fundamental question: How do you generate revenue? In these models, something new and interesting is invented, and is then turned over to the sales and marketing experts who figure out how to make money from it. But who pays for the fruits of your idea? The customer is a legitimate concern, but the answer dramatically differs by product and industry. Silicon Valley is perhaps the only place in the world where you *don't* need to answer this question, but you do need to fully develop how you are going to create value.

During the internet bubble of the mid- to late-1990s, Silicon Valley investors stopped hearing about business models altogether, adding to the allure of the startup culture. If you had an idea that involved the internet, you could build a company, add a "dot-com" to the name, go public, and sell your shares without ever worrying about how the business would make money. Every public offering upped the level of hysteria. In 1996, an average of one startup went public every five days, and 62 millionaires were being created every 24 hours.[1] But it didn't last long. The pendulum swung the other way, rationality returned, and investors demanded that entrepreneurs show how they were going to make money before agreeing to financially back ventures.

HOW THE IPO JUMPED THE SHARK

One of the greatest examples of investor hysteria gone awry was the rise and fall of Netscape. The company was originally founded as the Netscape Communications Corporation on April 4, 1994, by Jim Clark and Marc Andreessen with Kleiner Perkins Caufield & Byers as its investors. The company's first product was the web browser Mosaic Netscape 0.9, released on October 13, 1994, and renamed Netscape Navigator.[2] It was a groundbreaking and monumental innovation that allowed anyone unprecedented access to the World Wide Web.

A year later, Netscape went public on August 9, 1995, and in its first day of trading, its shares soared to $75 per share, a near record for first-day gains. The stock closed at $58.25 per share, which is not bad for a stock that opened at $14. Netscape's market cap was $2.9 billion.[3] This single day of hysteria made its founders and investors very rich.

But because the internet was in its infancy, Netscape's business model was untested. The company's strategy was to give away its browser for free but sell server software commercially at a low price. By encouraging a free trial of the product, Netscape was ahead of its competition and quickly obtained a critical mass of customers. In mid-1995, Netscape was the most widely used web browser, which caught the watchful eye of Microsoft, who licensed Mosaic to create Internet Explorer 1.0 and released it as part of the Microsoft Windows 95 Plus Pack. Three months later, Internet Explorer 2.0 was released as a free download to anyone, instigating the browser war. Microsoft used their now-famous strategy—"embrace, extend, and extinguish"—in order to gain leverage in the browser industry, meaning they would enter product markets involving widely used standards and extend those standards via proprietary capabilities to disadvantage their competitors. The "embrace, extend, and extinguish" strategy first entered the popular consciousness in the *United States v. Microsoft* antitrust trial, when Steven McGeady, vice president of Intel, testified that Paul Martiz, a Microsoft vice president, used the phrase in a 1995 meeting with Intel to describe Microsoft's strategy toward Netscape, Java, and the internet itself.[4]

Netscape could not compete with the elephant in the room, Microsoft, and it faced increasing criticism for the bugs in its products. In 1998, Netscape's fourth-quarter results showed a loss up to $89 million, including $35 million to pay for layoffs and office closures, according to a 1998 article in *The Economist*.[5] Investors were forced to push the company's fragile share price down by 21 percent. Netscape received more than half of its revenue from packaged software inclusive of its browser, but with the introduction of Internet Explorer and increased competition from Microsoft, they transitioned to "stand-alone" browsers. However, it was too late, as Microsoft had captured the public's loyalty. Netscape's stock decreased another 13 percent.

AOL acquired Netscape in 1999, in a pooling-of-interests transaction ultimately worth $10 billion. In an interview with *Business Insider* in 2009, Netscape co-founder Marc Andreessen discussed the sale, saying that in his opinion, AOL wanted to be considered "the ultimate Internet company."[6] If any investor or advertiser had to deal with something regarding the internet, they wanted to be at the front line of that interaction. So it made sense for AOL to buy Netscape in order to leverage itself as the internet provider.

In 2007, AOL announced it would no longer update the Netscape browser, and would stop supporting Netscape software products as of March 1, 2008, although the brand is still used to market a discount internet service provider.[7]

Like any evolution, business models goes through cycles like Netscape and Microsoft. Depending on the climate of the moment, business models become more or less crucial to attracting investors. The products and innovations for sale in Silicon Valley are rarely as simple as consumer products like food, which everyone needs and where there is a clearer path to profitability. As a result, Silicon Valley entrepreneurs such as the co-founders of Netscape have made fortunes without a proven business model. So even after the bursting of the bubble, the sense remains that, in Silicon Valley, a business model is important but not essential for a potentially huge financial payoff.

CREATING VALUE BEFORE MAKING MONEY

Eric Ries, author of *The Lean Startup,* thinks that not having a proven business model versus creating value is an essential distinction to make, because of common misconceptions about the Silicon Valley model. "The analogy that I use is, imagine that I have a business plan to open up a diamond mine. I'm going to dig into the ground and exhume diamonds, and then sell them," says Ries.[8] According to Ries, there are two big questions that underlie that business. Question number one is, If an entrepreneur digs into the ground in a certain place, are diamonds going to be there? And question number two is, If the entrepreneur has a giant pile of diamonds, would he or she be able to sell them for money? So Ries believes that one is the creation of the value and then one is the capture of that value. "Does a diamond mine that has diamonds have a business model, even if an entrepreneur hasn't actually sold a single diamond on the open market? I say the answer is yes. They are creating value but not yet capturing revenue," says Ries.

Consider the creation and acquisition of Instagram, the free photo-sharing program that allows users to take an image, apply a digital filter to it, and then share it on a variety of social networks. The story begins in 2010, with Stanford University graduate Kevin Systrom, who was working on a multi-featured HTML5 (the markup language that structures content for the web) check-in project on mobile photography, originally called Burbn. He began to build the prototype without any branding elements or design at all, just concentrating on its functionality and usability. After meeting a VC from Baseline Ventures and another from Andreessen Horowitz at a party, Systrom pitched his idea and within two weeks, he had raised a total $500,000 from both.[9]

Systrom recruited a Stanford friend, Mike Krieger, to help him develop the company. Together, they decided to focus exclusively on mobile photos. After developing a prototype of Burbn, they felt the app was too cluttered and overrun with features. One area where the app excelled was its distinctive feature that confined photos to a square shape.

So, they renamed the resulting program Instagram, to conjure the idea of an "instant telegram."

In December 2010, Instagram announced full photo support and sharing on Foursquare, a location-based social networking site for mobile phones, and quickly grew to a million registered users. After the impressive launch of Instagram, Kevin Systrom called on a fellow Stanford University Sigma Nu brother, Adam D'Angelo, former chief technology officer at Facebook. D'Angelo spent 30 minutes on the phone walking Systrom through all the basic things Instagram needed to do in order to get technically backed up. He made it clear that Systrom should spend time talking and getting to know the people around him, because one day, those people could be the ones to "press money into his palm."[10]

In February 2011, Instagram raised $7 million in a Series A round, the name typically given to a startup's first significant round of venture capital funding, from a variety of investors, including Benchmark Capital and serial entrepreneur Jack Dorsey. Instagram grew to 5 million users by June 2011, over 10 million by September, and in April 2012 announced its explosive growth to over 30 million users. All the while Instagram's extraordinary success grew without any revenue. In the fall of 2011, new reports stated that the company was seeking a $20 million valuation as it planned to go public after another round of funding. In April 2012, Sequoia Capital was said to be leading a $50 million funding round for the company, valuing Instagram at $500 million. Then, within that same month, Facebook announced their agreement to acquire Instagram for $1 billion in cash and stock, with plans to keep the company independently managed.[11]

THE MAGIC INGREDIENT

Silicon Valley businesses eschew traditional business models in favor of a newer model that relies heavily on experimentation in the marketplace. "What's different in the Valley is that we've found a quasi-scientific method for reinventing businesses and industries, not just products," said Randy Komisar, a partner at Kleiner Perkins Caufield & Byers and a lecturer on entrepreneurship at Stanford University.[12] The process for discovery has quickened, and companies in Silicon Valley are pioneering new business models to succeed.

Eric Ries believes that there are two key aspects of the Silicon Valley business model. First, equity ownership is paramount: "This is something that few people outside of Silicon Valley truly understand. Most people have a nineteenth-century idea of labor and management, where the more you have to pay to your workers, the less of a stake you have." Ries believes that Silicon Valley's fundamental value proposition, where no one has an insignificant stake in the outcome of a venture, is what leads to long-term gains. In a for-profit company where early employees actually own a stake, they all have a chance to become independently wealthy for life, and the philosophy prevails that whoever helps create value should share in it. Equity is a critical part of the Silicon Valley compensation package. "Almost everyone in the Valley who has made a lot of money has made it through this way of appreciating equity, long-term capital gains far beyond the traditional realm of salary, short-term bonuses, and financial shenanigans," Ries says. This is lost on many outside Silicon Valley, who don't believe in models based on deferred compensation.

Ries's second point mirrors a quote he likes to borrow from Tim O'Reilly, the author of *What Is Web 2.0?*: "The number one rule for startups is to create more value than you capture."[13] Silicon Valley companies think foremost about creating value, not necessarily about immediately making money—the thought of wealth must never get in the way of creating value. "If companies focus on creating the best company they can, the money will eventually follow," says Ries. Undoubtedly, many in Silicon Valley are there to get rich, and that is still important because it drives something to aspire to. Most VCs, however, are focused on building enterprise value for customers, and they are justifiably confident that there will be a financial payoff down the road. "I don't think there is any other way to take high-risk, disruptive innovation-type business, because they simply can't generate a lot of cash return quickly, as that is baked into the definition of disruptive innovation," says Ries.

He makes an interesting observation. However, if you are creating more value than you are able to capture, then you will most likely be acquired by a firm who can capture the value, as illustrated in Facebook's acquisition of Instagram. If you are able to capture the value you create, then it is likely you can grow into a Google or an Apple. One of two fundamental questions is, How do you make good decisions that will lead to creating value? The other queries: How do you know that you're creating real value and not just getting an inflated valuation? The answer to these questions lies in the business models themselves and how businesses or consumers value the product or service.

In the case of Silicon Valley business models, capturing value most naturally occurs in uncontrolled environments, unlike traditional business models that operate through predictability and a precise process. For example, out of the much-hyped business-to-consumer model (B2C), which mostly applies to internet-based businesses came the idea of the "freemium." The freemium model offers products or services for free but often charges a premium for advanced features, functionality, or virtual goods such as software, games, or web services. This really spun the B2C idea on its head, as innovators now had to quantify the assets of capturing an audience without any guarantee that any substantial revenue would ever be created from it, such as in the case of Facebook. Some of the restrictions to free products and services that require paid upgrades include limited capacity (e.g., a user can only read a limited number of articles on a news site); limited time (e.g., a user can only use the service for free for a certain period of time); and limited features (e.g., a user can only access a basic version of software), etc.

There are conflicting opinions about Facebook's business model. Did it address a revenue strategy early enough (or at all)? Should revenue in fact be secondary to capturing a vast audience? In the early stages of the company, monetizing Facebook was not terribly critical. The social network grew quickly and steadily and was able to capture angel investors and venture capitalists, but eventually it had to be monetized. Others, such as Eric Ries, see it from a different angle: "I don't agree with the criticism that Facebook didn't have a revenue strategy during the height of its growth. To me, the turning point of Mark [Zuckerberg]'s brilliance is when he turned down a billion dollar offer from Yahoo!. That is when I knew Mark had the data to support the value he had created."

And similarly, businesses like Facebook accumulate customer attention for free, which they can then resell to advertisers later. There's no question that customer attention is valuable; it's just unclear how much money you can get for it.

A CONSTANTLY SHIFTING CLIMATE

It must be emphasized enough how infrequently "home runs" like Facebook, Google, and Instagram truly occur, so a common strategy used in the Silicon Valley business model is the "pivot," when you actually rotate away from the original strategy or plan when it doesn't take hold. Pivoting means trying out new ideas, shedding the ones that don't work, and learning to move on. Changes can be as simple as re-pricing your product, or as complex as revamping your product line or service, reassessing your target consumer or customer acquisition strategy.[14] A pivot will most likely reveal previous findings about your customer, technology, and marketplace overall. But the key to a successful pivot is to quickly redirect based on these factors and use them to enhance your basic product and market fit, without compromising your company's credibility. Successful pivoting is crucial to adapting to and controlling issues as they arise.

"Pivot to me is not a four-letter word," says Tony Conrad, a partner in the early-stage venture capital firm True Ventures. "It represents some of the best methodology that the Valley has invented. Starting something, determining it's not working, and then leveraging aspects of [that] technology is extremely powerful."[15]

When asked about where he thinks the Silicon Valley business model is heading, Eric Ries responded,

> Today's model is going to be considered primitive in the future. I think we're on the cusp of a really dramatic revolution in how we manage startups. And I think when we look back 100 years at the way factories used to be managed compared to how they're managed today, it's like a joke. You can't believe how stupid the people of the past were; they're going to say that about us. Because we're just starting to work out a, frankly, better rational management systems for startups. And at the same time that's becoming a lot more important because the impact of the number of startups just getting started is going to be monumental. There are fundamental forces that made it possible for Silicon Valley to be a high tech software hardware set of businesses, with a specific set of business models, techniques, and capabilities that are about to crush every other industry in the world. So it is that kind of exponential change that we're going to have to get used to, that is moving into all

kinds of other businesses that currently think of themselves as stable. The disruption will be a thing coming.[16]

A WORD ABOUT FLAT MANAGEMENT

In order to build highly productive organizations, Silicon Valley leaders structure their companies in a way that the manager is seen as a team player and not as the "gatekeeper" above all. When a manager fails to communicate in a traditional company, it can debilitate the entire operation. But if the company sees its employees as a team, or family, the task and responsibilities are divided among everyone, thus avoiding single responsibility for failure.

Silicon Valley companies build autonomy and openness into their cultures. Every employee has access to all relevant information, as well as a voice in decision making. You will often hear of an employee establishing his or her own form of management that spreads throughout the company, then influences other Silicon Valley companies and, ultimately, becomes a new product. For example, in Google's early years, Larry Schwimmer, a software engineer, developed a simple productivity system for managing teams that became notorious at the company and continued to spread throughout Silicon Valley. In his system, called "Snippets," employees receive a weekly email asking them to write down what they did the previous week and what they plan to do in the upcoming week. Replies get compiled in a public space and distributed automatically the following day. The process has allowed Google to grow and still retain its flat organizational structure, because everyone can see what everyone else is doing, with minimal disruption to work.

A LAST WORD ABOUT SILICON VALLEY'S INCREDIBLE EMPLOYEE BENEFITS

Google has come a long way from the venture they started in a garage at a Los Altos home to their headquarters in Mountain View, California, known as the Googleplex. Although there are more than 70 offices in more than 40 countries around the world, Google encourages creativity and productivity by promoting the uniqueness throughout their offices. Many common features visitors can find at Google locations across the globe include: cafes and "microkitchens," whiteboards for old-fashioned brainstorming, pool tables and pianos, video games, Googler's sharing cubicles, cubes with three to five desks, yurts, used indoors as conference rooms, and "huddles," spaces set up for people to huddle and meet. Google believes that "it's really the people that make Google the kind of company it is,"[17] so it tries to maintain an open culture by creating a comfortable atmosphere where individuals can be contributors by sharing ideas and opinions. Every office design and employee benefit is strategically developed to support this notion of collaboration.

While employee benefits are not traditionally incorporated into the business model, in Silicon Valley it does create loyalty when leading employers fiercely compete for top talent. Below is Google's study:

Google from Cradle to Grave: Unrivaled Employee Benefits
Location: Mountain View, California
Year Founded: 1998

Professional Development
- Google's 20 percent time program allows any employee to spend a day per week on anything they want to work on outside of their job description.[18] Executives feel that this ignites innovation within Google, and simultaneously allows Google employees the opportunity to unleash the creative talent of their workforce.
- Weekly TGIF (Thank Goodness It's Friday) meetings occur where employees gather and put co-founders Larry Page and Sergey Brin through the grind of a Q&A session, where no question is off limits.[19]
- Google EDU is a unique program at the Googleplex that allows employees to take classes, taught by both professional instructors and fellow employees. The hundreds of offerings range from learning new coding languages to meditation to building emotional intelligence. Google also pays for supplemental education and advanced degrees.[20]

Food—Free, Organic, and Energy-producing
- Google offers over 30 individually themed cafes at the Googleplex—and all are free and organic.[21] Culinary options include the Asian-themed Cafe Jia and Cafe 150 that uses organic ingredients

locally grown within 150 miles of the Google campus. Charlie's Place, named after first head chef, Charlie Ayers, offers several stations of cuisine from sushi to vegetarian dishes. Yoshi's, formerly "The No Name" cafe, has been renamed in memory of one of the early employees' dogs that used to run around Google's first office.[22] Poultry dishes are all local, natural, and much of the produce is grown on small farms such as Alba Organics in Watsonville, Ecopia Farms in Campbell, and Knoll Farm in Petaluma.[23] Seasonal seafood is local, fresh, and supported by the Google Green Seafood Program, which uses stricter guidelines than those recommended by the Monterey Bay Aquarium.[24] Cafes are designed with collaboration in mind, offering long tables for people to come together and talk to one another.

- Google also grows food on campus. Employees have the resources to make informed choices about their diet and long-term health with the access to community gardens, cooking classes such as "Codes for Cooks,"[25] and cooking demonstrations from local chefs. The Google Food Program puts on five major events each quarter in Mountain View, including barbecues and themed "food" days. Besides the free food from Michelin-rated chefs, you'll find numerous Google snack rooms that offer fare including granola, chocolate covered pretzels, juices, and coffees.

Health and Wellness
- Google's healthcare plan includes onsite doctors, physical therapists, chiropractors, and unlimited sick days. Also included in health benefits is a Dependent Care Assistance Plan,[26] which allows employees to take a pre-tax deduction from their pay for eligible dependent care expenses.
- Massage is so built into the culture at Google that there are dedicated massage rooms in most every building, manned by certified massage therapists. One employee claims these rooms "look, feel, and smell like a real spa."[27] Employees receive a free massage on their birthday and free massages when managers and coworkers recommend them for doing an exceptional job. And if you need a nap after your massage, Google provides "nap pods": secluded, relaxing places to encourage proper amounts of sleep.

- Google employees are encouraged to stay active during the work-day with a state-of-the-art gym, discounted personal training, a swim-in-place pool, and a variety of sports clinics to help transition employees into Google's on-site sports leagues. Other fitness programs include "runners without shoes" and Weight Watchers, with meetings offered right on campus.

Maternity/Paternity Leave

- Google offers new parents five months for maternity leave and seven weeks[28] for paternity leave. At company baby showers that are held each month, employees get parenting tips, coupons, and credit for onsite massage, and "baby-bonding bucks," $500 deposited in their new parent account, which is expected to go toward services such as laundry, gardening, and cleaning in the first few months.[29]

Recreation

- In the summer of 2011, Google opened up its Garfield Sports Complex, which includes a soccer field, basketball court, two tennis courts, two bocce ball courts, two horseshoe pits, a putting green, and a roller hockey rink.[30] Bored with Garfield? Other recreation includes Frisbee golf, a bowling alley, and company bicycles, Capoeira, ping-pong tables, office razr scooters, billiards, foosball and video games.[31]

Culture

- Google provides regular cultural activities for employees off campus as well. In February 2012, for example, Google bought out the Cirque du Soleil Michael Jackson tribute at the Oakland arena, and gave free tickets and free transportation for the first 15,000 Googlers who wanted them.[32]

Transportation

- Employees have access to free shuttles that transport them to work from several areas around the Bay Area, including San Francisco over 30 miles away. Google executives say that it encourages employees to reduce their carbon footprint as the shuttle runs on 5 percent biodiesel fitted with filtration systems that eliminate any harmful emission including nitrogen oxide. Of course there is WiFi on the shuttle.

- Need a car? No problem. Google offers a car sharing program, GFleet, to employees once they get to the office using alternative modes of transportation. The GFleet is comprised of low-carbon-emission cars such as Chevrolet Volts, Nissan LEAFs, Mitsubishi iMiEVs, Ford Focus Electrics, Ford Transit Connect Electrics, and Honda Fit EVs.[33] If an employee is interested in buying a hybrid car with a gas mileage rating of at least 45 miles to the gallon, Google will offer that employee $5,000 to do so.[34]

Self-Powered Commutes that Translate to Charitable Giving

- Google's self-powered commute program encourages employees to get to work by walking, biking, roller-skating, skateboarding, scootering, or any other self-propelling method. In return, when employees self-power their commutes, they receive a digital stamp equivalent to real dollars that they can contribute to the charity of their choosing.[35]

On-site Errands and Concierge

- Google provides on-site services to make employee errands more convenient, such as on-site dry cleaning and alterations, laundry facilities, oil changes, a hair salon, bike repairs, ATMs and credit union services, a car wash, and a DVD rental.
- Google's corporate concierge team is also available to help Google employees with everyday tasks such as planning a dinner party, or unusual requests like finding a jewel-encrusted scepter for a special Halloween outfit.[36]

Google Day Care and Preschool

- Google's day care and preschool program, the Woods and the Wetlands, is an 18,500-square-foot center for 80 children.[37] The curriculum implements the Reggio Emilia approach, which believes that children are competent, resourceful, curious, and imaginative.[38] The program is not free, but initially Google subsidized it so that more of their employees could take advantage of the program, and kids would be provided with free breakfast, lunch, and snacks at the center.[39]

- Although Google hosts a "bring your kids to work day" and "bring your pre-K child to work day" with activities for parents and children, they also give employees the opportunity to bring their parents to work, to tour the Googleplex, attend workshops on how to use Google's search engine, and of course, parents are provided with lunch at one of Google's restaurants.[40]

Death Benefits

- Introduced in 2011, Google employees receive death benefits. If any Google employee passes away while employed by Google, their surviving partner would receive half their salary every year for the following decade. In addition, all stocks would be vested immediately, and children of the deceased would receive $1,000 a year until they are 19 or 23, contingent on whether they are full-time students.[41]

8 THE INVESTORS OF SAND HILL ROAD

Highway 280, Exit 24, Menlo Park, California

Draper Fisher Jurvetson, otherwise known as DFJ, a venerable venture capital firm in Silicon Valley whose offices lie at the foothills of the Santa Cruz Mountains on Sand Hill Road, was founded in 1985. Known as an "early-stage investor,"[1] the firm has capitalized on a handful of simple visions and products before they were household names, Hotmail and Skype among them, as well as complex technologies like Synthetic Genomics, a company developing "new scientific processes to enable industry to design and test desired genetic modifications."[2] DFJ now manages $7 billion in investments in a global network of partner funds, with a focus on "extraordinary entrepreneurs who set out to change the world."[3]

Tim Draper, the founder of DFJ, is a third-generation venture capitalist.[4] His grandfather, Gen. William H. Draper Jr., was the first West Coast venture capitalist. He cofounded Draper, Gaither & Anderson in Palo Alto in 1957, and started funding companies like Raytheon. General Draper served as the Undersecretary of the Army, and was most notable for his leadership role of the Marshall Plan after World War II, focusing on the economic reconstruction of Germany and Japan. The general partners of the firm were Rowan Gaither, founder of the Rand Corporation, and Frederick L. Anderson, a retired Air Force general, and included limited partners such as the Rockefellers, and the then-private financial services firm of Lazard Frères.

Draper, Gaither, and Anderson set much of the standards of the venture capital industry that exists today. Venture capital became a partnership where general partners managed the funds and invested anywhere from 1–10 percent of the fund, and limited partners put up the predominant investment in the fund, but collectively everyone shared in the economics once a start-up was sold or became a publicly traded company. The three men also laid the groundwork for how venture capitalists received compensation through management fees and a share of the profits after liquidity. The management fee, which was set between 1 and 2.5 percent of the total fund, was meant to cover the costs of doing business, of managing a fund, rather than creating meaningful wealth for the general partners. The carried interest or "carry" fee, a benchmark that set between 20 and 30 percent, was paid when companies became liquid, and limited partners had been paid back all of their investment

The general's son, William H. Draper III, graduated from Yale University in 1950, where he attended school with George H.W. Bush and became a member of the secret and powerful Skull and Bones society. After serving as a second Lieutenant in the Korean War, he attended Harvard Business School, and studied under professor Georges Doriot. Draper III started the venture capital firm Draper & Johnson Investment Company in 1962, and then founded Sutter Hill Ventures in 1965. He managed Sutter Hill until President Ronald Reagan appointed him Chairman of the U.S. Export-Import Bank in 1981, and then Undersecretary General of the United Nations in 1985. He returned to Silicon Valley and the venture capital world in 1995, and founded Draper International, concentrating on investments in India. He subsequently founded Draper Richards, which invests in early stage technology companies in the United States, as well as Draper Investment Company, which concentrates on seed investments in Europe and Asia. He remains the general partner of all three venture capital firms.

William Draper III's son, Tim, met John Fisher when they were officemates at the investment bank Alex, Brown & Sons. In 1985, Tim Draper left the bank to start his own venture capital firm, and six years later brought on John Fisher to help him raise a much larger fund to grow the firm. In late 1994, Steve Jurvetson, a then-second-year Stanford University business school student, sent a thoughtful letter to Draper and Fisher, and the two knew that Jurvetson would have the energy, intellect, and intuition to be a great third partner for the firm.

DFJ quickly became pioneers in the tech universe. Draper and Jurvetson coined the phrase "viral marketing" in a Netscape newsletter article.[5] After DFJ invested in Hotmail, Draper tried to encourage the founders to append an advertising message to every outbound email message that would read: "P.S. I love you. Get your free email at http://www. hotmail.com."[6] While the Hotmail founders took a pass on spreading the love, they did agree to include a promotional pitch with a clickable URL in every email message. According to a DFJ manuscript highlighting their investments, *The Riskmasters: A Dedication to the DFJ Entrepreneurs,* "Hotmail grew its subscriber base from zero to 12M users in 18 months, more rapidly than any company in any media in the history of the world."[7] They all realized that the key element of consumer branding is usage affiliation: Do I want to be a member of the group—in this case, my friends who already use this product?

Tim Draper cares deeply about spreading a global entrepreneurial message. He recognized early the benefits of dispersing venture capital around the country and then to the world, franchising DFJ to over a dozen states, including Alaska, Utah, and New York, and then internationally to China, Singapore, Ukraine, Russia, England, and Ireland (although he admits that he has had greater success in some places than others).

When his daughter, Jessica, was in elementary school, Draper started a program called BizWorld, a role-playing game to teach third- through eighth-graders about entrepreneurship. In the game, the students act as entrepreneurs in the business of manufacturing friendship bracelets.

They select executives from among themselves, while others apply for jobs, and pitch their teachers (who act as venture capitalists) for funding. The exercise culminates with finance day, where the students create income statements and balance sheets to determine which company has the highest valuation.

Tim Draper's latest endeavor is Draper University (DU), a boarding school for young entrepreneurs ages 21–24 who come from around the globe to learn the fundamentals of entrepreneurship in the heart of Silicon Valley. Tim insists that while there is value in traditional education, the system is far too rigid to cultivate aspiring entrepreneurs. "There is something missing in the current [education] system," Draper says.[8] After all, some of the world's leading entrepreneurs either dropped out of college or never even went, the most obvious being Steve Jobs, Larry Ellison, Mark Zuckerberg, Michael Dell, and Sir Richard Branson. Draper believes in educating these budding entrepreneurs in teams of five— groups large enough for individuals to provide value but small enough to ensure no one can hide. Classes range from traditional disciplines like accounting, law, and negotiation to creative exploration through activities such as painting, cultivating hydroponics, and guitar lessons. DU's young entrepreneurs are expected to give back what they've learned by going into the BizWorld classroom and teaching the next generation of entrepreneurs.

GEORGES DORIOT

Gen. Georges Doriot, a Parisian who immigrated to the United States to earn an MBA, is the father of venture capital as we know it. In 1946, Doriot, a Harvard business school professor along with Ralph Flanders and Karl Kompton, former president of MIT, founded American Research and Development Corporation (ARDC) in Boston, the first venture capital firm, and the first firm to invest in entrepreneurial soldiers returning from World War II.[9] ARDC was also the first institutional private equity investor, as it accepted funds from sources other than wealthy families. What solidified confidence in the venture capital model was in 1957, ARDC invested $70,000 in Digital Equipment Corporation (DEC),[10] a computer company that became a leading vender of software and peripherals, the devices that connect to a host computer.

After DEC's IPO in 1968, it was valued at $355 million, representing a return investment of over 500 times, or an annualized rate of return of 101 percent.[11]

HOW VENTURE FOUND ITS WAY TO SILICON VALLEY

Venture capital made its presence known in Silicon Valley before it even had a name, when an investment pioneer by the name of Frank Chambers raised $5 million in 1959 and founded Continental Capital Corporation. Chambers and his brother Robert were greatly influenced by Georges Doriot's teaching at Harvard. It is Frank's investment firm that became the predecessor for the kind of big-risk, big-reward financing that later fueled Silicon Valley's investment community, and it was Continental Capital that became the first Small Business Investment Company (SBIC). This program to create SBIC companies was authorized by the federal government in 1958, helping to stimulate the national economy through private equity investments for small business growth and expansion, a move that fueled the massive growth of venture capital firms seemingly overnight.[12]

Then there was Arthur Rock, who became renowned for finding a home and capital for the Traitorous Eight, as I mention earlier in the book. Rock joined forces with Tommy Davis in 1961. Davis, a lawyer and the president of Kern County Land Company, had raised $3.5 million from several of the founders of Fairchild Semiconductor to start the venture capital firm Davis and Rock in San Francisco. The firm's guiding mantra, "Back the Right People," inspired generations of venture capitalists to this day to invest more in the team than the idea. Davis and Rock created a hugely successful firm that invested in Scientific Data Systems, a company that was founded in 1961 by Max Palevsky, a veteran of Packard Bell, along with eleven other computer scientists.[13] The company was the first to employ silicon transistors and was an early adopter of integrated circuits and in 1969 was acquired by Xerox for $980 million. The partnership between the two men lasted until 1968, until Davis started a new partnership and formed the Mayfield Fund.

Besides Scientific Data Systems, Rock's two big home runs were his investments in Intel and Apple. Rock helped Bob Noyce and Gordon Moore capitalize Intel, and later admitted that this was probably the only company he invested in that he felt would undoubtedly be an enormous success, due to the talents of Noyce and Moore. However, Rock is probably most famously known for his apprehension about being an early investor in Apple. He balked when Steve Jobs, then a long-haired, flip-flop-wearing hippie, walked into his office and presented his idea. But Jobs was so articulate and dynamic that Rock quickly got over his jitters and became Apple's first investor.

In the 1960s, the early venture capitalists used to all gather once a month at the University Club in Nob Hill for the Western Association of Venture Capitalists, and share information about the ideas they were hearing from budding entrepreneurs. Often referred to as "The Group," in the 1970s, the venture capital community moved away from San Francisco and settled on Sand Hill Road in Menlo Park, a few blocks from Stanford University. In between San Francisco and San Jose, the location offered access to two major airports as well as pastoral properties down the road in Palo Alto, Los Altos, Los Altos Hills, Atherton, and Woodside. Sand Hill Road became the West Coast version of Wall Street.

SAND HILL ROAD

In 1972, Eugene Kleiner and Thomas J. Perkins opened a venture capital firm at 3000 Sand Hill Road. Kleiner was one of the Traitorous Eight, and Perkins was formerly a Harvard MBA who had also taken classes with Georges Doriot, and who had later worked for David Packard. The two men were introduced by famed San Francisco investment banker Sandy Robertson, who thought the two men would be a great team because they were the type of people who would play an enormous role in serving as active advisors in the companies they were investing in. The two were later joined by Frank Caufield, a graduate of the United States Military Academy at West Point, and Brook Byers, a former biotechnology entrepreneur, but what Kleiner Perkins Caufield Byers (KPCB) did differently was that they encouraged their associates to start companies on their own, an act that ultimately spawned some of the world's leading businesses such as Tandem Computers, America Online, Genentech, Netscape, Sun Microsystems, Google, Amazon, Verisign, and Symantec.

Kleiner and Perkins weren't finance guys, but entrepreneurs who had the experience to build out other companies. KPCB became the world's premier venture capital firm.[14]

Sand Hill Road became the de facto epicenter of venture capital. It became so renowned that, in 1997, according to venture capitalist Bob Pavey, a Japan Airlines pilot on its approach to San Francisco International from Tokyo tipped the wing of the plane so the Japanese business passengers could have an aerial view of the road. The bulk of venture capital firms that line the street cluster in a stretch less than a mile and a half long, extending in between Highway 280 and Sharon Heights Shopping Center. Many of the two- to three-story office buildings are not apparent at first, as they blend into the natural landscape of trees and hillsides.

Between 2100 and 3000 Sand Hill Road are over 80 of the world's most recognizable venture capital firms, including Andreessen Horowitz, Benchmark Capital, Charles River Ventures, Draper Fisher Jurvetson, Elevation Partners, Greylock Partners, Kleiner Perkins Caufield & Byers, Leapfrog Ventures, Lightspeed Venture Partners, Mayfield Fund, Menlo Ventures, Mohr Davidow Ventures, Morgenthaler Ventures, New Enterprise Associates (NEA), Oak Hill Venture Partners, Pequot Ventures, Redpoint Ventures, Sequoia Capital, Shasta Ventures, SVB Capital (Silicon Valley Bank), Tenaya Capital, The Blackstone Group, US Venture Partners, and Venrock Associates, among others.

In the mid-1990s, Sand Hill Road became the world's most expensive commercial real estate, at around $144 per square foot.[15]

HOW THE GAME IS PLAYED

Venture capitalists invest in startups with the hopes of having a high return on investment. The initial idea behind venture capital was for wealthy individuals—and later, institutional investors—to potentially double their returns from what they could otherwise receive in the stock market. Today, according to the National Venture Capital Association, the largest venture capital investors are pension funds (37 percent of investors); corporations (23 percent); foundations and endowments (16 percent); families and institutions (12 percent); and others (12 percent). Venture capital gradually became defined as "professionally managed, equity-like financing of young, growth-oriented private companies."[16]

A venture capital firm will strive to raise a ten-year fund, but invest a majority of it in the first few years. Once the initial fund is mostly invested into selected entrepreneurial ventures, the venture capital firm will seek to raise another fund. Of those investments, "three [of every ten companies] will be wipeouts, three will be poor returns, three will do well with a return, and one will hit a home run. It is the slugging average, not the batting average, that matters,"[17] says Bob Pavey, a long-term venture capitalist with Morganthaler. The expectation is to average five to ten times return on the invested capital over a period of five to seven years.

What makes the Silicon Valley venture capitalist unique is what he or she looks for in an entrepreneur. First and foremost, the interaction is extremely relationship-driven. One venture capitalist, who preferred not to be named, jokes that relationships between VCs and entrepreneurs last longer than many marriages, so there has to be a degree of chemistry from the start. Generally, the venture capitalist wants to know if the entrepreneur is capable, has realistic expectations, and most importantly, with market forces changing so rapidly, that they can quickly pivot if need be.

In his book *The Startup Game: Inside the Partnership Between Venture Capitalists and Entrepreneurs*, Bill Draper identifies the top ten avoidable mistakes of entrepreneurs:[18]

1. Creating overly optimistic projections about market size and customer acquisitions;
2. Underestimating timelines;
3. Trying to do everything yourself;
4. Failing to master the elevator pitch;
5. Not downsizing when necessary;
6. Being inflexible;
7. Not developing a clear marketing plan;
8. Building a board that consists only of friends;
9. Not taking action in a recession; and
10. Not knowing the right way to approach venture capitalists.

Venture capitalists gradually become the coaches of the entrepreneurs they select. Just like the world of professional sports, they choose which athletes get to play and when they play, and try to create the most favorable conditions for them. Without the attention and know-how of these coaches, many young entrepreneurs would spend a lot of time on the "bench"—squandering time, money, and energy on the wrong tasks. The proof is in the stats—after obtaining venture capital, most companies are measurably faster at bringing their product to market.

What gives Silicon Valley entrepreneurs a competitive edge in access to capital is partially geographic. Many Silicon Valley venture capitalists limit their investments to companies that are within a radius of a two-hour drive. According to the latest National Venture Capital Association report, the venture capital industry invested $3,945 per person living in Silicon Valley in comparison to $43 per person in the rest of the United States, including cities such as New York and Boston.[19] That is a 91:1 ratio. The reason for this? Because the relationship between venture capitalist and entrepreneur is paramount, and the mentoring must be assessable and preferably face-to-face. At any given time, a partner may be invested in up to a dozen companies, and needs to meet often with his or her management teams; that partner therefore cannot afford to spend too much time on the road. Co-investors, lawyers, accountants, and investment bankers who are an integral part of entrepreneurial success also must be managed. Shifting economic conditions and improved communications technology are changing the ways business can be done, however. In fact, Silicon Valley venture capital firms have increasingly begun looking abroad for investments in countries such as Israel, China, and India, but these investments will never be matched to their Silicon Valley counterparts.

VENTURE CAPITAL'S QUAGMIRE: CONTROVERSIAL TERMS AND RETURNS

The story that lingered nearly a decade later was that during the internet boom in the mid-1990s, deals between venture capitalists and entrepreneurs were allegedly being sketched out on paper napkins over lunch or coffee, but I could never find a VC willing to confirm this. It did resonate, though, that just about any entrepreneur could raise a few million dollars in capital if they breathed an idea of doing something online, and by the year 2000, total venture capital had reached its peak, with $99.2 billion in investments, mostly in online companies. Only a few years later, the venture capital world of Sand Hill Road had gained a reputation for being greedy instead of savvy, and many of the firms that opened up during the boom disappeared during the bust. In response, venture capitalists began to negotiate a broad range of new terms for this new world.

In 2002, *San Jose Mercury News* reporter Matt Marshall wrote an article entitled, "VCs Learning New Tricks to Weather the Downturn," about a report that two corporate partners at Fenwick & West, Barry Kramer and Michael Parker, had disseminated information to their clients concerning the broad range of terms VCs were trying to negotiate. Marshall wrote, "It [the Fenwick & West report] identified some of the preposterous terms that VCs were trying to build into their contracts, such as 'one arcane but high-octane clause, the so-called senior liquidation preferences.'"[20] Prior to the internet bust, if a startup was sold, VCs would demand that they be paid back first, before the co-founders and/or management ever saw a dime, which was perfectly reasonable. After the bust, in what can be best characterized as an overcorrection, VCs started demanding not only their initial investment back, but also double or even triple what they were owed. Kramer's and Parker's report forced questions about standardization, especially for entrepreneurs outside of Silicon Valley or the tech world. What started as a one-time report has now turned into a quarterly, "Silicon Valley Venture Survey," that not only provides standardization on terms, but also industry data including trends in venture capital investment, mergers and acquisitions, and IPO activity in addition to trends in secondary markets and corporate venture capital. It also includes any commentary on venture capital sentiment and performance comparisons to the NASDAQ.[21]

In May 2012, the Kauffman Foundation disseminated a scathing account on venture capital investments and their success in comparison to the public markets. Titled "We Have Met the Enemy . . . And He Is Us: Lessons from Twenty Years of the Kauffman Foundations Investments in VC Funds and the Triumph of Hope over Experience," the report pointed out that VC returns hadn't beaten the public markets for most of the previous decade, and even more damaging, it showed that the industry has not returned cash invested since 1997. "It's so easy to point the finger of blame directly at VCs—there are too many of them, they're raising too much cash, they're sitting on too much cash, they're investing too much cash, they're taking home too much cash . . . you get the idea."[22]

Eric Ries, however, sees a far greater problem to which venture capital turns a blind eye, a problem he calls *success theater*. "People are raising money and then using that money to make themselves look successful instead of creating value," says Ries. What Ries is suggesting is that just because an entrepreneur can raise venture capital does not ensure that they are on a path that will lead to success. "In my own work, I am really focused on trying to redeem as many people [entrepreneurs] as we can to steer them away from a hype-based economy towards an economy of real value creation, and in order to do that, I think we have to develop a scientific level of rigor around what are the indicators that a company will be successful in creating value and actually making progress . . . indicators that let us know that they are actually running valuable experiments."

In the research for this book, other venture capitalists have privately complained about the "Facebook effect"—a term not meant to refer specifically to Facebook, but to social media as a whole. Essentially, most VCs I interviewed feel that many of the limited partners of venture capital firms are starting to place unrealistic expectations on return on investment. Many of them don't want to wait around for the ten-plus years it often takes to see returns in true innovation or advancements in life sciences or more transformational technologies. This phenomenon of overnight success is relatively new, and will probably be around for good, but the reality remains that there are a small handful of Facebooks and thousands of companies that venture capital will invest in that will fail.

DEPENDING ON WHO YOU ASK . . .

If you ask Silicon Valley venture capitalist Marc Andreessen, a co-founder of Andreessen Horowitz, he believes that Silicon Valley is in year 12 of a 25-year boom. Of course, Andreessen Horowitz is one of the few venture capital firms that is yielding strong growth. In 2012, it returned its debut fund $300 million that was raised in early 2009, two times over, thanks to wise investments in Skype, Instagram, Fusion-io and Nicera that had auspicious acquisitions in companies such as eBay, Facebook, and VMWare.

Cambridge Associates, an independent research firm in Boston that specializes in investment advice, disputes the Kauffman Foundation findings and states as much in the title of its 2012 report, "U.S. Private Equity and Venture Capital Funds Handily Outperformed Public Equities in 2011 According to Cambridge Associates Benchmarks." The report finds that both private equity and venture capital generated double-digit returns for 2011, placing these performances well ahead of its public equity counterparts in what was a stormy year for the markets and the broader economy.[23]

According to the report:

> 2011 delivered a near record high in capital calls [a legal right that allows venture funds to demand a transfer of promised funds from investors] from LPs at more than $77 billion, but more importantly, a 25-year high in distributions to LPs, at nearly $94 billion; both are notable," said Andrea Auerbach, managing director and head of private investment research at Cambridge Associates. "The capital calls, particularly from the 2006 and 2007 vintage years, combined with a more moderate fundraising environment in recent years, should help to whittle away at the capital overhang of dollars committed but not yet invested. The record distributions likely reflect the long-awaited completion of realization events delayed largely due to the recession and buoyed by active M&A and IPO environments in 2011.[24]

Wherever returns truly lie, venture capital and liquidity in the marketplace will be impacted by economic conditions just like the public markets. Tim Draper calls it the Draper Wave, the highs and lows of venture capital since the mid-twentieth century, which mimic the natural slumps of the economy, and a resurgence of venture capital that follows in the wake of liquidity in the marketplace.

A RESURGENCE OF ANGELS

Immense prosperity in Silicon Valley has laid the groundwork for trickle-down wealth. As a result, budding entrepreneurs don't always have to immediately raise professional money. Local billionaires and million-aires often act as seed and angel investors. And there is no more prolific angel investor than Ron Conway.

In 1979, Conway, at the age of 28, went to work as the vice president of sales at Altos Computer Systems, a pioneering manufacturer of micro-computers. The company went public in 1982, and Conway became a multimillionaire. A few years later, he left, but when the company started falling apart, David G. Jackson, the founder and chairman, convinced him to return as CEO. In 1990, Conway sold Altos to Acer, a Taiwanese computer manufacturer, and consolidated his personal fortune such that he would never have to work again. Then, in 1994, Conway discovered a passion for investing in internet companies and tapped young, newly minted internet millionaires from Amazon, eBay, and Yahoo!, as well as high-profile individuals in sports, entertainment, and politics, to join his investment fund. Soon the roster included luminaries like Shaquille O'Neal, Ashton Kutcher, Arnold Schwarzenegger, and Henry Kissinger. Their collective star power proved very effective in harnessing the next generation of entrepreneurial talent.

SV Angel, Conway's current investment fund, has made more than 300 investments of sums between $50,000 and $200,000, mostly to startups still in their embryonic stages. Some of his biggest wins along the way include Groupon, Twitter, Zappos, Mint, AdMob, Square, Dropbox, and Airbnb, all of which have generated hefty revenues. Sure, there have been plenty of losing bets as well, but overall Con-way approaches his investments differently than the world of venture capital. According to a February 10, 2012, *CNN Money* article titled, "Ron Conway Is a Silicon Valley Startup's Best Friend," he doesn't sit on any of the boards of the companies he invests in, but rather pro-vides his entrepreneurs with access to a "who's who" of the tech world, as well as national media and traditional business figures. Conway's "SV Angel partner list," an 18-page document of more than 1,300 names, includes people like Larry Page, Sergey Brin, and top executives from Saleforce.com and Twitter, as well as top executives from the Washington Post Company, the Oprah Winfrey Network, and Wells Fargo. Being a part of Conway's world is a competitive advantage in itself—they call it the "Rontourage."[25]

THE GAME CHANGER—CROWDFUNDING

Crowdfunding web sites, such as Kickstarter and Indiegogo, may just change the whole game for entrepreneurs. Crowdfunding works by offering anyone the opportunity to post an entrepreneurial project they are working on, such as a citizen journalism website, a new tech gadget that works with the iPhone, or a documentary, and benefit from the collective willingness of others to financially support that project. The crowdfunding "investors" don't make money off the entrepreneur; rather, they back projects in exchange for some other tangible reward or opportunity, such as a producer credit on a film, lunch with the founder of the company, or original sketches from an art book.

Launched in 2008, Kickstarter has helped tens of thousands of entrepreneurs raise hundreds of millions of dollars by hosting projects and funding campaigns (all vetted and approved in advance) that can last up to 60 days with no charge to the entrepreneur. If the project meets its stated fundraising goal, Kickstarter receives 5 percent of the funds. Kickstarter has worked remarkably well for some, though so far the biggest winners most often come from established companies or are already high-profile artists with a following. For example, in March 2012, a video game project entitled "Double Fine Adventures" pulled in over $3.3 million, but the company's founder,[26] Tim Schafer, had an established fan club from prior video games that his company created. As of the writing of this book, Kickstarter's record-holder, with over $10 million raised, is the Pebble, a customizable watch that connects with smartphones to alert users of incoming calls, emails, and messages using Bluetooth technology. Kickstarter's revenue from this project was $500,000. [27]

The internet has proven to be an incredibly effective fundraising platform for those entrepreneurs who may not have geographic access to capital or need more time to work out kinks before pitching a project to outside investors. These sites also provide an entrepreneur with an opportunity to market and promote their product for free and, in the process, solicit feedback for how to improve it. Crowdfunding has grown so quickly that experts predict it will be a multibillion-dollar industry in five years. This should not negatively impact the venture capital community; rather, it should enhance it, as a sort of first-pass vetting to separate the winners from the losers—a home-run strategy for all.

9 THE SERVICES

GP Technology Partners, Palo Alto, California

In the 1970s and 1980s, Regis McKenna was the public relations force behind companies like Apple and Intel. One of McKenna's most notable accomplishments was turning into mainstream news the story about how Apple was founded in a garage in Los Altos by two young entrepreneurs. Because of his inventive storytelling strategies, McKenna was named one of the "100 People Who Made Silicon Valley What It Is Today" by the *San Jose Mercury News*.[1]

The first female entrepreneur who became a colossal success in Silicon Valley was Sandy Kurtzig. In 1971, she was 25 years old, married, working, and contemplating a career move to give her the freedom to work from home when she eventually had children. In 1972, with $2,000 from her savings account, Kurtzig started ASK Computer Systems, a software company that offered manufacturing and accounting management to medium-size and large firms, and time share options of the software for smaller firms that could not afford the software's six-figure price tag. Ironically named "Manman," the software helped manufacturing companies plan materials purchases, production schedules, and other administrative functions on a scale that was only previously possible on large, costly mainframe computers. ASK quickly dominated the market for manufacturing software and became one of the fastest-growing software companies in the United States.[2] In 1981, Kurtzig became the first woman ever to take a company public.[3] With ASK's valuation at $400 million, Kurtzig amassed a personal net worth of $67 million. Kurtzig's story was certainly an anomaly, especially in 1981, but she blazed the trail for other entrepreneurs to follow.[4]

Kurtzig once told McKenna, "If I need business advice, I call my friend Larry Sonsini. If I need technology or operations help, I call [then-president of Intel] Andy Grove, and if I need marketing advice, I call you."[5] Every entrepreneurial company in Silicon Valley owes their successes to others: advisors, investors, friends (and friends of friends), and service providers. "As the number of firms [service providers] increases, and the borders expand, the insider network culture of shared ideas and support remains critical for regional growth," said Regis McKenna.[6]

In any other sphere of influence outside of Silicon Valley, a "service provider" is often thought of as a necessary evil when conducting business; businesses need expensive services such as law or accounting firms who bill by the hour. In Silicon Valley, however, most of the service providers will defer fees, find a compatible fee structure based on the amount of capital raised, or forgo any fees for a small stake in the company. The Silicon Valley service provider becomes the cheerleading squad of an entrepreneur's ecosystem.

By design, Silicon Valley's service providers are mostly situated along the perimeters of Stanford University, existing as micro-clusters of relationships among themselves. On one side of Stanford you'll find the prominent law firms of Palo Alto, recognizable headhunters, investment banks on Page Mill Road, and innovative commercial banks on Hanover

Street, University Avenue, and other surrounding streets. On the other side of Stanford is Menlo Park, where the heft of the venture capital community has set up shop on Sand Hill Road. The service providers are accessible and interconnected, characteristics that Silicon Valley is known for.

Perhaps the most important relationship for the Silicon Valley entrepreneur begins with one's lawyer, because Silicon Valley lawyers are often the keys to entry into the ecosystem.

THE LAW FIRM

Name: Wilson Sonsini Goodrich & Rosati
Headquarters: Palo Alto
Street: Page Mill Road

In 1966, John Wilson, founder of the tech powerhouse law firm Wilson Sonsini Goodrich & Rosati, took a promising young lawyer, recent law school graduate Larry Sonsini, under his wing and taught him that they could build a firm on the unprecedented business model shaping up in what would come to be known as Silicon Valley. Wilson believed that, since they were in Gold Rush country where "new thinking" was part of the fabric, the law firm did not have to be cast in the image of those typical on the East Coast—or even those in San Francisco, for that matter. In the early days of Wilson Sonsini Goodrich & Rosati (WSGR), Larry Sonsini rubbed shoulders with people like Eugene Kleiner and Tom Perkins of the famed venture capital firm Kleiner Perkins, Bob Noyce, Wilf Corrigan, Pitch Johnson, and Arthur Rock, among others. They'd discuss among themselves what Silicon Valley could become and vowed to make it a place that would foster the creation of technology companies.

WSGR became an icon in Silicon Valley. They concentrated on cultivating relationships with the area's young technology entrepreneurs, providing them with both legal services and strategic business advice tailored to their needs. WSGR was the first firm in the world to take equity in the companies they were representing, but they set strict parameters so that there would not be any conflict of interest. This is a concept that, even decades later, remains foreign among the traditional

East Coast law firms. The firm's partners settled on providing a capital investment in exchange for up to 1 percent in any one company, and no individual partner or associate was allowed to privately invest. For that small percentage, the firm offered a proportional investment in a startup matched to seed capital. During their investment meetings, if WSGR partners learned about a promising concept, the firm would work to protect the idea first, and then network to get the entrepreneur in the door—as Sonsini is quick to note, "You never know who is going to be the next Google."[7] WSGR even offers a fixed-fee startup package for entrepreneurs, which also sets the firm apart from others, as up-front legal expenses for young companies can compromise other key areas, such as R&D, production costs, and marketing.

Looking back over the decades, Larry is proud of the vision they were able to realize and the firm's influence on Silicon Valley. While he was able to work with luminaries like Steve Jobs, Larry Page, Sergey Brin, and Elon Musk, to name a few, he and the firm are enormously gratified by the thousands of less-famous startup companies they helped get off the ground. Sonsini likes to recount how he took Coherent Radiation public in 1967, when he was just a year out of law school. Yet perhaps his favorite anecdote over the years stems from when he was helping Larry Page and Sergey Brin prepare the prospectus for Google's IPO, and the co-founders did something that had never been done before. Page and Brin were insistent on making it clear that Google was going to invest in many projects subsequent to its IPO and that many of them were likely going to fail. "So right there in the prospectus, Google admitted to many possible failures, but also encouraged investors to be there for the long haul and expect the company to take educated risks. I had not seen that before,"[8] Sonsini says with a wry laugh. But it's clear that, like Google, Sonsini believes that risk—and even failure—is a part of the human experience, and one that has helped fuel the growth of Silicon Valley.

THE BANK

Name: Silicon Valley Bank
Headquarters: San Jose
Street: Tasman Drive

Silicon Valley Bank emerged in 1983 at a time when startups were not well understood by the banking community. Bill Biggerstaff, Robert Medearis, and CEO Roger Smith launched the bank with 100 initial investors and two ideas in mind: supporting technical entrepreneurship and providing "outside-the-box" commercial banking services that young companies so desperately needed. Silicon Valley Bank instilled the notion that its employees speak the language of their entrepreneurial clients.[9]

The ties established between entrepreneurs and Silicon Valley Bank were unlike any other bank's relationships with newly established enterprises in the corporate lending market. The bank's executives understood that startup companies do not have revenue immediately, and learned to tailor its loans accordingly. By knowing its clients, their investors, and the business models of their companies, Silicon Valley Bank became adept at managing risk, and that afforded flexibility for the clients where traditional banks were more rigid.

In time, Silicon Valley Bank took on the role of helping to create Silicon Valley–styled "economic ecosystems" around the United States and the globe. It opened offices nationwide, and its bankers started traveling to Asia and Europe in the 1990s, sponsoring international missions to India, Israel, and China, and eventually bringing delegations of Silicon Valley venture capitalists abroad. These missions turned out to be some of Silicon Valley Bank's first steps to formalizing international relationships and catalysts to offer financial services in international regions. Today, Silicon Valley Bank has a full branch in London, is co-owner of a joint venture bank in China, and operates a Global Gateway group that helps U.S. companies do business overseas and helps foreign companies move more easily to the United States.

Silicon Valley Bank increases its clients' probability of success by helping them solve problems. When a client needs to find a way to make the next payroll, the bank will work with them. If an entrepreneur needs an introduction to investors or partners, bankers invite the heads of the company to pitch events or provide personal references, giving their clients great exposure. Large corporations looking for new innovative technologies to acquire or in which to invest can also make relevant connections through Silicon Valley Bank.[10]

Its focus and dedication to its clients has paid off. What started as a discussion at a poker game nearly 30 years ago has grown to an entity with more than $20 billion in assets and more than 1,500 employees globally.[11] It now provides commercial, international and private banking throughout 34 locations worldwide. *Forbes* ranks Silicon Valley Bank among America's Best Banks and *Fortune* recognizes the company as one of the best places to work in America.[12]

THE ACCOUNTING FIRM

Name: KPMG
Location: Santa Clara
Street: Freedom Circle

Everyone knows KPMG as one of the world's leading accounting and auditing firms, but its Silicon Valley office has some unique characteristics. First, it is home to KPMG's global technology practice. "KPMG's Silicon Valley office is part of this unique ecosystem and we constantly monitor market developments to continue to provide services and programs that support existing and emerging technology leaders," says Gary Matuszak, Global Chair, Technology, Media and Telecommunications, KPMG.[13] The practice meets the needs of Silicon Valley startups as well as larger technology companies driving disruptive technologies to market, but sets fees that match each client in the stage they are in, so younger startups have a chance to get off the ground. KPMG's team of technology professionals is a fast-moving, globally connected unit that can provide insight on issues unique to technology companies.

Additionally, as the cycle of technology innovation is speeding up and unfolding in other parts of the world, KPMG's Silicon Valley office recognizes the need to connect Silicon Valley with other hubs. "We have launched the KPMG Global Technology Innovation Center that is designed to identify and assess the business impact of disruptive technologies," says Patricia Rios, Global Director, KPMG Technology Innovation Center.[14] As it develops, the center will network leading technology intellectuals, including entrepreneurs, Fortune 500 technology executives, venture capitalists, and KPMG professionals, to draw on their collective insight about disruptive technologies. The center is headquartered in Silicon Valley, with plans for offshoots in other cities including Cambridge, Massachusetts, and Bangalore, India. The global network is expected to include China, Israel, Japan, Korea, Singapore, Russia, Canada, and the United Kingdom, among other countries.

THE INVESTMENT BANK

Name: GrowthPoint Technology Partners
Location: Palo Alto
Street: Page Mill Road

Composed of former engineers, technologists, and entrepreneurs, GrowthPoint Technology Partners is not your typical investment bank. The firm, which specializes in the technology sectors of consumer internet, mobile, hardware, enterprise, and cloud, has the depth of knowledge in the underlying science and innovation that will power the next generation of apps, services, and technology platforms. Based upon their decades of experience dealing with corporate development executives, they can anticipate how different technology sectors will evolve and what types of companies are a good fit for acquisition.[15]

The firm's location allows them to gauge the heartbeat of Silicon Valley. "The majority of leading global technology companies are headquartered at GrowthPoint's doorstep in Silicon Valley and the team has completed hundreds of transactions with them. We are believers in cluster theory—that there is a positive feedback loop between smart entrepreneurs, creativity, world-class investors, and the whole ecosystem almost self-perpetuating itself," says managing director Markus Salolainen.[16]

Recently, GrowthPoint opened new offices in London and Tel Aviv, which gives them an on-the-ground presence in other key technology centers. "We have always viewed technology as a global business and Europe in particular has proven to be a very important market for us given the breadth of innovation and entrepreneurship we see in the major technology centers. Historically, a significant percentage of our clients have had European origins. Having people on the ground with the same passion for technology and know-how to make the right combinations come together is what matters," says GrowthPoint co-founder and managing director John Cromwell.[17]

Adds managing director, Laurie Yoler:

> The thing that makes me love what I do most is seeing an entrepreneurial team that we have had the pleasure to work with thriving, scaling, and growing in a new larger platform. We work with our clients for many months—sometimes years—and get a chance to explore many potential strategic opportunities for strategic partnerships to accelerate their growth. Sometimes that means taking in a new investment, and sometimes that means the company gets offers to be acquired. The process can be stressful and the hours can be long, so it is important that we work together as a team to ensure their success. After a successful transaction, when I talk to clients months or years later, I love when I hear their excitement with the team, product, and technology thriving and surpassing their growth expectations with the help of a new strategic partner that we helped them find. That is the greatest reward of all.[18]

THE DESIGN CONSULTANT

Name: IDEO
Location: Palo Alto
Street: Forest Avenue

The company that would become IDEO (pronounced "eye-dee-oh") has roots in Silicon Valley dating back to 1978. As mentioned earlier, IDEO was co-founded by David Kelley, a product designer and engineer trained at Stanford and Carnegie Mellon. IDEO began in Palo Alto as many startups do: in a small office among friends.[19] A year later, Kelley met Steve Jobs and began designing the first commercial mouse for Apple's new computer, Lisa. The creation of this early icon of the digital era, along with inventions such as the deodorant stick, the standup toothpaste dispenser, and other grocery store items, would prove to set the tone for IDEO's innovative culture: collaborative, iterative, hands-on, human-centered, forward-thinking. Over the following three decades, IDEO designers found more and more applications for this approach to problem solving, often called "design thinking" or "human-centered design."

In Silicon Valley, many CEOs and emerging tech leaders have experienced IDEO's human-centered design approach firsthand. It is defined by IDEO designers as "a deeply human process that taps into abilities we all have but get overlooked by more conventional problem-solving practices. It relies on our ability to be intuitive, to recognize patterns, to construct ideas that are emotionally meaningful as well as functional, and to express ourselves through means beyond words or symbols. Nobody wants to run an organization on feeling, intuition, and inspiration, but an over-reliance on the rational and the analytical can be just as risky."[20]

IDEO continues to push the boundaries of design. It recently launched OpenIDEO.com, an online platform for collaboration where anyone can sign up to participate in design challenges for social good. The OpenIDEO community, which now includes more than 35,000 members, has taken on design problems such as how to restore vibrancy in cities, improve health in low-income communities, and better connect food production and consumption. In addition to new platforms like OpenIDEO, the firm continues to grow its global capabilities around digital design, organizational design, and the tackling of deep, systemic challenges.[21] The award-winning firm is ranked number 16 on *Fortune*'s 2012 list of the "100 Most-Favored Employers" by MBA students, and is consistently listed as one of the most innovative companies in the world.[22]

THE INCUBATOR

Name: Y Combinator
Location: Mountain View
Street: Pioneer Way

In Silicon Valley, incubators are a fantastic way through which entrepreneurs can quickly enter the ecosystem, whether they have an idea or not. By definition, incubators are "programs designed to support the successful development of entrepreneurial companies through an array of business support resources and services, developed and orchestrated by incubator management and offered both in the incubator and through its network of contacts."[23] Often referred to as the "alternative MBA," incubators provide budding entrepreneurs a soup-to-nuts menu of everything an entrepreneur would need—mentorship, advice, introductions, trainings, pitch sessions, and, in many cases, seed funding. By all accounts, the top Silicon Valley incubator is Y Combinator, who, in 2005, sought to develop a new model of startup funding, which is unusual for a startup to do. Twice a year, Y Combinator invests no more than $20,000 into a large number of startups, has them move to Silicon Valley for three months if they are not local, and works endlessly to get each company in the best shape possible to pitch to investors during "Demo Day," where entrepreneurs showcase their companies.[24] "The best way to find out if a product will work is to [quickly] launch it," says Y Combinator co-founder Paul Graham."[25]

Y Combinator has also developed a reputation for incubating stellar companies among some of Silicon Valley's most leading investors. Sequoia Capital invested in Y Combinator funds, and Andreessen Horowitz, Yuri Milner, and Ron Conway have guaranteed $150,000 in funding to each startup that Y Combinator backs.[26]

After a company launches, the business relationship continues as Y Combinator works with each company on corporate development activities such as strategic partnerships and even acquisitions. Here's the remarkable part. As of September 2012, there are 200 companies with whom Y Combinator has worked to raise venture capital or become acquired that total $8 billion in value.[27] While the data may be a bit skewed by greater successes such as Airbnb and Dropbox, it is still a remarkable figure. Some of Y Combinator's largest acquisitions have included 280, Heroku, OMGPOP, Loopt, Cloudkick, Zecter, Wufoo, and Reddit. Irrespective of its high valuation, what may be the greatest value a startup gains from being part of Y Combinator is the access to its network, which is made of hundreds of companies who are now willing to support their entrepreneurial colleagues.

THE HEADHUNTER

Name: Egon Zehnder International
Location: Palo Alto
Street: Page Mill Road

For over two decades, Egon Zehnder International has helped build out many leading companies in Silicon Valley by vetting top talent for executive and board searches.

In particular, Martha Josephson, a partner in Egon Zehnder's Global Head New Media Practice, is making tremendous inroads in placing more Silicon Valley women on corporate boards, specifically Google women. Over the last 15 years, Josephson has placed Google executives, past and present, such as Shona Brown, Francoise Brougher, and Nikesh Arora, on the boards of PepsiCo, Sodexo, and Colgate. She says, "There is a process that occurs at Google that makes these executives board ready. They have seen something scale very dramatically, and they have in their minds all the factors that allow that scaling to occur, and this is what a lot of other companies want to tap into."[28]

Josephson and her colleagues are seeing a new trend in corporate board recruitment. Many Fortune 500 companies that are consumer-oriented are looking for younger Silicon Valley board candidates who have come out of technology and social networking companies. For example, Google or Facebook executives bring a lot of insight and experience but don't necessarily represent the traditional profile of a corporate board member. Josephson feels this is especially important in Silicon Valley where, as new business models are being introduced, there may not be that "obvious benchmark" candidate.

Egon Zehnder doesn't solely provide a service to the executives of Silicon Valley, but consultants participate in supporting a vibrant talent market by facilitating connections and knowledge. "We all learn it here, and those shared experiences bring us closer as colleagues. It's been interesting as many of our clients seek to plug into the Silicon Valley ecosystem of talent—not just for the skills but also for the network connectivity," says Lindsay Trout, a consultant at Egon Zehnder.[29]

10 THE MEETING PLACES

Buck's Restaurant, Woodside, California

Woodside, California, is a small town in Silicon Valley within the jurisdiction of San Mateo County. It still looks like a pre–Gold Rush Western town, with a blink-and-you-miss-it main street. With a population just over 5,200,[1] it is home to some of the country's top billionaires, including Larry Ellison, John Doerr, Gordon Moore, Thomas Siebel, Ken Fisher, Scott Cook, and Jim Breyer. Woodside even has some movie and television credits under its belt: scenes from *Bicentennial Man, The Wedding Planner, The Game, Lolita, George of the Jungle, Heaven Can Wait, Harold and Maude,* and *Rent* were all shot there. The estate home at Filoli Gardens stood as the backdrop of the Carrington mansion on *Dynasty.*

On Woodside Road, right in the center of town, is an eclectic restaurant called Buck's.[2] Its mantra is "Real Food for the Human Race," and it's one of the gaudiest establishments imaginable, filled with knick-knacks that have absolutely no continuity or theme. When you walk through the wooden front door, you are overpowered by the towering eight-foot-tall, green aluminum replica of the Statue of Liberty. Instead of her proudly raised neoclassical torch, this Mexican-made Lady Liberty bears a hot fudge sundae. There is an invasion of flying machines overhead, and dizzying displays of notorious deals done on paper napkins, license plates, magazine covers, and tchotchkes that adorn every inch of wall space. The owner of Buck's, Jamis MacNiven, has an affinity for "stuff," and this well-known love gives people license to continue to supply him, hoping that their contributions will become part the legendary décor. In true MacNiven style, Jamis named the restaurant Buck's after the town drunk, Leo Buckstaber.

Buck's Restaurant is a world-renowned institution. MacNiven claims that the most important deals in internet history, such as the launching of Netscape and Hotmail, happened there. On any given day, you can catch some of the most recognizable faces in venture capital and entrepreneurship, such as Larry Ellison and Elon Musk, eating a meal. Buck's also has been frequented by politicians such as Israel's former prime minister and current president Shimon Peres and then-French President Nicolas Sarkozy. Newt Gingrich and his then-staffer (and future wife), Callista, were at Buck's the day he publicly announced the separation from his previous wife, Marianne. Buck's has become so famous that delegations from around the world will stop for lunch and claim to MacNiven that they represent their country's version of Silicon Valley. A restaurant in Hong Kong, called Jamis, even tried to replicate Buck's model, hoping to attract the local venture capital community.

Buck's rose to prominence in the mid-1990s during the dot-com boom, when a handful of billionaires moved into the tiny town. Buck's is neutral territory for the entrepreneur and funder alike, and good for business. So much happens at Buck's that MacNiven put in extra power outlets for laptops or cell phone chargers, just so entrepreneurs could sit for as long as they needed. There was even a time when a patron was so engrossed in his work that he blew past closing time, so MacNiven just let him sit there and continue to work, and opted to forgo turning on the alarm that night.

Buck's is also a famous power breakfast spot (Silicon Valley is truly a breakfast town—everyone starts early). On February 14, 1992, a small blurb in *Info Week* mentioned that Bob Metcalfe, founder of 3Com, was having breakfast there. *The Economist* wrote about powerhouse venture capitalist John Doerr, who had breakfast at Buck's in 1993, and it was this mention that put Buck's on the map.[3] By 1994, three camera crews had swung by Buck's to see what all the fuss was about, and by 1995, MacNiven had hosted over 100 media outlets.

THE PLACES WHERE SILICON VALLEY'S LEADERS AND RISING STARS CONGREGATE

Stroll along Woodside Road, Santa Cruz Avenue in Menlo Park, University Avenue in Palo Alto, Main Street in Los Altos, or Castro Street in Mountain View, and at some point you're likely to run into someone like Mark Zuckerberg, Larry Page, Sergey Brin, or a high-profile venture capitalist such as Marc Andreessen. The distinguishing nuance about Silicon Valley leaders is that you have direct access mostly due to the casual manner in which business is conducted—the hierarchy and the entourages just don't exist in Silicon Valley. And the twist of fate is that often, many of these leaders will be just as engaging and interested in you as you are in them, probably one of the central reasons for Silicon Valley's extraordinary success. There are a handful of organizations, restaurants, and coffeehouses where, on any given day, the probability is higher that a familiar face will make an appearance.

The Churchill Club

Named after Winston Churchill, the Churchill Club was established with one basic premise: "Allow important people to say important things."[4] The goal of the Churchill Club is to provide a place where individuals can start meaningful conversations that spark ideas. The club hosts 30 to 40 events a year where notable leaders from Silicon Valley and around the world share the stage and discuss hot topic issues going on in the world, uncensored and unscripted.

Founded by Rich Karlgaard, publisher of *Forbes* magazine, and Tony Perkins, the former chairman and editor-in-chief of Red Herring Communications, the club held its first meeting on November 12, 1985, with Robert Noyce as the inaugural speaker. From then on, the Churchill Club became Silicon Valley's largest business and technology forum with 7,500 members, attracting the world's most acclaimed speakers.[5]

Karen Tucker, chief executive officer of the Churchill Club, believes that a culture of freely exchanging ideas is a key ingredient in Silicon Valley's secret sauce. "People who are obsessed with innovation in Silicon Valley want to discuss their thoughts with like-minded others. Visitors from other places are sometimes shocked at the openness here. Also, you never know who will show up at the gatherings. Larry Ellison [CEO of Oracle] and Ed Zander [former CEO of Motorola] spoke at the Churchill Club in September 2009. During audience Q&A, Scott McNealy [former CEO of Sun Microsystems, a company Oracle was in the process of acquiring] paid a surprise visit to ask a few humorous questions from the back of the room. The audience was delighted by their impromptu exchange."[6]

Tucker shared one of her favorite moments at Churchill Club: "When then–Google CEO Eric Schmidt and famed filmmaker James Cameron spoke at an October 2010 event, their wide-ranging conversation revealed a common interest in technology, maps, and deep-ocean exploration. Schmidt observed, '97 percent of the ocean is not mapped in detail.' Cameron quipped, 'This must drive you crazy.' Schmidt replied, 'It does!' Fun exchange aside, it was fascinating to see how Silicon Valley and Hollywood interests are converging."[7]

TechNet

While Silicon Valley doesn't make a habit of putting tremendous energy into Washington's battles, TechNet has been incredibly effective at galvanizing the technology community in Silicon Valley and around the world on issues that impact the growth of the technology and innovation economy. Founded in 1997, Kleiner Perkins Caufield & Byers venture capitalist John Doerr initially brought together a group of leading tech CEOs to lobby the executive and legislative branches of the federal government. Some of the leading founding companies included Cisco,

Apple, and Google, and TechNet later expanded outside of Silicon Valley to include companies such as Dell and Microsoft.

TechNet works on both sides of the political aisle to promote focused public policies that strengthen innovation as well as create private sector initiatives that help ignite U.S. competitiveness and economic leadership. It accomplishes this through financially supporting political candidates who are strong on technology and innovation issues and hold industry-based initiatives that educate thought leaders and the public about technology policy issues. Today, TechNet represents over 100 member companies, universities, and service providers that collectively have over 2 million employees and approximately $800 billion in revenue.[8]

AlwaysOn

AlwaysOn (AO) is the leading event and media brand that networks Silicon Valley globally. It is the place to go for anyone who is interested in getting insights into the Silicon Valley innovation and venture capital world. Tony Perkins, founder and editor of AlwaysOn, explains that "Silicon Valley no longer describes a geographical area, but is this global ecosystem of entrepreneurial-minded people as the Global Silicon Valley." AO offers conferences on need-to-know topics and brings together specific industries with venture capital through its traveling summits, which include the Silicon Valley Innovation Summit (technology), OnMedia (media), OnHollywood (entertainment), and GoingGreen (clean tech).

Sequoia Capital's Michael Moritz once commented, "The currency of Silicon Valley is information—and the sooner you have it, the more valuable it is!"[9] AlwaysOn provides an editorial component that bridges some of the most influential executives and venture capitalists around the country to weigh in on major topics in addition to top trends in the digital media, on-demand computing, and greentech industries. Bloggers include Mark Cuban, chairman of HDNet and owner of the Dallas Mavericks; Fred Wilson, partner at Union Square Ventures; Marc Benioff, founder and CEO of Salesforce.com; Steve Blank, serial entrepreneur and professor at Stanford University; Joe Schoendorf, partner at Accel Partners; Paul Deninger, vice chairman of Jefferies & Company; and William Sahlman, venture capital professor at Harvard Business School. "AlwaysOn is a major driver of the very revolution it blogs about every day—the open-media revolution—a place where readers can stand up and have their say, and the most innovative and forward-thinking ideas have the best chance of rising to the top.

Alley to the Valley®

On November 12, 2010, 25 women in entrepreneurship, venture capital, and private equity from the East Coast gathered in the ballroom of the Rosewood Hotel to meet with 25 of their Silicon Valley counterparts to figure out how to bridge the distance between them. The heavy hitters at that initial summit included venture capitalists Theresia Gouw Ranzetta of Accel Partners, Maria Cirino of .406 Ventures, Amanda Reed of Palomar Ventures, and Nanon de Gaspe Beaubien-Mattrick of Beehive Ventures; private equity funders such as Cia Buckley of Dune Partners; and executives such as Barbara Byrne of Barclays Bank, Karen White of Syncplicity, Janet Hanson of 85 Broads, and Linda Law, a real estate developer, and keynote addresses by Sheryl Sandberg of Facebook and Somaly Mam of Somaly Mam Foundation, a human rights organization. The summit was so popular that it expanded to multiple events a year, building a vast community.

Alley to the Valley® networks women around the world, through its summits and its online community that focuses solely on deal flow and dealmaking. The combination of the intimate setting and the high ROI dealmaking process espoused at the meetings was once described by one attendee as "summer camp for smart women."[10] The summits take place in both Silicon Valley and New York, and pop up in other U.S. and global cities depending on innovation trends. The goal of Alley to the Valley® summits is for participants to bring three specific "asks" and "offers" topics to the table, including: investment, strategic partnerships, exit strategies, corporate board seats, and connections. The highly accomplished attendees either directly respond to these requests or leverage their very powerful networks to bring each attendee's level of business to the next level.

Women 2.0

Women 2.0 began as a side project for Angie Chang and Shaherose Charania in 2006, after they realized there was a lack of women in the room at many networking business and tech events. Over the years, what began as panels, workshops, and an annual conference has grown into a digital media site and social platform for current and aspiring female founders of technology ventures.

What Women 2.0 has really become known for is its PITCH Conference, which brings together 1,000 women—from product managers and founders of early-stage startups to executives of late-stage tech companies—who have dedicated their professional lives to shaping the future of technology. The conference is an opportunity for attendees to learn from the product innovation leaders who built Flickr, Facebook, Zipcar, TaskRabbit, LARK, and more. Many of the speakers and panelists are from female-led companies, most of whom have secured millions of dollars in venture funding.

Women 2.0 grew into Women 2.0 Labs, offering a pre-incubator five-week program for engineers, designers, business developers, and marketing professionals to brainstorm high-growth technology ventures. Both men and women are encouraged to attend and bring their ideas, passions, and startup questions for industry leaders to answer. At Women 2.0 Labs, entrepreneurs receive hands-on experience with potential team members and have the opportunity to moonlight in teams at the co-working space to demo their latest prototype.[11]

The Indus Entrepreneur, Silicon Valley (TiE)

The year 2012 marked the twentieth anniversary of TiEcon Silicon Valley, an event hosting an audience of entrepreneurs, investors (angels and venture capitalists), seasoned corporate executives, and professionals for the purposes of networking and deal flow. Recent conferences have featured some of the most respected speakers in the industry, including Larry Page (CEO, Google), Steve Ballmer (CEO, Microsoft), Tony Hsieh (CEO, Zappos), Ted Turner (philanthropist, businessman), Eric Schmidt (chairman, Google), Larry Ellison (CEO, Oracle), Narayana Murthy (co-founder, Infosys), Peter Thiel (venture capitalist), Dr. Irwin Jacobs (co-founder and former chairman, Qualcomm), and Aneesh Chopra (first Federal CTO).

Ben Davidson, the VP of business development at OEM Group, IRON Systems, Inc., has attended these events for eight years. Although TiEcon is Davidson's favorite event, he attends at least one conference per month, networking with successful entrepreneurs and TiE charter members, high-profile entrepreneurs, and professionals. "There is no place on earth like TiE" due to the value of the conference, says Davidson.[12] It was at the TiEcon event "My Story: Inspiring Journey of an Entrepreneur" featuring Sheng Liang (CTO, Citrix) where Davidson met an enormous group of influential executives including a division head from Cisco, a senior director from HP, the CTO of Citrix, the general manager from Meru Networks, two Sand Hill Road venture capitalists, a senior vice president at Silicon Valley Bank, and three entrepreneurs with whom he discussed his latest venture, and received constructive feedback.

In celebration of TiEcon's twentieth anniversary, a new program for entrepreneurs was introduced: the TiE Youth Forum, which showcases youth entrepreneurs, guiding them to entrepreneurship as a career option. The high school and college students who are lucky enough to attend learn about life's lessons from world-famous entrepreneurs, and network with distinguished business professionals who often serve as mentors to the budding entrepreneurs. The mission of the TiE Youth Forum is to instill in youth that entrepreneurship is the leading driver of innovation and job creation, and inspire them to create companies rather than just exploring the safe route of a four-year degree and a 9-to-5 job.[13]

Hua Yuan Science and Technology Association (HYSTA)

In 1999, a group of Chinese entrepreneurs created HYSTA, hoping to bridge between Silicon Valley and China. Today, HYSTA has become an integral part of the Chinese business community in Silicon Valley, bringing together like-minded Chinese professionals through multiple events per month. Two of HYSTA's largest events include the Annual Conference and the invitation-only CEO Summit.

The HYSTA Annual Conference draws more than 2,000 participants to discuss trending topics such as China's influence on the global economy, specifically as it relates to activities such as intellectual property, trade, and innovation. Attendees are introduced to some of Silicon Valley's most influential Chinese business leaders from technology companies including VMware, Yahoo!, Cisco, Tencent, Salesforce; keynote speakers such as Harry Shum, corporate vice president of Microsoft; and investors and venture capitalists from notable firms such as DFJ Dragon, The Hina Group, GSR Venture, Walden International, and Keystone Ventures.

Every year a select group of highly qualified professionals are invited to the CEO Summit at an exclusive, tranquil location to exchange stories and discuss common topics including global business trends, opportunities, and issues concerning both China and the United States. Attendees often walk away from the summit having made many important business interactions. At the 2011 HYSTA Pebble Beach Summit, Jerry Yang, co-founder and former CEO of Yahoo!, and Jack Ma, chairman & CEO of Alibaba, were on their way to making a deal. After Ma returned to China, his discussion with Yang quickly accelerated into action. Yahoo soon invested $1 billion in Alibaba, which manages Yahoo!'s operations in China. HYSTA continues to play a key role in nurturing the relationships between Chinese and American business leaders throughout Silicon Valley and China.[14]

Other notable organizations that bridge Silicon Valley and Asia are: Chinese American Semiconductor Professional Association (CASPA), Silicon Valley Chinese Engineers Association (SCEA), and Silicon Valley Taiwanese American Industrial Technology Association, (TAITA).

Rosewood Hotel/Madera Restaurant

Location: Menlo Park
Road: Sand Hill Road

"Great things are done when man and mountains meet," William Blake, the American poet, said.

Walk into Menlo Park's Rosewood Hotel, and despite the humming of business deals from the world's most powerful venture capital firms that surround it, you'll feel an immediate zen-like calm. The resort is nestled into some of Silicon Valley's most spectacular landscape, with the Santa Cruz Mountains as the backdrop, fragrant gardens surrounding it, and affable staff who make everyone feel like a Silicon Valley mogul. Just west of Stanford University, the Rosewood becomes the central meeting place for anyone who is serious about doing business in a "see and be seen" style.

The Rosewood's renowned restaurant and lounge, Madera, has become known as the "VC watering hole." Almost every morning, at table 13, you'll find Harry Kellogg, vice chairman of Silicon Valley Bank, with his back to nature so he can see all of Silicon Valley's movers and shakers. Tech executive Vivek Ranadive and venture capitalist Tim Draper praise the hotel as a place to take clients from out of town and give them a taste of Silicon Valley. It has been named one of the "Best Business Bars in America" by *Entrepreneur* magazine, and Madera has been awarded a Michelin star.[15]

The restaurant's chefs use sustainably harvested seafood and meats from surrounding areas, in addition to locally grown produce from farming communities in Palo Alto. Executive chef Peter Rudolph taps into traditional methods of dining with cutting-edge cooking techniques performed in wood-burning stoves. Madera partners with seven local farms, from which an estimated 75 to 80 percent of their food comes directly from these farms. For the chefs and kitchen staff, the restaurant is not just a business, but also a chance to create delicious food with the freshest ingredients and an opportunity to give back to the community.

"I think one of the secrets of Madera is that we created an environment where Silicon Valley feels comfortable to come and conduct business in a casual manner. It's like anything; you get inspired by being around amazing people. I know who comes here, I know what they do. And when you know that something big is happening, it's pretty inspiring to be around the dealmakers. These are the people who are leading the current trends in the world right now, and that in itself is inspiring in a very human way," says chef Rudolph.[16]

The Village Pub

Location: Woodside
Street: Woodside Road

The amazing thing about the Village Pub is that it has become one of the area's finest restaurants, but due to its location, you will find people dressed in everything from couture to blue jeans—all perfectly acceptable.

And while high-profile deals take place here as well, people often come for the extraordinary creative food. The Village Pub takes its culinary philosophy one step further by establishing a unique relationship with SMIP Ranch—SMIP is an acronym for *sic manebimus in pace,* Latin for "thus we will remain in peace"—which produces pesticide, herbicide, and fertilizer-free produce solely for the Village Pub. Chef Mark Sullivan and his partner Tim Stannard put up seed money in 2002 to create SMIP Ranch Produce, in exchange for being able to use its produce.[17] The Village Pub has an exclusive relationship with SMIP, in which the ranch grows the vegetables to the chef's specifications. Now, the Village Pub no longer gets produce from SMIP Ranch for free, but pays for its vegetables as a customer.

The ranch, located in the hills above Woodside, provides approximately 80 percent of the Village Pub's produce. SMIP and the Village Pub's collaboration with the landowners and farmers allows them to demonstrate their allegiance to the global effort for earth stewardship and safe, sustainable food while providing guests with the freshest ingredients possible.

Executive chef Dmitry Elperin crafts the menu daily around a list of fresh-picked produce. "The farm comes to us. It's challenging and it gives me a chance to be creative. It's such a difference using an ingredient fresh from the ground. The taste is incomparable." says Elperin.[18] The restaurant's menu of contemporary American cuisine represents a vision from farm to table, producing food that is fresh and unique. Chef Sullivan supports this vision as he puts his creativity to use by getting his hands dirty each week at the ranch, hand-picking ingredients for the day's menu.

Dutch Goose

Location: Menlo Park
Street: Alameda de las Pulgas

The Dutch Goose opened its doors in 1966 and became a favored gathering place for venture capitalists, Stanford students, and even Little Leaguers. "You can come in at any given time, and see your buddies, everyone calling each other by their first name, it's that type of atmosphere that makes people feel like they are at home. It's the community and customers that makes the Goose what it is today, not necessarily the burgers or brews," says owner Greg Stern.[19]

Enter into this hole-in-the-wall burger joint littered with peanut shells and you may find Bill Campbell, the chairman of Intuit, or Chad Hurley, the co-founder of YouTube, brokering deals in the surrounding booths. It has a laid-back atmosphere where anyone can enjoy the burgers and the renowned smoked brisket sandwich. It is a favorite of the Stanford alumni crowd as well those who want to catch a football or basketball game on one of its seven plasma TVs.

For Stern, the Dutch Goose is a really special place. When he was five years old, he used to head over there with his dad after tee ball games for a burger and fries. He told his dad, "One day, I'm going to buy this place." On October 1, 2005, that dream of owning the Dutch Goose came true.[20]

Coupa Café

Location: Palo Alto
Street: Ramona Street

Nancy Coupa opened the first Coupa Café in 2004 off University Avenue in Palo Alto with her two children, Camelia and Jean Paul, after learning how to brew the perfect cup of Venezuelan coffee from her native country. It is the only restaurant in Silicon Valley where you can enjoy Venezuelan crafted dishes and single-estate Arabica coffee beans. Today, Coupa Café has four other locations on Stanford's campus, where her children graduated.

On any given day, you will find venture capitalists and entrepreneurs inspired by the deal-making interactions. "I've seen people hand out business cards while waiting in line at the registers, basically offering startups money," says Jean Paul.[21] And entrepreneurs go to Jean Paul. In early 2011, Coupa Café helped test the product Talkbin, a customer service tool for restaurants, and Jean Paul gave the founders feedback to create new features and enhancements. Venture capitalists respected Jean Paul's perspective, and contacted him to find out if the technology was really useful for restaurateurs. Later that year, just five months after its founding, Y Combinator's fund backed Talkbin, which was later acquired by Google for an undisclosed sum. To date, Jean Paul estimates that he's advised more than 40 startups, including Five Stars Card, Reference.me, Bling Nation, Bump Technologies, and RewardMeApp, all technology products in the restaurant or reward space.[22]

"It's a great place to see and be seen," says Jules Maltz, a venture capitalist at Institutional Venture Partners. "A table is so difficult to get. But people still flock there. Whenever I meet an early stage company selling to restaurants or small businesses, I always tell them the best place to demo it is Coupa because of all the VCs there."[23]

Chef Chu's

Location: Los Altos
Street: North San Antonio Road

In the week after her 2012 Wimbledon victory, Serena Williams played the Bank of the West tournament at Stanford and won. One of her first stops thereafter was Chef Chu's. Serena tweeted, "I'm at Chef Chu's restaurant in Palo Alto Ca. This place is insanely good! Thanks Chef! I love it!!!"

Chef Chu (the restaurant is actually in Los Altos, not Palo Alto as Williams tweeted) has a rock star following. Adorning the entry wall of the restaurant are photos of the chef and some of the most important political figures of the twenty-first century—Presidents George H. W. Bush and Mikhail Gorbachev, Prime Minister Margaret Thatcher, and Secretary of State George Shultz. Some of the biggest names in popular culture have also dined there, such as Justin Bieber and *Dancing with the Stars*'s Cheryl Burke. People such as Gordon Moore claim it is their favorite restaurant, and the late Steve Jobs made regular stops there. Since the restaurant's opening in 1970, it has been an institution, whether one is making a deal there or celebrating one.

Beyond serving consistently fantastic Chinese food, owner Chef Lawrence Chu is emblematic of the highly successful Silicon Valley immigrant entrepreneur. Raised in Taiwan, Chu first came to the states with an opportunity to design the Taiwan pavilion at the World's Fair in Seattle in 1963. He later moved his family to the Bay Area and worked at the restaurant Trader Vic's, making more money in one day than most people he knew back in Taiwan made in a month. "It made me realize how lucky I was to be able to try to make it in America," says Chu.[24]

When Chef Chu's first opened its doors in the location of a former laundromat, it was a fast food place with a menu of about 12 entrees and a kitchen consisting of about $5,000 worth of used equipment. While his customers raved about the food, they shared that they wanted something more of a sit-down, family-style restaurant. So Chu did what any Silicon Valley entrepreneur does: He pivoted. He abandoned his fast fast food food approach, and lived up to his customers' desires.

Over four decades later, you'll still find Lawrence Chu running around the kitchen, but you'll have to walk past the rows of people either waiting for takeout or dining in for one of its famed dishes. In true Silicon Valley fashion, Chu is open and nurturing, and shares his secrets in both recipe books and Tuesday-night cooking classes. He even hosts annual foodie adventures to China and Taiwan, exploring a different region each year.

11 THE LIFESTYLE

The Dish, Stanford University

Fern Mandelbaum, a venture capital partner at Monitor Ventures and an advisor to many startups, likes to walk the Dish several times a week, the 3.5-mile loop of daunting hills and beautiful views located in the Stanford foothills. A 150-foot satellite dish—built in 1966 by the Stanford Research Institute, but paid for by the United States Air Force—situated on top of a hill gives the area its name. The Dish originally monitored the chemical composition of the atmosphere, but later was used to communicate with satellites and spacecraft.

Mandelbaum often conducts business meetings during her hikes. She insists that taking a meeting out of the boardroom and onto the pavement is a really great way to get to know someone. "I can tell what an entrepreneur is like when they climb the first hill,"[1] says Mandelbaum. Metaphorically or otherwise, the initial hill that Mandelbaum refers to can be intimidating even for the most conditioned athletes. "Because you are changing the dynamics of how people are used to conducting business, entrepreneurs will open up about everything, from their family life or how they like to spend their time outside of work,"[2] says Mandelbaum. An entrepreneur's personal life and interests are something that Mandelbaum finds really critical in being able to evaluate whether this is the type of a person she wants to invest in. "I once had a potential board member show up in heels, not realizing that we were going to truly walk the Dish. I was very impressed, as she actually walked the entire Dish all dressed up," Mandelbaum reminisces. "I guess you can say that walking the Dish is my version of the golf course."[3]

Silicon Valley is about striving to do business in a more casual, balanced way, and while she acknowledges there is an appropriate time for formality, Mandelbaum particularly enjoys informal interaction. "I have coached my son's baseball team with other venture capitalists, and often set the groundwork for deal flow in the middle of an inning. I get business done whether I am in the office or not, and often more effectively outside of the office," she says.[4] While not everyone in Silicon Valley has a similar flexibility and mindset, Mandelbaum is emblematic of the lifestyle that very much shapes the region's quality of life. And because much of it is free, it is accessible to all.

Bill Davenhall, an expert in health and human services, comes to the conclusion that where you live impacts your health: "Throughout our lives we spend our time in numerous places, at work, home, outside, traveling, etc. But have we ever considered that our health is dependent upon more than the food we eat and our genetics?"[5] Research shows that a healthy diet and exercise will keep our hearts healthy and blood pressure down, but many people don't focus on their environment to dictate how healthy they are. Geographical information and geomedicine support the hypothesis that in order to maintain good health, we need to be aware of our environmental surroundings. "Many of the barriers to better health, like smoking, crime, and poor food choices, are not present in Silicon Valley. Here, we have ample and beautiful areas to exercise, safe areas to walk in, and the best organic food in the world. The natural beauty and the can-do spirit of the valley fill our souls so we don't have to find satisfaction through food alone. We are lucky to live in a place where we have a downhill advantage to better health," says Dr. John Morton, a bariatric surgeon at the Stanford School of Medicine.[6]

The Silicon Valley lifestyle is unique, and once newcomers experience it, most can't ever imagine going back to their former way of life. There are five factors that define the quality of life in Silicon Valley: weather, health and wellness, outdoor activity, farmers' markets, and sustainability.

WEATHER

The Forecast: Paradise

Silicon Valley lies inland and is surrounded on three sides by mountain ranges. The area, from San Jose in the south to Palo Alto in the north, has some of the most optimum weather in the world, with more than 300 sunny days a year. The average temperature in Silicon Valley ranges between 42 and 60 degrees Fahrenheit in January, and between 57 and 84 degrees in July. Temperature fluctuations between night and day can vary as little as 10 to 12 degrees, meaning that its climate does not experience huge temperature drops or rises like some other parts of California. The highest temperature ever recorded in San Jose was 114 degrees in June 1961; the lowest was 20 degrees Fahrenheit in December 1990.[7]

Because of the topography, the Peninsula is somewhat more sheltered from rain, giving it a semi-arid feel with a mean annual rainfall of 14.4 inches. Some other parts of the Bay Area can get about three times that amount, yet Silicon Valley is strangely devoid of high humidity.[8]

"I believe the wonderful weather we enjoy contributes to better health by promoting more outdoor fitness," says Morton. "We know more exercise leads to better cardiac health and less stress. Also, the famous 'can-do' attitude can be attributed in part to the days of sunshine—more sun, more fun and less depression."[9]

In comparison, drive a mere 30 minutes north to San Francisco, and experience a range of microclimates due to proximity of the mountainous terrain and the more harsh conditions off the Pacific Ocean and San Francisco Bay. According to the National Weather Service, when it can be an average temperature of 80 degrees in San Jose, it can be 65 degrees in San Francisco, on the same day.

HEALTH AND WELLNESS

The Googles and Facebooks of Silicon Valley have responded to the mounting evidence that links health and wellness to productivity, creativity, on-the-job performance, and overall happiness. As mentioned earlier, Google offers on-site doctors, gyms, masseuses, physical therapists, and chiropractors, in addition to unlimited sick days, nap pods, and hammocks. There is fierce competition to employ top-notch chefs who are religious about healthy meals, particularly those that are less than 600 calories. The Google cofounders have even gone to the extreme of color-coding the healthiness of menu options in conjunction with the Harvard School of Public Health's healthy eating pyramid, where healthier items are at direct eye level and easier to reach. Google also hosts health-related and spiritual speakers, from Dr. Mehmet Oz to Vietnamese Buddhist monk Thich Nhat Hanh.[10]

Facebook also codes their food, and there are posters plastered all over its 57-acre Menlo Park campus encouraging employees to take full advantage of its yoga and boot camps. And the wellness extends to newer Silicon Valley startups as well, and while they can't compete with the extreme health and wellness benefits that Google can offer, it is quite common for startups to offer a monthly wellness stipend, subsidized visits from a massage therapist or acupuncturist, consultations from a nutritionist, a zen room where employees can chill out, and biking and running groups.[11]

Because of Silicon Valley's optimum weather and bike-friendly road conditions, residents incorporate more physical activity into everyday life through alternative modes of transportation. Yen Lee, a Canadian native who moved to Silicon Valley, is an entrepreneur and cycling devotee. Every day you will find Lee cycling to work and wearing shorts, two things that are unheard of in Canada.[12]

Stanford University encourages students and faculty to cycle to campus with their "commute club," making it desirable to bike due to Stanford's safety stations on campus, which provide bike registration services, free bike safety check-ups, and bike pumps. For its efforts, Stanford won the 2012 League of American Bicyclist's (LAB) Platinum award.[13]

Apple, Google, Stanford University, and the Silicon Valley Leadership Group actively participate in the Silicon Valley Bicycle Coalition's annual "Bike to Work Day." This program advocates alternative transportation for the entire Silicon Valley community, promoting biking, transit, regional transit, walking, and even carpooling. In 2012 Mark Jones of the Metropolitan Transportation Commission reported that an energizer station set up on the Google Campus in Mountain View had accommodated more than 1,500 bike-riding employees on Bike to Work Day.[14]

OUTDOOR LIFESTYLE

You've probably heard the story before: In Silicon Valley, you can be surfing at the beaches in the morning and skiing in the late afternoon. Well, it's true. Whether one takes advantage of it or not, Silicon Valley's active, year-round, outdoor lifestyle includes a combination of activities from pristine beaches to the stunning mountain ranges that line the coast of the Pacific Ocean on the west and the Sierra Nevada on the east. When Silicon Valley wants to get away from it all, here is a sampling of activities that one may engage in, all in a reasonable commute distance:

Hiking

There are thousands of miles of hiking trails that are literally at the back doors of Silicon Valley neighborhoods. The Midpeninsula Regional Open Space District is a greenbelt system that works to protect the unparalled beauty of over 60,000 acres of open space. Depending on where you live in Silicon Valley, you could go from your home to the grocery store, and on the way pull your car off the side of the road and walk a quick hike at one of the 26 Open Space Preserves that run along the Silicon Valley Peninsula, some that are even interspersed in between neighborhoods such as Los Altos Hills and neighboring Portola Valley.[15]

Biking

The Alto Velo Bicycle Racing Club meets in downtown Los Altos and offers weekend rides that originate from Peet's Coffee on State Street in Los Altos at 9:00 A.M. After riders grab their morning cup of java, they prep for the scenic, but pounding, 45-mile routes, in packs of dozens of cyclists. The club has nearly 200 members including U.S. Olympian Karen Brems (aka K. Kurreck), a Women's World Time Trial Champion and Master Women's World Cyclecross Champion; U.S. Olympian Christine Thorburn; Women's National Road Champion and World Cup race winner Katheryn Mattis; and John Elgart, Masters National Champion in numerous disciplines, among other national and state champions. Alto Velo also does an hour-long weekday ride beginning at noon that meets at Page Mill and Old Page Mill Road, a 22-mile loop of interval training and road racing experience for those who want to feel the intensity of a peloton.[16]

Camping

Big Basin

Big Basin Redwoods State Park is California's oldest state park, established in 1902. It has become a popular destination for introducing young schoolchildren to camping. The park is home to 18,000 acres of old growth and recovering redwood forests with a mixture of conifer, oaks, chaparral, and riparian habitats. There are 146 campsites spread throughout four campgrounds that offer tent cabins, private one-room cabins, backpacking camps, trail camps, horse camps, and traditional tent camping.[17]

Little Basin

Once a private retreat for Hewlett-Packard employees, Little Basin is a favorite team-building location for Silicon Valley companies. Located in the Santa Cruz Mountains a short drive from Silicon Valley, Little Basin, a 534-acre campground, sits in a majestic redwood forest and is surrounded by miles of hiking trails and camping sites.[18]

Horseback Riding

All along the Peninsula, there are stables and riding centers. One of the more popular centers is Spring Down Equestrian Center, located on 12 pristine acres in Portola Valley, which offers riding lessons for kids as young as three years old and adults of any skill level. They have over 50 show-quality and safe horses to accommodate novices and experts alike, and programs ranging from Mommy/Daddy & Me sessions, drill teams, seasonal camps, and riding packages. Several times a year, Spring Down hosts a three-day clinic for riding students featuring Nick Karazissis, one of the most successful trainers on the West Coast. For a fee, Karazissis guides students through three days of lectures, demonstrations, and instruction as he perfects individual riding techniques.[19]

Sailing

The Sequoia Yacht Club (SYC) has been active in boating for 70 years. SYC is located at the Redwood City Marina, and is a proud member of the U.S. Sailing and training facility affiliate of the American Sailing Association and the Yacht Racing Association of San Francisco Bay. SYC hosts and sponsors a variety of racing events including the Redwood Cup, Winter Series, and Single-handed Racing in addition to a number of races that are held in conjunction with South Bay Yacht Racing Association and the Pacific Inter Club Yacht Association. SYC has an active cruising fleet and an award-winning junior sailing program that teaches sailing for all ability levels.[20]

Surfing

Mavericks is a world-known surfing competition held at Pillar Point Harbor at the Village of Princeton By the Sea in Half Moon Bay, approximately 30–40 minutes west of Silicon Valley. It takes place every year between January and March, and is an invitation-only event: It's far too dangerous for anyone who is not experienced in big wave surfing. World-class surfers Mark Foo and Sion Milosky died in 1994 and 2011, respectively, during the competition. Because of the presence of an unusually shaped underwater rock formation, at this time of year and with the right weather conditions waves can routinely crest over 25 feet and top out at 80 feet. The competition is announced about 24 hours in advance, and surfers fly in from around the world literally overnight.[21]

Mavericks is a favorite competition among most of the world's best big wave surfers, including Jeff Clark, the first person to surf Mavericks;

Jeff Rowley, the first Australian surfer to paddle in to a 50-foot wave at Jaws Peahi, Hawaii[22]; and Kelly Slater, 11-time Association of Surfing Professionals (ASP) World Champion.[23]

For the rest of us not ready to compete at Mavericks, the Bay Area is notorious for all levels of surfers. The area has been called one of the most unusual places on the planet to surf, "mainly for its unpredictability with incredible views."[24] In San Francisco, at surfing destinations such as Fort Point, surfers can be spooked by the Golden Gate Bridge, often feeling dwarfed by the massive architecture and the surrounding hills. South Ocean Beach is also another favored surfing spot in San Francisco, especially for more intermediate and above-level surfers, but be prepared to possibly have your board broken in half due to the largely unpredictable waves and challenging turns. Outside of San Francisco, and less than an hour's drive from Silicon Valley, are other surf destinations such as Santa Cruz and Capitola.

Wine and Music

Napa Valley and Sonoma County became visible on the vintner's map as a premium wine region in 1976, when a California wine defeated a French wine in a blind taste test during the "Judgment of Paris" wine competition.[25] Napa and Sonoma are two of the premier travel destinations in the world, and are in Silicon Valley's backyard. The pastoral landscape is a day trip from Silicon Valley and offers anyone a great time whether you are interested in wine tasting, dining at one of its renowned restaurants such as French Laundry, enjoying a mud bath at Calistoga, or just taking in the Tuscan-like scenery.

While Northern California's wine country is globally renowned, Silicon Valley's climate supports local wineries as well. One of the more treasured wineries is the Mountain Winery in Saratoga, California, which presents a spectacular view of Silicon Valley and, looking out toward the east, the Diablo Mountain Range. In 1905, French immigrant Paul Masson built a chateau and winery as a private getaway and entertainment venue for his famous guests such as Charlie Chapin, John Steinbeck, and Herbert Hoover. Today, the heritage continues on a grander scale. The Mountain Winery produces an estate chardonnay and pinot noir in addition to a collection of wines from the Mountain Winery Series. Beyond the wines, the Mountain Winery houses a 2,500-seat state-of-the-art enter-tainment amphitheater for a summer concert series featuring artists such as B.B. King, Daryl Hall & John Oates, the Go-Gos, and Lynyrd Skynyrd.

Skiing

The Sierra Nevada Mountains are what attracted early settlers to Silicon Valley, and one of its jewels is Lake Tahoe. Less than a five-hour drive from Silicon Valley, the mountain range receives about 400 inches of powder snow each year, with the ski season often lasting as late as June.[26] Lake Tahoe offers seven world-class ski resorts, all surrounding the majestic lake: Heavenly, Kirkwood, Alpine Meadows, Sierra, Mt. Rose, Squaw Valley, and Northstar. While there are closer ski resorts to Silicon Valley, Northstar is consistently ranked as one of the best ski-in, ski-out facilities in the country, where you can just put on your ski gear and ski outside of your front door. During both the winter and summer seasons, Northstar Resort offers a multitude of activities beyond skiing, including: outdoor ice or roller skating, a fire pit, gondola rides to ski runs or hiking trails, tubing, and live music in the Village. One of its unique features is the Cross Country, Telemark + Snowshoe Center that hosts a sundeck and teaching center where anyone can learn. Along the trail, skiers can stop by one of the many warming huts for hot chocolate or tea, with picnic tables to rest and enjoy the scenery.

FARMERS' MARKETS

Silicon Valley boasts a "farm to table" virtue, making farmers' markets an ingrained part of the lifestyle. There are over 26 farmers' markets throughout the year including California Avenue in Palo Alto, State Street in Los Altos, Redwood City Farmers' Market, Old Macdonald's Farmers' Market in San Jose, Castro Street in Mountain View, Vallco in Cupertino, Campbell Farmers' Market, and Menlo Park Farmers' Market.

Certified Farmers' Markets, established in 1977 by the California Department of Food and Agriculture, exempts farmers from packag-ing, sizing, and labeling constraints, allowing small farmers to market their products without the added expenses of commercial preparation. This simple idea is intended to bring fruits and vegetables to shoppers who lack accessibility to them. The National Farmers' Market Directory reported in their annual report that the United States has increased 17 percent since 2010, with California being the nation's leader in farmers' markets with 729 locations.[27]

SUSTAINABILITY

In 2001, the California Environmental Protection Agency, Santa Clara Valley Water District, Silicon Valley Leadership Group, Silicon Valley Environmental Partnership, and Sustainable Silicon Valley formed a collaborative partnership to work on resource conservation issues. A variety of project initiatives resulted that have significantly impacted conservation in Silicon Valley.[28]

Water

Because Silicon Valley exists in a semi-arid climate with a growing population, water conservation is a top priority. About half of the water in Santa Clara is imported from outside the county, and supplies continue to be limited due to regulatory restrictions and a growing pressure on the state's water delivery system. The District's Water Use Efficiency (WUE) Program, which includes water conservation, water recycling, and desalination programs, reduces demand on existing imported and local water supplies. From 2000 to 2009, Silicon Valley's gross per capita consumption dropped 18 percent, and by 2010, 3.6 percent of the total water consumed in Silicon Valley was from recycled sources, the highest recycled consumption level since measurement began in 1999.[29]

Electricity

Since 1998, electricity consumption per capita has fallen 7 percent in Silicon Valley, compared with 2 percent in the rest of California. The growth of solar panels both at homes and in companies has played a large role in electricity sustainability. According to the 2012 Silicon Valley Index, the region's solar capacity increased by 41 percent from 2010 to 2011, compared to 21 percent statewide. The residential sector accounted for 60 percent of the solar capacity added in Silicon Valley, and increased substantially in the commercial sector by 2,127 percent. Santa Clara's Neighborhood Solar Program raises money from members to upgrade facilities in the community, and helps nonprofits and schools with the cost and installation of solar panels. The first solar electric system funded by the Neighborhood Solar Program was installed at Haman Elementary School in Santa Clara in October 2004.[30]

Car Charging Stations

Silicon Valley, home to Tesla Motors and Google Car, fuels the drive for electric charging stations throughout the Bay Area. Xatori, a Palo Alto–based company, makes an app called "PlugShare" that helps drivers of electric vehicles (EV) find public charging stations, and claims that Northern California ranks first for EV ownership, but lags behind Portland, Oregon, for the number of public charging stations per 100,000 residents. Many of Silicon Valley's municipalities and workplaces have made installments for employees and visitors to utilize, such as the city of Palo Alto, the city of San Jose, Google, Netflix, YouTube, and SAP. "As a leader in Silicon Valley, we feel it's important to live the principles of sustainability, which are also core to our corporate strategy—both in serving our employee base and helping our customers," said Barbara Holzapfel, managing director of SAP Labs North America.[31]

Recycling

This practice is built into the fabric of Silicon Valley, so much so that a convenient curbside recycling collection program, for both general household recycling and yard trimmings, is provided to all residential customers in Santa Clara County for no additional charge. Since 2009, San Jose is one of the ten emerging sustainable cities to watch, making the Global Top 10 list of progressive and environmentally conscious models for 2012.[32] It is the city's plan to aspire to reach zero waste through its curbside programs, civic recycling, and the construction, demolition, and diversion programs. Such programs are helping San Jose divert 70 percent of its total waste stream from landfills, and San Jose is now the nation's recycling leader among cities of its size. These programs are currently being analyzed for ways to improve recycling rates through increased education and participation, better processing of the collected materials, and expanding recycling programs to include new waste streams such as food waste in schools, events, and city facilities. The city of San Jose is so serious about its zero waste plan that it is now a bag-free city—if you don't bring your own bags to the store, you are charged up to a quarter per bag.

12 THE BENCH

THE COMPETITIVE ADVANTAGE OF BEING RAISED IN SILICON VALLEY

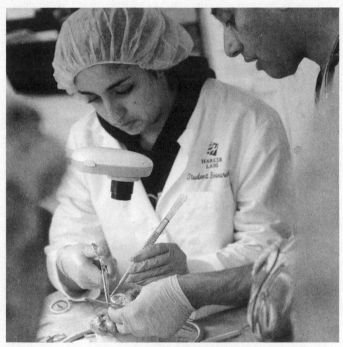

Saira Ahuja (grade 12), working with
Dr. Murali Dharan, The Harker School

Heidi Roizen—who has been a highly successful entrepreneur, venture capitalist, Stanford adjunct professor, and corporate board member—is one of those people who represent the nerve center of Silicon Valley. She's described that way by many of Silicon Valley's highly accomplished not because of her success, wealth, or her personal relationships with people such as Bill Gates, but because she happens to be the reason that so many influential people in Silicon Valley know one another. Just check out her LinkedIn page: It's a who's who of Silicon Valley. There are two things that surprise you about Heidi Roizen. First, Roizen retains that rare combination of confidence you admire and humbleness you greatly appreciate. She admittedly has little respect for people who self-flagellate and agonize. "When something goes wrong, you own it, think about why it happened, take constructive steps to make sure it doesn't happen again, and move on," Roizen says.[1] Second, she isn't the least bit pretentious, and is quite willing to openly discuss her childhood.

Roizen's early years saw some big financial and lifestyle swings. Her father, Joseph Roizen, emigrated from Romania to Canada and then California—first living in Los Angeles and then Silicon Valley. Joseph was an engineer who worked for Ampex. He was part of the team that invented color videotape, and he ran the international video operations group, so Heidi and her older brothers experienced the lifestyle of children of an executive would, including traveling to Europe.

When Roizen was about ten years old, her parents split up. Her much older brothers were already away at college, and her father was still travelling extensively for his job, so she lived alone with her mother, Gisela, who decided to move the two of them to Nevada. Soon after, her father started a business venture, which failed, and he faced some very difficult personal and financial circumstances. As Heidi's mother was not working at the time, and they were living off spousal and child support Joseph was providing, it was a tough time for the family.

At 13, Heidi and her mother lived in a motel on El Camino Real in Palo Alto, a major thoroughfare that runs throughout California. She learned how to pay utility bills and file federal taxes as her mother, who had only an eighth-grade education and struggled with administrative tasks. Gisela worked a minimum-wage job at the high school cafeteria, and dinners at home often consisted of whatever was left over from school that day. Eating out at Denny's once a month was a big deal. While Heidi had a roof over her head and never went hungry, she learned the lessons of living on a very tight budget, and any miscellaneous things like clothes and extracurricular activities, such as athletics or cheerleading, she had to fund by working.

To earn money, Roizen came up with the idea of putting on puppet shows for children's birthday parties. She went after business with determination, advertising her puppet shows in the classified section of the *San Jose Mercury News*. Roizen's bookings went from the occasional party to up to six shows a weekend, and she was earning $30–$35 a show, and pulling in between about $500/month, a large sum of money for a 17-year-old in the mid-1970s. While her "no extra money" existence had its challenges, Heidi learned the values of personal determination, responsibility, and hard work, and how to make the seemingly impossible possible through creativity and drive.

Roizen graduated as the valedictorian of Leigh High School in 1976, and explored every possible academic scholarship so she could put herself through school. She attended Stanford University, majored in English, and quickly discovered that she was no longer the smartest kid in the room. In fact, she started out as a pretty average student, until her college sweetheart died in a plane crash. Her world rattled, Roizen realized that she had fallen into the trap of following the "future spouse" route, was somewhat drifting in school, and needed to get her act together. She took extra courses, graduated early, and entered the job market, becoming the editor of the company newspaper for the early technology company Tandem Computers. She later returned to Stanford for her MBA.

Her exposure to technology entrepreneurs in Silicon Valley and then at Stanford, coupled with her growing passion for personal computers, put her on the entrepreneurial track once again. Stanford friends such as Tim Draper, Jeff Raikes, Alain Rossmann, and Doug Burgum, among others, were pursuing entrepreneurship, and Roizen was inspired and encouraged to do the same. She also benefited from the know-how of her older brother Peter, who had developed a reputation as a genius programmer. Heidi and Peter went into business together and started T/Maker, an early software application for personal computers. Twelve years later, at the age of 36, Heidi sold her company for $20 million.

Roizen believes that there is no better place to be raised than in Silicon Valley. "It is a meritocracy that is very diverse—both great conditions for any underdog to succeed," says Roizen. "No matter what socioeconomic class you are in Silicon Valley, you have exposure to the startup culture. If you are driven, creative, tenacious, and willing to work hard, I believe you can find the team and the opportunity to be successful. I'm very grateful that I was born here, to a certain extent in the right place at the right time. But, I also worked a lot of hard years to make my dreams a reality."[2]

A COMPETITIVE ADVANTAGE

What gives Silicon Valley kids a competitive advantage? Among the many young people I interviewed for this chapter, the one common thread was the exposure to the world of technology, entrepreneurship, and venture capital that not only gave them early adoption of innovations that are changing the world, but also enthused them to their chosen career paths following in the footsteps of high-profile innovators and product developers who were sometimes their moms and dads. "With companies such as Apple and Google in your back door, there is an infectious nature that inspires you to want to do your best," says Anshul Samar, a young entrepreneur and Stanford University student.[3] "There was a greater expectation that is placed on you when you are surrounded by excellence,"[4] says Channing Hancock, a product developer at a technology company. But there are deeper factors as well. To the newcomer coming to Silicon Valley, there is an apparent hyper-engagement of parents, specifically fathers, who often prioritize their children not just in the coaching of extracurricular activities, but also in side-by-side learning. There are preschools, such as Bing Nursery School on the campus of Stanford, that offer an early design-thinking curriculum, and private schools such as the Nueva and Harker School that are design-, science-, and technology-centric. Finally, there are novel approaches to how kids spend time, such as bypassing traditional East Coast sleep-away camps and opting for the plethora of science, math, and technology day camps that are offered around the Bay Area, and new questions being raised about the value of a four-year degree that are allowed to bubble up and simmer, only in Silicon Valley.

IT ALL BEGINS AT HOME

One of the first things visiting friends and relatives often notice about Silicon Valley is the high engagement of fathers in their children's lives. Visit a park within a ten-mile radius of Stanford University and you will see just as many fathers pushing swings and strollers as mothers. Go to the grocery store or the school drop-off or pick-up and witness a plethora of dads helping to take care of errands, carpools, and school functions. This suggests Silicon Valley families are more aligned in their priorities, and this fosters a greater integration between work and family.

Rod Strickland has been a partner at the law firm of Wilson, Sonsini, Goodrich & Rosati since 2000. He is also chairman of the board at Bowman International where his kids go to school, and coach of their soccer, basketball, and baseball teams. "I just enjoy being around my kids, but if I had had my children at 25 versus at 35, I would not have had the flexibility that I do," says Strickland. "My work is immensely rewarding, but the advancements of technology make it so that I don't have to be in the office as much, but I am never disconnected." Every Saturday morning, Strickland has a routine of having breakfast with his kids, and then they'll spend the rest of the day doing something outdoors. He also plans an annual camping trip to Lassen Volcanic Park where it is just him and his daughter and son. "I have to say that I am unremarkable, as I look at my law partners and then friends who are at venture capital firms. We all spend highly engaged time with our kids. We all coach our kids' teams,"[5] he says.

Silicon Valley kids learn what their parents do, and they also learn what their friends' parents do. When venture capitalist Sue Siegel volunteered at a counseling event at her son's school, she learned that "every single junior in his high school class knew what a venture capitalist was. Entrepreneurship is so embedded here. It's what everyone talks about. If you don't participate, you're on the outside," said Siegel in a *New York Times* article called, "The Risk-Taking Edge of West Coast Women."[6]

Bowman International School's predominant feeder preschool is Google's Children's Center at the Woods, so the elementary and middle school children who attend Bowman come to school "talking about the product launches that their moms and dads are engaged in at Google, Apple, and other leading technology firms," says Mary Beth Ricks, the head of school at Bowman International.[7]

These unique opportunities not only expose Silicon Valley's children to the startup culture, but also the innovative educational philosophies and practical real-life experiences that prepare them for a twenty-first century economy. It all begins before kindergarten at Bing Nursery School, on the campus of Stanford University.

BING NURSERY SCHOOL

At three and a half years old, one of our twin boys, Dominick, refused to learn Mandarin at his preschool and suddenly insisted that we only speak Spanish at home. Unfortunately my husband and I speak very broken Spanish, at best. When we inquired why he refused to learn Mandarin, he looked us point blank in the eye and emphatically commanded, "I am not a Chinese boy, I am a Hispanic boy, and I only want to speak Spanish." Neither my husband nor I are Hispanic, but Dominick had anointed himself Hispanic, would only eat rice and beans for lunch and dinner, and insisted that if we got a dog, the dog's name was going to be Mrs. Hernandez, paying homage to his then–piano teacher. We couldn't really argue with his comprehensive approach, or his convictions.

When Dominick was four years old, he started walking around the classroom during lessons at his Montessori preschool. Dominick easily disengaged from learning when something didn't interest him, and was nearly impossible to reach when he did anything related to science. We didn't know how to best calm his mind, so we had him evaluated by a specialist who diagnosed him with having "an extreme curiosity and need for constant mental stimulation,"[8] but also "a heightened sense of justice and advanced moral development." He once scurried up to a homeless man who was digging in the garbage can and asked him, "Why are you digging in the trash?" When the disheveled man didn't respond, Dominick persisted, "Can I help you?" Homelessness became something that plagued him at four years old.

The specialist told us that we needed to move homes because Dominick needed a large yard to explore. She recommended that we throw away all toys except for books, blocks, and LEGOs, and—lastly—strongly insisted we move Dominick to Bing Nursery School on the campus of Stanford University. "But that's play," I immediately responded. "You want us to pay for our child to play?" Besides not having any connection to Stanford, which would benefit us in the admissions process, I had mixed feelings about separating him from his twin brother, Drake, who was thriving in a Montessori education. In the end, we took the specialist's advice and moved him to Bing, and within two weeks we saw a remarkable transformation in our son. He was happier, calmer, and had developed a bond with one of his teachers, Mark Mabry, who would sit with Dominick for long periods of time and support his interest in designing things. Every time I picked up Dominick from Bing, Mabry would brief me on what Dominick did that day, including reports such as: "He started building a road using the large hollow blocks, starting from the classroom door all the way out to the sand area . . . and as other children became interested in what he was up to, he explained his plan and all of a sudden found himself collaborating with many eager volunteers." Anecdotes like this gave me insights on Dominick's mindset, which according to Mabry were pretty unusual for his age. "Dominick seems to be quite a cerebral child. I feel like he has a very intuitive grasp of spatial relationships and does a lot of thinking and planning before implementing his ideas," he remarked.

Bing Nursery School was founded as a laboratory school in 1966 with a grant from the National Science Foundation and a matching gift from Dr. Peter S. Bing, who was an undergraduate at Stanford at the time, and his mother, Anna Bing Arnold. The original mission of the school was to provide a sound educational environment for young children, a laboratory setting for research in child development, and a chance for undergraduate and graduate students to observe children in the classroom. But it has developed into "a national treasure"[9] with methods that are studied by educators and media outlets around the world. Its core curriculum is based on free play, free for a child to do what he or she wants to do and when they want to do it, and consists of five basic materials: sand, blocks, paint, clay, and water, all in spacious classrooms that include half-acre play yards. Children enjoy freedom of movement and choice; the only structured activities are snack and story times. The underlying play-based philosophy is designed to help children learn to self-regulate. Play is what develops design capacities and the love of learning in our brains. Jennifer Winters, Bing's director of school, says, "In the magical world of play, children act out what is on their minds; they practice life as they know it, on their own terms. In play, children make their own rules, and the rules change depending upon many factors, none of which necessarily make sense from the adult perspective. It is through play that we can foster a love and a passion for learning that can last a lifetime."[10] Having first-hand experience at Bing Nursery School, it's easy to see how these methods shape the next generation of inventors and entrepreneurs.

THE NUEVA SCHOOL

On the majestic Pre-K-through-8 campus of the Nueva School in Hillsborough sits a 3,500-square-foot facility called the Innovation Lab, otherwise known as the I-Lab, where students research and develop design-thinking skills as early as kindergarten. The lab features robotic arms, 3D printers, flexible worktables, and bins and bins of repurposed materials like paperclips, cylinders, and Popsicle sticks for rapid prototyping. Students can often be found working on mechanical toys, electrical switches, and model solar houses. They are also challenged to extend the design thinking process to areas of social entrepreneurship and have developed innovative approaches to water conservation, green building, and access to health resources. Students work collaboratively and independently, and many return to the I-Lab every chance they get, including during recess.

With over 45 years of experience in inquiry-based applied learning projects, the Nueva School is a leading pioneer in teaching design thinking and engineering. The faculty share knowledge with their peers at other schools during Nueva's biannual Innovative Learning Conference and annual Design Thinking Institute. According to the Nueva website, "The power of design thinking comes from practicing and gaining confidence in different types of thinking, which includes both mindsets and specific techniques that foster creative and critical thinking. For example, the underlying mindsets for interviewing involve putting one's own thoughts and preferences to the side, going for depth (versus breadth), and listening with both heart and mind. Critical to this type of work and learning is developing the mental abilities to navigate from one way of thinking to another, based on a project's needs."[11]

Students refine and grow their skills at all ages. Second-graders build bridges while fourth-graders are challenged to design green buildings and maximize sustainability within a budget. Fifth-graders work on engineering catapults as well as "peace projects," to create something that would promote peace in the world in some way. Eighth-graders have designed knee braces and LED-illuminated clothing, as well as public issue campaigns and community service projects. Nueva's approach emphasizes empathy and deep curiosity, critical thinking, and the synthesis of information, an ability to quickly and confidently delve into unknown areas and develop questions and hypotheses, and an appreciation for working collaboratively. Students are taught to be flexible in their learning, to suspend judgment in order to expand their thinking, and to take risks, create, and seek feedback without fear of failure.

The school's motto, "Learn by Doing, Learn by Caring," is reflective of its mission to inspire a passion for lifelong education through applied learning and systems thinking. Using a constructivist model, the curriculum emerges from the students' interests and connects them to real-world explorations for class themes. For example, in third grade, "three questions form the basis of the program: How does geography affect the way people live? How are people's choices shaped by geography? How do people express their beliefs in their daily lives?" At the basis of Nueva's success is that teachers are considered "coaches" and "guides" who help students reach their full potential in arts, science, technology, and creativity.[12]

One graduating eighth-grader remarked, "Nueva has taught me that when we are presented with a question, we are presented with an opportunity—an opportunity to thrive, to grow, to learn. Nueva has taught me to let my passions lead me, be who I am, and not follow someone else's path."

THE HARKER SCHOOL

The Harker School[13] in San Jose, offering preschool through twelfth grade, has held the number-one ranking in the world since 2006 for a school its size (between 300 and 799 students) in Advanced Placement test scores in Computer Science, Psychology, Chemistry, and Calculus, according to The College Board for Advanced Placement.[14] The label given by the *San Jose Mercury News,* "The It School for the Next Einsteins,"[15] is evident in the number of science winners the school can claim. Harker consistently produces semifinalists and finalists in the Intel Science Talent Search, the nation's oldest and most prestigious science competition, and the Siemens Competition.

Classes at Nichols Hall, Harker's $25 million, state-of-the-art science and technology center, foster a culture of structured inquiry and scientific discovery. Students can engage in college-level subjects including organic chemistry, biotechnology, environmental science, electronics, and after-school programs in robotics as well as advanced research labs. Anita Chetty, the Science Department chair, feels that schools must provide an advanced science and math curriculum if students want to succeed in Silicon Valley later in life. "I love the fact that our chair of the Computer Science, Dr. Eric Nelson, doesn't just teach robotics, but he insists that students build their robots in the context of an entrepreneurial venture," says Chetty.[16] Students will conceive a company, starting with a business plan, then select a CEO and president, and develop the business within a budget just like a real company.

"We have a student body that is incredibly motivated and passionate about STEM education, so we are fortunate to be able to act on their curiosities," says Chetty. Throughout the academic year and during the summers, Chetty takes students to conduct field studies in Costa Rica and the Galapagos Islands; she will soon be adding a trip to Tanzania. "Every trip is designed to have an academic, research, and community service component, where at the end of the trip students are required to present their findings," she says.[17] As she plans the Tanzania curriculum, titled "One Health: The Interplay of Animal, Environmental, and Human Health," she wants to emphasize the connectivity between rangeland management and human health. She insists that this is what an authentic education is all about: "I don't want our students to just read or hear about someone else's experiences, I want them to experience it for themselves."[18]

One of the cornerstones of Chetty's tenure is the annual Harker Research Symposium, which completes the research cycle, allowing students to share the findings of their original research with the Harker community. With poster sessions, formal talks, workshops, corporate exhibits, and keynote speakers featuring Nobel laureates, leading Silicon Valley CEOs, venture capitalists, and Stanford research doctors, adult attendees comment that the event is no different from any national science conference they might have attended. Student participants not only practice presentation skills, they also pass on their newfound knowledge and inspire the next generation of Harker student researchers.

The teaching staff at Harker is evenly split among Ph.D.'s and pedagogues, who all hold an incredible passion for the subjects they teach. Chetty, like many of the Harker faculty, still maintains relationships with former students, many of whom are now doing post-doctoral work. One student in particular, Surbhi Sarna, a 2003 graduate, raised venture capital and invented a medical device for early detection of ovarian cancer. She recently called Chetty and said, "I don't know what you put in the water at Harker, but many of us [alumnae] feel like we can change the world . . . and I haven't come across anyone else outside of Harker who feels that way."[19]

Jennifer Gargano, the assistant head of academic affairs, says, "I think a big part of our special sauce is the students. We attract students who are motivated to learn, with the right intentions. They want to learn and improve the world and know that it is hard work and focus that will allow them to achieve their goals. We have a community where students positively encourage one another to do their best and do it with the right intentions. It is just part of the culture."[20] Chris Spenner, Harker's physics and research teacher, attributes the school's success to much more, due in part to the freedom and creativity that the teaching staff is allowed. "I can go beyond the AP curriculum, adding subjects like special relativity. [The students are] so advanced in math, I can do multivariable calculus . . . I've taught at other schools and never seen anything like this," he commented in a *San Jose Mercury News* article.[21]

CREATING FUTURE INNOVATORS

Passion is the key ingredient in creating innovators of the future. According to Tony Wagner, the author of *Creating Innovators: The Making of Young People Who Will Change the World*, there are seven survival skills young people will need to be successful in a twenty-first century world:[22]

1. Critical thinking;
2. Collaboration;
3. Agility and adaptability;
4. Initiative and entrepreneurship;
5. Oral and written education;

6. Access and information; and
7. Curiosity and imagination.

In a *Wall Street Journal* op-ed, "Educating the Next Steve Jobs," Wagner writes that he believes that in "conventional schools, students learn so that they can get good grades. My most important research finding is that young innovators are intrinsically motivated. The culture of learning in programs that excel at educating for innovation emphasize what I call the three P's—play, passion and purpose. The play is discovery-based learning that leads young people to find and pursue a passion, which evolves, over time, into a deeper sense of purpose."[23]

In Silicon Valley, one discovery-based program that has received accolades from the parents who send their kids there is Quantum Camp, a K–12 education program that teaches advanced science and math education for the twenty-first century. It was started by two former high school science teachers, Dr. Michael Finnegan and Ryan Nurmela, neither of whom lasted long in the Oakland public school system. Finnegan says that he was teaching the same old things that he learned in high school, but the world had changed dramatically since then and those changes weren't reflected in the curriculum. "We were absolutely baffled by what was being taught or not being taught in the schools, and made a pact to do something."[24] The unique course structure at Quantum Camp allows students to take classes such as computer engineering, global math, designing math, advanced physics, astrophysics, and Euclid's elements either on a class-by-class basis or as a year-round curriculum.

Even Finnegan admits that as a kid he loved science but hated his science classes, and this admission comes from one who has a Ph.D. in material sciences and a passion for synthesis and the peculiar properties of titanium dioxide nanoparticles. He decided to tap into the innate curiosity all humans share and co-founded Quantum Camp to offer science and math in a way that will stimulate innovation, so his students won't face the same educational humdrum that he did.

Ryan Nurmela, who is a credentialed mathematics and physics teacher and has developed an extension of the mathematical foundation Object Theory, a theory in mathematical logic concerning objects and the statements that can be made about objects, firmly believes "that through an amazing curriculum, students of all socioeconomic and learning backgrounds can learn far more than what our current educational system is designed to deliver."[25] Nurmela and Finnegan call their education system QED: "QED pedagogy creates a space where students can self-actualize in the context of a classroom. Whether they are learning mathematics, science, history, language arts, or any other subject, students deserve the chance to reach their highest level of self in an environment where learning, collaboration, and problem solving become part of who they are as a person."[26] The four cornerstones of QED are: 1) contextualization (to immerse students in relevance and meaning); 2) conceptual flow (to build excitement and momentum); 3) moment of discovery (to place the student into the act of creating their own knowledge); and 4) application (to help students reach a level of mastery).

EARLY INTRODUCTIONS INTO A TWENTY-FIRST CENTURY WORKFORCE

In the summer of 2011, I met Anshul Samar, who was entering his senior year of high school at Bellarmine College Preparatory School. His polished determination immediately impressed me, and I soon found out where it came from. In fourth grade, he came up with the idea for the chemistry card game Elementeo in response to his parents' dissatisfaction with the lack of learning in most games. He credits his parents for his creativity. When Samar and his younger sister, Shailee, were nearly school-aged, his mother would take them on adventures, often as part of programs organized through classes or museums, and exposed them to all things creative. "My dad also started this program at my elementary school, Collins, in which parents would come and run clubs teaching kids things from languages to website design. One of these clubs was 'Dissecting Machines' in which we took apart computers, computer mice, and other contraptions. I remember a lot of fun things that we would do, many of them around being creative, writing or making something of our own," remembers Samar.[27]

His entrepreneurial father was in the process of launching Extensio, an enterprise software company, at a "very impressionable time . . . I would hear him talk about the mechanics of launching a business around our house," Samar says. He also credits growing up in Silicon Valley for the idea to try entrepreneurship at such a young age. "Being in Silicon Valley, the energy is just there. So many people were doing cool things.

Apple was in the neighboring building of my middle school [Lawson Middle School in Cupertino]." One thing Anshul was persistent about was that he didn't want to wait to get into the world of startups. "I would be playing a lot of games, and there was not a lot of learning in them, so I'd brainstorm with my parents about creating something fun and educational."

In middle school, Samar worked on a project personifying the elements of the periodic table, assigning each element a character and a personality so that it could be a fun board game for kids about chemistry, a game he named Elementeo. He worked with artists in Argentina, Michigan, and Southern California to create each periodic character. His father later taught him about cash flow, profit-and-loss statements, and the difference between a C and an S corporation. In sixth grade, Samar applied for a grant from the California Association for the Gifted, and won $500. "This was incredibly motivating for me because they not only validated my idea of Elementeo but believed in what I was doing," says Samar.

In 2007, he attended TiEcon in Silicon Valley and showcased Elementeo, and from the press he received, he was tracked down by venture capitalists in San Francisco about taking in capital. In seventh grade, Samar was making a presentation about his marketing and revenue strategy for Elementeo before a group of venture capitalists. After many meetings with the venture capitalists, the two sides mutually agreed not to head down the venture capital path, in part because Samar wanted to focus on his schooling, but these venture capitalists became great advisors to him.

Shortly thereafter, Amazon, Exploratorium, and the MIT Museum Store came to Samar about selling Elementeo, and he then marketed his game to other small specialty toy stores and catalogs nationwide. The first generation of Elementeo quickly sold out, and his second generation is now available. He now speaks about game-board design at conferences such as TEDx, which is an independently organized TED event, and gifted summits such as the Davidson Young Scholars, a national K–12 program for profoundly gifted children. In Fall 2012, with many successes already under his belt, Samar matriculated to Stanford as a freshman.

By the time Channing Hancock graduated from Henry M. Gunn High School in Palo Alto in 2006, she had already worked at four startups, including Facebook and the mobile media company Mozes. At Gunn, Hancock was on the student executive council as well as student body president, yearbook copyeditor, and co-founder of the *Partisan Review*, a publication that stimulated political debate at Gunn.

Hancock believes that having so many internship opportunities at some of the world's most innovative companies inspired her to approach college very differently than the average student.

> Because I had real experience in the workplace, I knew what sort of skills and accomplishments were valuable and focused more on the experiences I had in college instead of obsessing over grades. I chose an interdisciplinary field of study because through my internships, I learned that working at the intersection of multiple disciplines was valuable and personally rewarding. I graduated with a degree in bioinformatics, essentially a combination of the core of biology, chemistry, statistics, and computer science.[28]

Hancock, who is now married, has since moved to Singapore to work in product development at a tech company. She feels that it is vital to have working experience in Asia to understand the differences between the markets there and in the United States. "I do hope to get back to Silicon Valley one day, but I want to work at helping American companies penetrate Asian markets, so this is where we want to be right now," she says.

Hancock also believes in the benefits of being raised in Silicon Valley:

> There's something special about being in Silicon Valley, and I think a lot of it is immeasurable and intangible and difficult to articulate. Growing up in the Valley, you have different expectations of success, in addition to providing value and living meaningfully. I went to public schools—although I joke they were as or more rigorous than private schools—and everyone around you was also accomplished, doing interesting things, and that was infectious. Yet, my story is unremarkable: There were tons of other kids in my class doing similar things. Obviously, having world-famous companies and universities in your backyard opens up opportunities that might not otherwise be available, but the biggest difference between Silicon Valley and other similar

areas I've observed is that those companies are willing to give anyone who is hardworking and a real contributor a chance, whether they be high-schoolers or Ph.D.'s.[29]

THE THIEL FELLOWS

The debate rages in Silicon Valley over whether extremely bright students should bypass college in pursuit of their innovative passions. Venture capitalist Peter Thiel sees such potential that he is offering $100,000 over two years for the brightest to bypass the Ivy League and jump into entrepreneurship before they even graduate from high school. Thiel feels that the growing costs of tuition, with little guaranteed payoff after graduation, is not only a bad investment, but doesn't teach the practicality of how to run a business. "Increasingly, technology creates unprecedented leverage for young people to do influential groundbreaking work," Thiel said in a *San Jose Mercury News* article, "No college? No degree? No problem for young entrepreneurs at Palo Alto startup looking to make it big in Silicon Valley." In the article, reporter Mike Cassidy writes, "Is it better to go to college, become traditionally educated, and then go out and make your mark in the world? Or is college for losers, a four-year wasteland that only slows innovation because the up-and-coming boy geniuses are busy reading Homer when they could be slinging code?"[30]

A member of the first class of Thiel Fellows is Laura Demming, who, as of the writing of this book, is an 18-year-old partner at Floreat Capital (she matriculated to MIT at 14), a specialty life science venture capital firm. Demming's passion is her life's work in anti-aging science, researching the genes responsible for aging in hopes of extending human life. Demming was eight years old when she discovered the concept of death over a conversation with her mother, and knew what she was meant to do in her life. Her mother tried to explain to her that all people die eventually, but she felt she needed to find a way to stop death. At the age of 12, she started working in a genetics lab under the guidance of Dr. Cynthia Kenyon, a pioneer in anti-aging technology. Kenyon's lab at the University of California, San Francisco, played a huge role in furthering Demming's interest in the field. She spent hours at the lab and would often sit in on lectures about genetics and biochemistry, never losing interest in the field of biotechnology. Demming and Dr. Kenyon were astonished when they used age-defying therapies and discovered a way to get worms to live longer. Demming feels that this discovery will help her to unlock the key to extending the human lifespan. In an interview with Gary Goldman, CEO of the Daily Brink, Demming talks about that life-changing experience: "Life is incredible, but death is inevitable. I already knew biology was fantastic fun. But that moment, for me, made science more than fun. It made it into a power that could save lives. And I couldn't imagine doing something more fascinating or important."[31]

Today, Demming and her co-founders at Floreat Capital focus on companies that specialize on anti-aging technology and identifying pioneering science that could hold the promise of addressing late-onset medical conditions. They welcome proposals from early-stage companies and laboratories with translational research in this area, and work with scientists and entrepreneurs to advance enterprises that can translate research into effective preclinical drug development programs. In an interview with MIT's *Technology Review,* Demming says, "The cool thing about Silicon Valley is that, though people might be skeptical of youth, they don't actually know that you're not smart enough or capable enough to make it work."[32]

With college costs skyrocketing and no end in sight, the question has to be raised: Is technology the great equalizer of the twenty-first century? While undergraduate years can have value far beyond academic nourishment, is there a better way to prepare today's generation for a twenty-first-century economy? Peter Thiel's methods may be meant for only a small subset of the brightest of the young adult population, but he is forcing a long-overdue conversation. The nation is desperately in need of innovation, and it can't afford to wait while its brightest innovators finish college, he insists. Besides, "years of experience aren't so important in a meritocracy."[33]

EPILOGUE
CAN SILICON VALLEY
BE REPLICATED?

Transporting Silicon Valley's unique culture to the world

I n the mid-2000s, global demand for solar panels was booming, driven by supportive policy in Japan and Germany. A kilogram of highly purified silicon—the raw material for solar panels, and essentially purified sand—was selling to the highest bidder for ten to fifteen times the cost of production, around $300–$500/kilogram. Production facilities that traditionally supplied the raw material for the shiny metal blocks to the semiconductor industry cost up to $1 billion to build. The semiconductor industry is continually fitting more computational power on less silicon substrate, but the solar industry needs more silicon for each solar panel. The boom in solar demand caught the polysilicon industry by surprise, and prices for the material increased tenfold.

At that time, there were only six major manufacturers of polysilicon worldwide: two in Europe, two in the United States, and two in Japan.

China had two manufacturers as well, but they were much smaller players, state-owned, and producing for their own semiconductor applications and domestic consumption. The first of China's manufacturers, Dongfang Electric Emei Semiconductor Material Company (or simply Emei Semiconductor), was founded in 1964 and seen as having the best technology in China. They adapted their designs from Russian polysilicon reactors imported during a time of congenial relations between the two nations. As the market for polysilicon heated up in 2006 and 2007, Emei Semiconductor was slow to react.

But other private and state companies quickly noted the opportunities in the polysilicon market by looking for new industries to profitably enter. Within two years of the initial boom in 2006, Chinese polysilicon companies announced plans to produce more than 200,000 tons of polysilicon per year, more than four times the capacity of the six industry leaders at that point in time.[1] But efficiently and cheaply producing high-quality polysilicon is very complicated, and in the end, less than one-tenth of the polysilicon was eventually produced. In order to be successful, the new entrants needed to get their hands on the technological know-how.

One of the companies faced with this challenge was the Chinese company, Golden Concord Limited Poly Energy Holdings (GCL). GCL was an independent power producer with over 30 cogeneration, biomass, incineration, and wind plants, and they were eager to enter into the solar industry. They hired away two of Emei Semiconductor's top engineers, who brought with them the technical know-how and plans for producing high-quality, low-cost polysilicon. GCL invested over $1 billion in their production facilities and by 2009 was one of the largest producers of polysilicon in the world, surpassing four of the six original incumbents of the industry in just three short years. They are now the largest manufacturer of polysilicon worldwide and have since moved into other components of the solar value chain, producing wafers, cells, modules, and entire utility-scale solar projects.

Emei Semiconductor was left far behind in this game, barely increasing its production capacity and missing the polysilicon boom. They were particularly unhappy that two of their engineers defected, and they sued them and GCL for infringement of intellectual property, and insisted that both the technology and engineers be returned. The challenge was that while Emei Semiconductor lay in the foothills of the western mountains of Sichuan province, GCL's operations lay more than 1,500 kilometers away on the east coast of China, in Jiangsu province, whose government had a vested interest in the success of GCL's already large investment in polysilicon. Various agencies of the two provinces disputed the issue for a number of months before they found a resolution: The two engineers would be returned to Sichuan province for prosecution, but GCL—and Jiangsu province—would be allowed to keep the technology and become the largest producer of polysilicon in the world, a telling illustration of the mechanisms of knowledge-transfer and IP protection in China.

CAN SILICON VALLEY BE REPLICATED?

One of the most highly anticipated questions pressing the global world is, Can Silicon Valley be replicated, and if so, what would it look like? Many cities, regions, and countries around the world have announced or implemented plans to create a Silicon Valley of their own. At the writing of this book, 11 cities use Silicon in the name, but I suspect there will be many more that will pop up. Even Iraq's minister for digital wants to create Silicon Baghdad. Currently, the 11 are:

- *Silicon Alley* of New York
- *Silicon Hill* in Washington, DC
- *Silicon Beach* in West Los Angeles
- *Silicon Forest* in Washington County, Oregon
- *Silicon Hills* in Austin, Texas
- *Silicon Valley* of Zhongguancun in Beijing
- *Silicon Valley* of India in Bangalore
- *Silicon Roundabout* in East London
- *Silicon Cape* in Cape Town, South Africa
- *Silicon Slopes* in Park City, Utah
- *Silicon Wadi* in Haifa, Tel Aviv and Jerusalem, Israel

The answers to whether Silicon Valley can be replicated are diverse, highly contextual, and dependent on shifting policies and regional balances.

There is, no doubt, a competitive advantage of being in Silicon Valley that, first and foremost, benefits from favorable federal laws such as flexibility of labor regulations, the familiarity and comfort of U.S. banks to lend to young companies with little collateral, and the lack of heavy government regulation that would typically favor the interests of established banks, companies, and labor unions. Some argue Silicon Valley and the Bay Area is "just the right size."[2] With 800,000 people in the city of San Francisco and 7 million in the Bay Area, many feel that networks are broad enough to incorporate many different people, but also intimate enough that most are only separated by one or two degrees.[3]

As Paul Graham put it in his essay on "How to Be Silicon Valley," you need two types of people to create a hub of technology innovation: "rich guys [and gals] and nerds."[4] The rich provide the start-up capital, and the nerds—who I prefer to identify as the "super smart"—provide the ideas and elbow grease. The former is the water and the latter the soil. The super smart are drawn to the area by top universities such as Stanford and UC Berkeley, and they remain for career opportunities and quality of life.

When contemplating the creation of a Silicon Valley, Alley, Beach, or Hills somewhere else in the world, what makes the original so tough to replicate is the culture itself. It is a web of interactions, stimuli, connections, and recombinations. It is a culture that thrives on creative destruction and gets bored with the norm.

Another critical ingredient is the depth and breadth of the talent pool. Richard Florida, an urban studies theorist, wrote that "more than half of all the Silicon Valley startups launched over the past couple of decades have had an immigrant on their founding teams."[5] The immigrant population in Silicon Valley and influx of global talent and perspective is a critical human factor to its commanding position in global technology innovation. And while I mostly focus on the Indian and Asian populations earlier in this book, there are many aspiring European entrepreneurs in Silicon Valley and the Bay Area as well. According to a briefing in *The Economist* on European entrepreneurs, there are about 50,000 Germans in Silicon Valley, and an estimated 500 startups with French founders.[6] One of the things many of these entrepreneurs agree upon is the freedom to fail. "If your company goes under in France," says Dan Serfaty, the French founder of Viadeo, a fast growing business-networking website, "you don't get a second chance."[7]

Paul Graham and others also point to Silicon Valley's toleration of odd ideas, contraptions, and big dreams.[8] The future of markets and technologies often lies in seemingly crazy ideas and visions. One only needs to think of the original dreamers who concocted the personal computer, the internet, or online shopping to understand how dramatic the transition from vision to reality can be, especially in terms of economic and social implications.

There is also a strong local market for the products being produced. Nowhere in the United States boasts such a tech-savvy and tech-hungry population as that of the Bay Area. These people live and breathe internet platforms, tech-enabled startups, social media, and big data. A fast-moving startup thrives from staying close to its users and customers.

Finally, Silicon Valley is as much a culture as it is a religion, one that is self-reinforcing through its success and uniqueness, and in which the whole exceeds the sum of the parts. For those trying to replicate it in other parts of the world, it is reassuring to know that if the fundamental elements fit together, a dynamic will begin to unfold among these elements which will likely strengthen over time and create new hubs of innovation and excellence around the world.

The last critical ingredient of any vibrant ecosystem is time. Every ecosystem and culture needs time to develop, work out the relationships between its various parts, and find its own character and place in the world. Many like to point out that Silicon Valley's reputation as a hub for technological innovation has been growing for more than 50 years, but others, such as Carlos Baradello, founder and manager of the Silicon Valley Immersion Program at the University of San Francisco, believe that its roots and entrepreneurial spirit lie far deeper. He argues convincingly that "the Valley's entrepreneurial mindset has been 165 years in the making," starting with the Gold Rush of 1848.[9] Then, westward expansion attracted people who were willing to risk everything for the chance to strike it rich. They were "independent and individualistic," risk-taking, tolerant of diversity, willing to fail on the way to success, and driven.

THE ENTREPRENEURIAL ECOSYSTEM ELSEWHERE

Innovators such as Jack Ma from China and Masayoshi Son from Japan have received global recognition, and Chinese companies such as Baidu and Tencent are starting to be seen as competitors to innovation leaders such as Amazon, Apple, Facebook, Google, and Microsoft. Europe has a few entrepreneurial success stories as well, but they are further between. Sir Richard Branson's Virgin empire is the most well-known, and the wealthiest success story is that of Spain's Amancio Ortega. Austria has Dietrich Mateschitz, who founded the energy sports drink Red Bull, and France has Xavier Niel, who started a mobile phone revolution with the introduction of extremely low prices. Sweden has Ingvar Kamprad, the founder of IKEA, but most of these examples—with the exception of Branson—fly under the radar, avoiding media, preferring to be humble and modest.

A 2012 Organization for Economic Co-Operation and Development (OECD) report titled "Entrepreneurship at a Glance" reveals that it takes, on average, 12 times as long to set up a company in Europe as it does in the United States—and costs four times as much.[10] In the "Doing Business 2012" survey, the International Finance Corporation reports that it costs a company six times as much to set up a business in Eastern Europe and Central Asia, than in the United States.[11] The OECD report also concluded that the American legal system is more favorable to new business ventures than virtually most other OECD countries. In European countries, for example, it is challenging to get seed funding or to start over after a failed venture. In Germany, it can take 6 years to get a fresh start due to bankruptcy, and in Britain it can take 12 months after debts have been paid before companies or entrepreneurs can start again. Additionally, payment in the form of stock options is not as prevalent a practice, and being listed on stock exchanges without many years of stable operations and even several years of profits is challenging. This, without a doubt, limits the capital sources for high-tech startups.

While global governments are boosting policies to bolster entrepreneurship, it is unimaginable that any place will be able to exactly replicate and supplant Silicon Valley. But many believe it is possible to create a similar dynamic in other parts of the globe, perhaps focusing on different industries. Gary Matuszak, global chair and U.S. leader of KPMG's technology, media, and telecommunications practice, pointed out that "the key takeaway" from his organization's survey is that other countries "underestimate what it takes to create the environment we have in Silicon Valley."[12] As it happens, there are some dynamic ecosystems growing globally. Efforts are underway in Israel, China, and Chile, which are explicitly modeled after Silicon Valley.

Israel

Israel is the ecosystem that most resembles Silicon Valley in its startup fervor. In the last few years, Israel has become a hub of technological innovation in computer science, software, and semiconductors, although a majority of new investments have shifted to new media, internet, and mobile platform applications. If you look at the number of software companies alone, it is disproportionately vast in comparison to the overall population.

Donna Petkanics, a corporate partner at Wilson, Sonsini, Goodrich & Rosati, who represents many Israeli startups, says that Israel has been ripe to take off for the following reasons:

> They have an extremely entrepreneurial culture and a work ethic that is similar to Silicon Valley. These entrepreneurs are very flexible in working across time zones, especially as they often have Silicon Valley VCs on their boards. Israel has developed an ecosystem like Silicon Valley's that is supported by the presence of major venture funds and venture debt lenders to provide the capital, as well as the local arms of accounting firms that are familiar with startups and can coordinate with their colleagues on U.S. accounting norms. Even as a Silicon Valley–based law firm, we are able to provide legal services seamlessly. These Israeli startups have been very successful in growing their businesses and achieving successful outcomes for the founders and venture investors.[13]

In 2009, Dan Senor and Saul Singer co-wrote a book called *Start-Up Nation: The Story of Israel's Economic Miracle*. A Council on Foreign Relations blurb on their book raised the seminal question that most people want to know: "How is it that Israel—a country of 7.1M people, only sixty years old, surrounded by enemies, in a constant state of war since its founding, with no natural resources—produces more start-up companies than large, peaceful, and stable nations like Japan, China, India, Korea, Canada and the United Kingdom?"[14] As of 2011 some 60 Israeli companies were listed on NASDAQ, more than those of any other foreign country.[15] As of June 2012, two Israeli companies, Check Point Software and Perrigo, are listed on the NASDAQ–100.[16]

Senor and Singer argue that much of Israel's success lies in the compulsory military service and immigration. Since almost every 18-year-old Israeli man and woman is required to serve in the Israeli Defense Forces (IDF) for two years, almost every Israeli gets exposure to deeply complex military technology. The authors believe that due to the IDF's non-hierarchical environment, there is a high value placed on creativity and intelligence, even if it means that some rules are broken. Additionally, children raised in an environment where they have to remain strong in the face of the enemy, and later are indoctrinated into the mindset that "no mission is impossible," can create a very determined and unflappable culture.[17]

Then, there is Unit 8200, the technology division of the IDF's Intelligence Corps—its alumni have founded some of the most successful high-tech companies in Israel, such as Check Point, Metacafe, Nice, and Comverse. Unit alums claim that they accumulate technology intel that is most desired as an entrepreneur and as an employee. "There are job offers on the internet and wanted ads that specifically say 'meant for 8200 alumni,'" commented Ziv, a Unit alumnus who only shares his first name, in a *Forbes* article entitled, "The Unit."[18] Instead of valuing where someone went to school, the question, "Where did you serve in the army?" is what inquisitive employers want to know.

Israel's immigration laws policy plays a vital role in its economic growth. Immigrants by definition are willing to take risks and to start over, just for a chance at a better life. The State of Israel is composed of 90 percent immigrants or descendants of immigrants. From welcoming survivors of the Holocaust to absorbing scientists and engineers who fled the former Soviet Union in the mid-1980s and beyond, Israel has disproportionately benefited from the highly educated who have chosen to migrate there.

China

Unlike democratic societies, it is the Communist Party of China's (CPC) Central Committee that dictates industry growth in addition to the specific business activities that companies partake in to maximize efficiency and eliminate internal, domestic competition. Its "12th Five-Year Plan"[19] that began in 2011 (its first five year plan was 1953–57, and there have been subsequent five-year plans since) aims to accelerate the transformation of the economy towards "inclusive growth" such as services and scientific developments that benefit a greater proportion of Chinese citizens. No longer does China want to be known as the world's manufacturing plant, but rather seven strategic emerging industries have been targeted for growth: next-generation information technology, biotechnology, new energy, energy conservation, clean energy vehicles, new materials, and high-end manufacturing equipment. These industries are expected to attract 5 trillion Renminbi (RMB, the currency of the People's Republic of China, approximately $787 billion) of central government investment by 2020.[20]

Reports on the ability of the rising giant in the East to become the new global hub of innovation are conflicted, however. To say that China only knows how to cut and paste would be to overlook the dynamic that is fueling its rapid development. The country boasts a number of highly successful homegrown companies that have adapted business models of companies in other countries to the needs of their domestic consumers. Yet, one of China's most prominent angel investors, Xu Xiaoping, recently proclaimed in a talk at the Yale Club of Beijing that it will take at least another 20 years before China will no longer need to send its students abroad to become creative and innovative.[21] Still, "the Chinese government is offering incentives, including tax holidays for select industries such as software and integrated circuit companies, and tax breaks for research-intensive businesses. The sub-industries that continue to draw attention in China and abroad include cloud computing, internet, smart devices and other similar subsectors," according to Egidio Zarrella, Clients and Innovation Partner, KPMG China.[22]

China's most well-known effort to establish its own Silicon Valley focuses on the city district of Zhongguancun, where Peking University and Tsinghua University reside, along with the all-powerful Chinese Academy of Sciences. Zhongguancun is a prime example of government trying to "create" a Silicon Valley, rather than figure out how to let one grow.[23] Indeed, perhaps the biggest issue that faces Zhongguancun as a viable competitor to Silicon Valley on the global stage is the fundamentally different role that government plays in China. As just one indication of this top-down approach, Vice Premier Li Keqiang announced in March 2012 the Chinese government's intention to spend RMB 1 trillion ($158 billion) in 2012 alone on research and development to encourage domestic innovation.[24] This type of spending is coupled with policies aimed at convincing foreign companies to move more of their global innovation activities to China.

The problem with Zhongguancun, however, is that it has substantial weaknesses. The immigrant talent pool is thin, and quality of life in Beijing is questionable. Competing interests of government determine rule of law, and smaller private sector innovators will continue to experience difficulty in asserting IP rights vis-à-vis larger established players with better connections to government.[25]

In China, industries are often consolidated by the government into favored hands, rather than by market forces. In early 2010, when GCL decided to enter the silicon wafer business and needed to rapidly build up production capacity, Konca Solar, at the time a highly successful silicon wafer factory, was a natural fit. But instead of letting the two companies work out an agreement, the local government in Jiangsu province approached the founder and major shareholder of Konca Solar and asked him to sell his company to GCL. Not only was the local government a minority shareholder in Konca Solar, they also held the power to reissue the annual permits for factory operations. The founder had little choice but to sell his company to GCL and exit the business. And as we saw in the example of Emei Semiconductor and GCL, even 50-year-old state-owned enterprises can face challenges in asserting their IP rights.

Another example is Tencent, whose recent launch of Weixin 4.0 is seen as a "prime example of the homegrown combination of copying, remixing, and innovation that Tencent executes to perfection."[26] Then there is Huawei, a networking and telecommunications equipment company, now considered the world's largest 4G provider. Yet, Huawei has been accused of and sued by Cisco for patent infringement for stealing its IP and router technology, even down to the very flaws that exist in Cisco's routers.

Another difference between Silicon Valley and China is how investors exit their investments in startups. In the former, a majority of startups are acquired by the larger established firms—such as Google, Cisco, and Facebook—as part of an explicit innovation outsourcing strategy. In China the larger, more established companies tend to react to startups by copying their ideas, developing them in-house, and using their dominant market position to marginalize the startups. There is a clear preference for building in-house rather than acquiring external capabilities, removing a major exit option for startups in China.

Ultimately a more nuanced look across different industries and markets is necessary to determine whether or not China can replicate Silicon Valley. Chinese companies are highly innovative in their own markets, and a recent *McKinsey Quarterly* article points out that Chinese companies are particularly good at innovation in "commercialization," i.e., they take imperfect prototypes to market quickly and let the markets tell them how to develop their products. By comparison, western companies tend to go through numerous internal iterations to perfect their products before first market introductions.[27]

In certain industries, such as PC and router manufacturing, this makes Chinese companies highly competitive in the global marketplace, as evidenced by the dominant presence of Lenovo and Huawei in each of these product categories, respectively. But in more culturally dependent product markets, such as internet commerce and social media, it is hard to imagine a RenRen or Baidu replacing Facebook or Google on the global stage. One important trend that gave Chinese companies increased leverage in the innovation race was the shift of manufacturing to China and Asia. As argued by Andy Grove in a widely cited 2010 *Businessweek* article, certain types of innovation happen close to manufacturing.[28] Chinese companies have proven themselves highly adept in "process innovation" and one of the world's leaders in this area. Small, step-like innovations and improvements in manufacturing processes are key to leading in this field, and this process is one of the reasons why they've recently risen in prominence in the solar manufacturing industry.

But the window for China to take advantage of their current manufacturing prowess may be limited. As Vivek Wadhwa argues in a *Foreign Policy* article, rapid advances in artificial intelligence, robotics, and 3D printing will result in an entirely new generation of machines and models of production, shifting the balance back toward made-to-order, local manufacturing, and making the current model of mass manufacturing in China for the world soon obsolete.[29]

Perhaps this discussion is best summarized by the news that Chinese company Lenovo—with its global headquarters in Zhongguancun, Beijing—is now poised to overtake one of the original Silicon Valley icons, Hewlett-Packard, as the largest PC maker in the world. Regardless, this would be the first time in the past several centuries that a Chinese company has been number one in a global technology sector. At the same time, Apple's fastest growing market for its innovative products is China itself, and Silicon Valley has long since moved on to other areas of dominance in search engines, social media, and big data. It would seem that Chinese companies have overtaken the past, but not yet the future of Silicon Valley.

Chile

In the last couple of years, Chile has garnered a great deal of media attention for its government program, Start-Up Chile, which gives $40,000 in free equity funding (no strings attached) over six months, office space in an incubator environment, and a 12-month visa to successful applicants, since all of its initial applicants were directed to foreigners. Launched in March 2010 with the goal of funding a thousand startups by 2014, Start-Up Chile has since received over 1,600 applications from 70 different countries. Perhaps tellingly, the majority of applications have come from the United States. As of April 2012, the program tally was 500 entrepreneurs, 220 foreign startups, 180 locals employed, and 143 employed abroad. In July 2011, after gaining critical mass of foreign applicants, the program opened itself up to Chileans as well, receiving 600 domestic applications of which 80 were selected for funding.[30]

Although it is too early to draw conclusions on the success of the program, it is interesting both in its thrust and initial developments. According to *Businessweek*, the first $8 million in venture capital money was raised not from Chile, but rather from Argentina, Brazil, France, the United States, and Uruguay.[31] Indeed, the program has become a magnet for startups that target the Latin American market, as well as Latin American entrepreneurs with global ambitions, strengthening Chile's bid to become the entrepreneurship and innovation hub in Latin America.

Early commentators on the program have pointed out that Start-Up Chile has benefited from the presence of global companies located in Chile's capital, Santiago, underscoring the importance of a globally savvy talent pool. However, graduates from the program have also commented on the challenges it faces. There is a lack of venture capital money in Chile, with most of domestic seed funding coming from CORFO, the Chilean Economic Development Agency. So startups seem to migrate back to their backers' countries of origin. For example, of the 87 teams from the 2011 class, approximately half of them stayed in Latin America, with 40 percent of them moving to Argentina and Brazil, where small incubators and seed funding already exist.

One interesting misconception is that the $40,000 in funding is handed over to the startup founders after submitting a business plan. In fact, each company needs to apply for reimbursement for expenses to tap into the $40,000, so they need to first spend the money and wait for the program administrators to approve their expenses. This is somewhat different to the general concept of startup funding, and points to the government hand behind the program: It's hard to imagine government officials or their sponsored programs simply handing out one lump sum in the same way as angel investors—the money comes from taxpayers. Another challenge is the fact that bankruptcy proceedings in Chile can drag on for years, rather than the matter of months they take in the United States. This greatly increases the cost of failure for entrepreneurs.

Compared to the United States, Chile's economic development and wealth is more concentrated in the hands of certain families, making it more difficult for independent entrepreneurs to be successful. At the same time, entrepreneurs coming from the established families will more likely focus on traditional business opportunities, such as infrastructure development, rather than on riskier startup ventures like internet platforms or new product innovations. This challenge points to the benefit of a merit-based economic rewards system in stimulating innovation through private sector startups.

Start-Up Chile has clearly already been successful in highlighting Chile as a country that is keen to foster innovation and private sector economic growth. It has attracted both talent and external funding to Chile; entrepreneurs will certainly remember the jumpstart given to them by the Chilean government even if they move abroad to other countries in pursuit of funding.

But the program has also highlighted the challenges faced by trying to replicate the Silicon Valley ecosystem in a new environment. There is the relative lack of successful entrepreneurs who can provide seed funding and mentor the next generation; a dearth of a venture capital community and service providers such as legal, tax, and accounting firms that can play key advisory roles; and a deficiency of economic and political resources in the hands of established families who would be more inclined to take risks in innovation. It will take time to slowly change the dynamics, but at least the Chilean government has taken the first positive steps in this direction, as well as a leadership role to South America in the promotion of regional innovation.

KEEPING PACE WITH INNOVATION

The greatest challenge for innovation no matter where anyone is located will be the ability to keep pace with geopolitics. For example, the demand for clean technologies to accompany economic development in China and Asia, coupled with the expansion of manufacturing in those regions provide a fertile ground for innovation given the right political, legal, and social frameworks. Each region can take the lessons learned from Silicon Valley and apply them to their own markets, focusing on local needs.

Local demand for products and services will continue to be critical. One example is how Bollywood has been able to assert itself vis-à-vis Hollywood in both India and South Asia due to a large domestic market. And governments will continue to play a defining role in shaping demand, as evidenced in the development of the internet and communication technologies in China. A local consumer will give domestic companies an advantage, but ultimately serves as a global disadvantage as they struggle to adapt to different rules abroad.

Proponents of the Silicon Valley culture argue passionately that government bureaucrats can and should provide the necessary legal framework for startups to succeed (uncomplicated registration of new ventures, free flow of talent, favorable tax treatment, etc.), but that they should otherwise "stay away!"[32] The difference in mindset of entrepreneurs and bureaucrats could not be greater. Whereas angel investors are usually successful entrepreneurs who help pick other budding entrepreneurs with great potential and provide advice and connections, bureaucrats often have few relevant connections, minimal buy-in (i.e., no personal investment), and little industry experience.[33] As such, bureaucrats are ill-equipped to pick the winners and losers, and such efforts will lead to not only a waste of resources, but more importantly will cause U.S. businesses to fall behind in the global race of innovation.

Linda Glenn, a guest lecturer at Singularity University, believes that one of the greatest barriers to growth of technology is the lack of a common lexicon between entrepreneurs, stakeholders, policy makers, and implementation agents. Glenn provides the following example about how the definition of "nanotechnology," which has been very challenging to settle on, could trigger scientific discrepancies depending on how it's used.[34] In late 2010, the International Organization for Standardization (ISO) adopted the "Methodology for the Classification and Categorization of Nanomaterials." Yet the United States has yet to recognize this particular schema, which would make it easier for everyone to speak one another's language. Using nanotechnology in medicine as an example, the FDA must determine whether the medical product falls within the category of "drug" or "device" or "cosmetic"; depending on the classification, treatment by the FDA will be very different.

In addition to the establishment of a new lexicon for the new relationships that are being created as a result of new technologies, we should be considering the possibility of legal reform. How can the legal system deal with exponential change? The creation of specialized science or technology courts is also necessary, in which the judges have ongoing education and training to recognize and deal with these new legal issues and categories that arise from emerging technologies. Another important element to keep in mind is the rule of law with respect to intellectual property, particularly in contrast to the story of Emei Semiconductor and GCL, which shows what happens when right is determined via power struggle and regional leverage, rather than by a clear set of rules that places companies on a (relatively) level playing field regardless of size and location.

CONCLUDING THOUGHTS

Silicon Valley is essentially a one-industry town, freeing the region of the distractions of multiple economies. Instead, all of its energy and resources go toward creating the best possible high-tech economy. And of course, the defining outgrowth of high tech is innovation.

Silicon Valley's framework of innovation rests on three pillars: advancements in technology, tolerance of risk and failure, and the brainpower of its people. Stanford University started as a borderless partner with industry and the community at large, then grew into one of the world's leading research universities. Bright people came who were attracted to the lifestyle, but who also disdained the traditional East Coast hierarchies. Venture capital followed, swelled, and flourished, and the resulting new business models fostered creative destruction and democratized the playing field for anyone with a good idea and the stomach for the process. This evolving culture then attracted other brilliant minds in entrepreneurship, engineering, and management, creating an entrepreneurial ecosystem that trades in meritocracy, openness, and collaboration, and which accepts failure as part of the journey.

There is nothing inherently special about the people in Silicon Valley—it's the way they interact and collaborate that makes the magic. Whether out of altruism or self-interest, the net effect of the Silicon Valley business model is an emphasis on giving back, wealth at the top that actually does "trickle down," and an acknowledgment—still overdue in other corners of corporate America—that great companies and ventures grow from the hard work of many indispensable people, not just the vision of a handful of CEOs.

Of course, it's impossible to purely replicate Silicon Valley, which was the right place at the right moment of history (the tech boom, as well as a handful of other transformational innovation cycles), and has fully embraced that good fortune to create a market niche it will dominate for the foreseeable future. But other communities can certainly learn from Silicon Valley's commitment to continuous innovation and a culture of creativity—those quintessential twenty-first-century values so key to remaining competitive not just in technology, but in finance, education, and every other human endeavor. It is this culture that will produce the next round of life-changing products, services, and improvements in everything from healthcare to transportation to alleviating poverty. It's a deep well of potential we're only beginning to tap into, and the more it spreads outside Silicon Valley and around the world, the better off we'll all be.

ACKNOWLEDGMENTS

This book has been six years in the making. There are scarce moments in one's life that are life-changing and, for me, moving to Silicon Valley was one of them. In true Silicon Valley form, there are so many people who took an interest in my transition from Washington, DC, and who schooled and helped me navigate this foreign land that I had embarked upon.

In addition to moving to Silicon Valley, there were three other events that were the primary basis for this book. Pamela Ryckman's *New York Times* article, "The Risk-Taking Edge of West Coast Women," which reported on Alley to the Valley and my move from the East Coast; Dr. Deborah Gruenfeld and Lisa Sweeney, who approached me about a Stanford business case study of my transition to Silicon Valley and finding opportunity here; and a panel discussion I gave at a *More* magazine conference, where my speaking agent and former editor both said, "There's a book here!"

In truth, the writing of this book, as with any book, was arduous and challenging. My company was going through a pivot while I was in the researching and writing stage; there were many 4:30 A.M. awakenings so I could effectively attend to both demands. On weekends, I'd try to rise hours before my children woke up so they wouldn't feel neglected in the process. Still, there were many weekend days when my children would ask, "Do you have to work on your book again?"

I'll never forget one of the first conversations I had with my editor, Emily Carleton, at Palgrave Macmillan. She commented, "It is amazing that no one has written about Silicon Valley in this context." I soon figured out why. Emily, your command of Silicon Valley is beyond astonishing considering that you have not spent significant time here. I have enormous gratitude to you, Emily, as you persuaded me to reposition the book, and, because of that, you have helped me develop a new platform that I am wildly passionate about. You are a brilliant writer to boot.

In writing this book, I was humbled by how much time and interest many of the ecosystem founders contributed. Thank you to Larry Sonsini and Tim

Draper, who instantly invited me to sit down with them and learn about their version of the Silicon Valley mindset and founding histories.

I owe Vivek Wadhwa an enormous amount of gratitude, not only for your own expertise and iconoclastic style, but also for tolerating my incessant badgering to speak with even more Silicon Valley experts. If you had not invited me to sit in at one of Singularity University's (SU) executive education programs, I am not sure that this book would have been the same. What I learned at SU did change my life, and my only issue was that once I experienced SU, I wanted to spend all my time there instead of taking care of the business at hand. Thank you to many on the SU staff, most especially Robin Farmanfarmaian for your responsive diligence to my inquiries, to SU's co-founder Dr. Peter Diamandis, and many of SU's leading scientific experts, including Andrew Hessel, who inspired me to think about the next big thing in science and technology.

To Frank Spencer, whose talented, futuristic mind would stretch my thinking, so that after hours of stimulating dialogues, I'd have to pull my mind back into the present. To Doug Henton, who shares my love of economics, and helped me to understand the unique economic immunity of Silicon Valley.

To Stanford University, for serving as the most inspiring backdrop. All these years later, I still walk around campus in awe, and I am fortunate that my young children have experienced the benefits of Stanford, including the opportunity to attend Bing Nursery School, Math Circle, and Stanford gymnastics. Dr. William Miller and Marguerite Gong Hancock were so gracious and inviting in allowing me to learn from their experiences at the Stanford Program for Regional Innovation and Entrepreneurship (SPRIE).

A huge debt of gratitude to Anita Chetty, AnnaLee Saxien, Anshul Samar, Barry Kramer, Ben Lauring, Bob Pavey, Donna Petkanics, Eric Ries, Fern Madelbaum, John Swan, Kanwal Rehki, Heidi Roizen, Jack Boyd, Jamis MacNiven, Jennifer Winters, Jerrold T. Brandt, Dr. John Morton, Jonathan Levav, Jordan Newman, Kenwal Rehki, Leslie Berlin, Lindsay Trout, Liz Wiseman, Luis Buhler, Luis Meiia, Mark Bercow, Martha Josephson, Michael Finnegan, Neesha Bapat, Pam Dickenson, Raj Desal, Dr. Richard Swanson, Russ Hancock, Michael McWhinney, Steve Blank, and Tatiana Chapira, who all contributed in one way or another. To Stefan Kratz, whose experiences in China helped importantly shape my insights on China's entrepreneurial climate. To Patricia Rios at KPMG, whose innovation report gave momentous intuition into what the rest of the world thinks about Silicon Valley.

There were so many people who added sunshine to my day when I occasionally felt besieged by the simultaneous tasks of running a company and researching and writing a book. To Suzy Ginsburg, whose energy and cheerleading approach to life inspires me on so many levels. To Pamela Ryckman, what a pleasure it has been to get to know you and be on this journey simultaneously. To Mallun Yen, who provided the expertise and context on intellectual property. More notably, how I value (and miss) our long runs, especially as we strategized on business and life.

To my agent, Claudia Cross, who has stuck with me throughout the years and has had to endure vast proposals that align with my myriad of passions. Claudia, you have been a support system—often a muse—in times of uncertainty.

To my assistant, Jamie Danno, who was unflappable during this very intense process of book research and writing. Your "can-do" attitude will serve you well throughout your life. To April Daniels Hussar of our BettyConfidential staff, thank you for your passion for Betty and for always rising to the task. Of course, thank you to Francine Gani—none of this would be possible without you.

To my father, who must have instilled my curiosity for science. To my mother, whose unconditional love has supported me throughout the many peaks and valleys in life. And to Mitch, for being the Renaissance man that you are. We love having you in our lives.

To my incredibly loving and supportive husband, Dino Piscione, who not only goes along with whatever I want to do or wherever I want to travel, but also has to tolerate being married to someone whose curiosity often causes her to have her head in the clouds in deep thought. And to our three remarkable children, Drake, Dominick, and Dayne Alexandria, who inspire us to be better people every day.

PHOTO CREDITS

Part I: An East Coaster Goes West
Courtesy: The Author

Chapter 1: Why You Should Care about Silicon Valley
Courtesy: Singularity University

Chapter 2: Why Silicon Valley Exists
Courtesy: Los Altos History Museum

Part II: Silicon Valley Ecosystem and Culture
Courtesy: Artwork created by Jamie Danno

Chapter 3: The University: Stanford
Courtesy: Linda A. Cicero, Stanford News Service

Chapter 4: A Population of Highly Motivated People
Courtesy: The California Historical Society

Chapter 5: The Cycle of Innovation
Courtesy: Tesla Motors, Inc.

Chapter 6: The Unique Profile of the Silicon Valley Entrepreneur
Courtesy: The Author; photo by Asa Mathat

Chapter 7: What Makes Silicon Valley Business Models Different
Courtesy: Box, Inc.

Chapter 8: The Investors of Sand Hill Road
Courtesy: Jamie Danno

Chapter 9: The Services
Courtesy: GP Technology Partners

Chapter 10: The Meeting Places
Courtesy: Jamie Danno

Chapter 11: The Lifestyle
Courtesy: Jamie Danno

Chapter 12: The Bench
Courtesy: The Harker School

Epilogue: Can Silicon Valley Be Replicated?
Courtesy: Artwork created by Jamie Danno

NOTES

PART I: AN EAST COASTER GOES WEST

1. Morgan Brennan, "America's Most Expensive Zip Codes," *Forbes*, October 12, 2011, accessed August 21, 2012, http://www.forbes.com/lists/2011/7/zip-codes -11_land.html.
2. Karrie Jacobs, "Saving the Tract House," *New York Times Magazine*, May 15, 2005, accessed September 10, 2012, http://www.nytimes.com/2005/05/15 /magazine/15TRACT.html.
3. "Residential Real Estate | Top 400 Sales Professionals," *The Wall Street Journal*, 2009, accessed August 20, 2012, http://online.wsj.com/ad/top100individual volume_2009.html.
4. Juliet Chung, "Russian Investor Buys Silicon Valley Mansion for $100 Million," *The Wall Street Journal*, March 15, 2011, accessed August 20, 2011, http://blogs.wsj.com/developments/2011/03/30/russian-investor-buys-silicon -valley-mansion-for-100-million/?mod=WSJBlog.
5. Lauren McSherry, "Maxed out: Los Altos Hills Ponders How Big Is Too Big?" *Los Altos Town Crier*, November 9, 2005, accessed August 21, 2012, http:// www.losaltosonline.com/index.php?option=com_content&task=view&id=136 21&Itemid=46.
6. Interview with Marc Andreessen, PBS, first broadcast June 27, 2012, Executive Producer Charlie Rose and Yvette Vega.

CHAPTER 1: WHY YOU SHOULD CARE ABOUT SILICON VALLEY

1. Nick Bostrom, "Superintelligenence, Answer to the 2009 Edge Question: 'What Will Change Everything?'" 2009, accessed June 25, 2012, www.nick bostrom.com/views/superintelligence.pdf.
2. Edward Cornish, *Futuring: The Exploration of the Future* (Maryland: World Future Society, 2004), 12.
3. Dr. Peter Diamandis, phone conversation with author, June 28, 2012.
4. Ray Kurzweil, *The Singularity Is Near* (New York: Viking Penguin, 2005).
5. Ray Kurzweil, Singularity University lecture, NASA Research Park Building, Moffett Field, CA, April 11–13, 2012.
6. Bruce Upbin, "Wait, Did This 15-Year-Old from Maryland Just Change Cancer Treatment?" *Forbes*, June 18, 2012, accessed September 10, 2012, http:// www.forbes.com/sites/bruceupbin/2012/06/18/wait-did-this-15-year-old-from -maryland-just-change-cancer-treatment/.

7. Valerie Strauss, "Meet Jack Andraka, 15-Year-Old Researcher," *Washington Post,* September 18, 2012, accessed June 29, 2012, http://www.washingtonpost .com/blogs/answer-sheet/post/meet-jack-andraka-15-year-old-cancer-researcher /2012/09/18/049a81f4-01a1-11e2-9367-4e1bafb958db_blog.html.

8. "Intel International Science and Engineering Fair: Winners," *Intel.com,* 2012, http://www.intel.com/content/www/us/en/education/competitions/international -science-and-engineering-fair/winners.html?cid=cim:ggl.

9. Gordon E. Moore, "Cramming More Components onto Integrated Circuits," *Electronics Magazine* 38, (April 19, 1965):1–4.

10. Peter H. Diamandis and Steve Kotler, *Abundance: The Future Is Better than You Think* (New York: Free Press, 2012), 9.

11. Ibid.

12. Michio Kaku, *Physics of the Future: How Science Will Change Daily Life by 2100* (New York: Double Day, 2011).

13. Diamandis and Kotler, *Abundance,* 9.

14. Vijay Govindarajan and Chris Trimble, *Reverse Innovation* (Boston: Harvard Business Review Press, 2012).

15. Alex Perry and Nick Wadhams, "Kenya's Banking Revolution," *Time,* January 31, 2011, accessed June 28, 2012, http://www.time.com/time/magazine/article /0,9171,2043329,00.html.

16. David Rose, lecture, Singularity University, Moffett Field, CA, April 12, 2012.

17. Dr. Peter Diamandis, phone conversation with author.

18. "Did Dave Carroll Lose United Airlines $180m?" *The Economist,* July 24, 2009, accessed October 2, 2012, http://www.economist.com/blogs/gulliver/2009/07 /did_dave_carroll_cost_united_1.

19. Mark Tran, "Singer Gets His Revenge on United Airlines and Soars to Fame," *The Guardian,* July 23, 2009, accessed October 2, 2012, http://www.guardian .co.uk/news/blog/2009/jul/23/youtube-united-breaks-guitars-video.

20. "How to Set Syria Free," *The Economist,* February 11, 2012, accessed September 21, 2012, http://www.economist.com/node/21547243.

21. Frank Spencer, interviews with author, April–August 2012.

22. "Personal Income and Outlays, August 2012," *The US Department of Commerce Bureau of Economic Analysis,* September 28, 2012, accessed October 2, 2012, http://www.bea.gov/newsreleases/national/pi/pinewsrelease.htm.

23. Frank Spencer, interviews with author, April–August 2012.

24. Jon Pittman, lecture, Singularity University, Moffett Field, CA, April 8, 2012.

25. *The State of Independence in America,* MBO Partners, Workforce Index, September 2011, accessed July 12, 2012, http://www.mbopartners.com/state- of-independence/docs/MBO-Partners-Independent-Workforce-Index-2011 .pdf.

26. Frank Spencer, email conversation with author, April 18, 2012.

27. Department of Economic Social Affairs, Population Division, United Nations, "World Urbanization Prospects: The 2011 Revision," March 2012, accessed September 10, 2012, http://esa.un.org/unpd/wup/pdf/WUP2011_Highlights .pdf.

28. Ayesha Khanna, "Generative Cities: The Future of Urban Intelligence," *PSFK Need to Know Magazine,* no. 1 (2012).

29. Doug Henton, phone conversation with author, April 16, 2012.

30. William F. Miller, "The 'Habitat' for Entrepreneurship," thesis, Stanford University, July 2000, accessed June 28, 2012, http://www.kaahlsfiles.com/thesis /thesis%20papers/3%20Low/Miller.pdf, 5.

CHAPTER 2: WHY SILICON VALLEY EXISTS

1. As told to Jerold T. Brandt at AlwaysOn Kick-off breakfast at KMPG, June 27, 2012.
2. "Frederick E. Terman," 1997–2012 Stanford University, accessed October 2, 2012, http://engineering.stanford.edu/about/bio-terman.
3. History of Stanford, "The Birth of the University," Stanford University website, accessed October 2, 2012, http://www.stanford.edu/about/history/.
4. The Founding Grant, Leland Stanford Junior University, "About Stanford University," November 1885, accessed October 3, 2012, http://www.stanford.edu/dept/visitorinfo/basics/about.html.
5. Ibid.
6. Theodore Roosevelt, "Remarks at Leland Stanford Jr. University in Palo Alto, California," May 12, 1903. Gerhard Peters and John T. Woolley, *The American Presidency Project,* accessed June 29, 2012, http://www.presidency.ucsb.edu/ws/?pid=97726.
7. Stanford Facts: The Founding of Stanford, Stanford University website, 2012, accessed June 28, 2012, http://facts.stanford.edu/founding.html.
8. Lee De Forest, Space Teleobaphy, U.S. Patent 879,532, filed January 29, 1907 and issued February 18, 1908.
9. Dag Spicer, email with Jamie Danno, research assistant, October 5, 2012.
10. Keith Venter, "Moffett Field History: Laura Thane Whipple," NASA Ames Historic Preservation Office, accessed October 2012, http://historicproperties.arc.nasa.gov/history/history3.html.
11. Ibid.
12. *West Coast Navy Airship Base, Sunnyvale, CA* (video), Moffett Field Historical Society Museum.
13. NASA, "Hanger 1: Moffett Field Naval Air Station HAER NO. CA 335," 2006, accessed January 31, 2013, http://historicproperties.arc.nasa.gov/downloads/hangar1_haer_ca335.pdf/.
14. Keith Venter, "The USS Macon," NASA Ames Historic Preservation, accessed October 2012, http://historicproperties.arc.nasa.gov/history/history5.html.
15. National Ocean and Atmospheric Administration, United States Department of Commerce, "Wreck of Airship USS *Macon* Added to National Register of Historic Places," February 11, 2010, accessed July 8, 2012, http://www.noaanews.noaa.gov/stories2010/20100211_macon.html.
16. Keith Venter, "Moffett Field: From Lighter than Air to Faster than Sound to Outer Space," NASA Ames Historic Preservation, accessed October 2012, http://historicproperties.arc.nasa.gov/history/history2.html.
17. Keith Venter, "World War II and LTA Blimps," NASA Ames Historic Preservation, accessed October 2012, http://historicproperties.arc.nasa.gov/history/history9.html.
18. Keith Venter, "A New Era for Moffett Field," NASA Ames Historic Preservation, accessed October 2012, http://historicproperties.arc.nasa.gov/history/history13.html.
19. "Frederick Terman," PBS Online, 1999, accessed June 28, 2012, http://www.pbs.org/transistor/album1/addlbios/terman.html.
20. Steve Blank, "Secret History of Silicon Valley," video emailed to author by Steve Blank, 1:04:45, July 12, 2012, http://steveblank.com/secret-history/.
21. Ibid.
22. Ibid.

23. Ibid.
24. Gene Bylinsky, "California's Great Breeding Ground for Industry," *Fortune Magazine,* June 1974.
25. Christophe Lécuyer, *Making Silicon Valley: Innovation and the Growth of High Tech, 1930-1970* (Massachusetts: MIT Press, 2005), 135.
26. HP Corporate Archives, "Dave Packard Biography," 2004, accessed July 10, 2012, http://www.hp.com/retiree/history/founders/packard/dave.pdf, 2.
27. Pierpont David Gardner, "William Redington Hewlett," *The William and Flora Hewlett Foundation,* June 2003, accessed July 10, 2012, http://www .hewlett.org/about-the-william-and-flora-hewlett-foundation/william-and -flora-hewlett-and-the-hewlett-foundation/william-redington-hewlett.
28. "Model 200A Audio Oscillator, 1939," HP website, 2011, accessed July 10, 2012, http://www.hp.com/hpinfo/abouthp/histnfacts/museum/earlyinstruments /0002/index.html.
29. Ibid.
30. Russell H. Varian and Sigurd F. Varian, *A High Frequency Oscillator and Amplifier* (Maryland: The American Institute of Physics, 1939).
31. E. L. Ginzton and Russell Varian, "An Early History," *Varian Associates,* accessed July 10, 2012, http://www.cpii.com/docs/files/Varian%20Associates%20 -%20An%20Early%20History.pdf.
32. Silicon Valley Engineering Council, "1993 Hall of Fame Recipients," accessed October 1, 2012, http://www.svec.org/print.html?id=60.
33. Paul Siffert and Eberhard Krimmel, *Silicon: Evolution and Future of a Technology* (New York: Springer, 2004), 25.
34. "The Nobel Prize in Physics 1956," Nobelprize.org, accessed January 31, 2013, http://www.nobelprize.org/nobel_prizes/physics/laureates/1956/.
35. C. Joseph Touhill, Gregory J. Touhill, and Thomas A. O' Riordan, *Commercialization of Innovative Technologies: Bringing Good Ideas to the* Marketplace (New Jersey: John Wiley & Sons, September 20, 2011), 2-6.
36. Christophe Lécuyer and David C. Brock, *Makers of the Microchip: A Documentary History of Fairchild Semiconductor* (Massachusetts: MIT Press, 2010), 33.
37. Chong-Moon Lee, William Miller, Marguerite Hancock, and Henry Rowen, *The Silicon Valley Edge* (California: Stanford University Press, 2000), 164–165.
38. Lee et al., *The Silicon Valley Edge,* 165.
39. Lécuyer, *Making Silicon Valley,* 135.
40. Lee et al., *The Silicon Valley Edge,* 166.
41. Ibid., 167.
42. Ibid., 168.
43. Ibid., 172.
44. Ibid., 180.
45. Ibid., 159.
46. Jim McCormick, "A Brief History of Silicon Valley," *Silicon Valley Economic Development Alliance,* 1995, http://people.seas.harvard.edu/~jones/shockley/sili _valley.html.

PART II: SILICON VALLEY ECOSYSTEM AND CULTURE

1. Tony Perkins, author attended AlwaysOn Kick-off breakfast at KPMG, June 27, 2012.
2. Bert Sperling, "Cost of Living in Santa Clara California," Sperling's Best Places, 2010, accessed July 10, 2012, http://www.bestplaces.net/cost_of_living/city /california/santa_clara.

3. Joshua Brustein, "For Tech Start-Ups, New York Has Increasing Allure," *New York Times,* May 27, 2012, accessed October 8, 2012, http://www.nytimes.com/2012/05/28/technology/for-tech-startups-new-york-has-increasing-allure.html?pagewanted=all.

4. Marguerite Gong Hancock, in-person meeting with author at Stanford Graduate School of Business, April 10, 2012.

CHAPTER 3: THE UNIVERSITY: STANFORD

1. Karen Bartholomew, Claude Brinegar, and Roxanne Nilan, "A Chronology of Stanford University and Its Founders," Stanford Historical Society, 2001, accessed July 12, 2012, http://janestanford.stanford.edu/biography.html.

2. Ibid.

3. Bill Yenne, *The History of the Southern Pacific* (Nebraska: Bison Books, 1985), 10–11.

4. Bartholomew et al., "A Chronology of Stanford University and Its Founders."

5. Julie Cain, "Rudolph Ulrich and the Stanford Arizona Garden," *Sandstone & Tile* 17, no. 2 (Spring/Summer 2003), 3, accessed July 20, 2012, http://histsoc.stanford.edu/pdfST/ST27no2.pdf.

6. Suzanne and Stephen Eschenbach, "What You Don't Know About Leland Stanford's Horses," *Stanford Magazine,* September/October 2005, accessed July 14, 2012, http://alumni.stanford.edu/get/page/magazine/article/?article_id=34389.

7. Stanford University, "The Birth of the University," About Stanford University, accessed July 12, 2012, http://www.stanford.edu/about/history/.

8. Eschenbach, "What You Don't Know About Leland Stanford's Horses."

9. Ibid.

10. Cantor Arts Center at Stanford University, "The Stanford Collection."

11. Theresa Johnston, "Grief's Beauty," *Stanford Magazine,* July/August 2009, accessed July 10, 2012, http://alumni.stanford.edu/get/page/magazine/article/?article_id=29959.

12. Stanford University, "The Birth of the University."

13. "Truth and Lies at Harvard," *Stanford Magazine,* November/December 1998, accessed July 23, 2012, http://alumni.stanford.edu/get/page/magazine/article/?article_id=41534.

14. Stanford University Libraries & Academic Information Resources, "Frequently Asked Questions," *Stanford University Archives,* accessed July 23, 2012, http://www-sul.stanford.edu/depts/spc/uarch/faq.html.

15. Stanford University, "The Birth of the University."

16. Ibid.

17. National Archives and Records Administration, "Biographical Sketch of Herbert Hoover 1874–1964," June 20, 2001, accessed July 19, 2012, http://www.ecommcode.com/hoover/hooveronline/hoover_bio/stan.htm.

18. Steve Staiger, "Timothy Hopkins: The Ironic Journey of Palo Alto's Founder," *Palo Alto Weekly,* April 28, 1999, accessed July 22, 2012, http://www.paloaltoonline.com/weekly/morgue/spectrum/1999_Apr_28.HISTORY.html.

19. Martin Kenney, *Understanding Silicon Valley: The Anatomy of an Entrepreneur Region* (California: Stanford University Press, 2000), 19–20.

20. Stanford Engineering, "Frederick E. Terman (1900–1982)," 1997–2012, accessed July 19, 2012, http://engineering.stanford.edu/about/bio-terman.

21. Stanford University Real Estate, "Stanford Research Park," accessed July 10, 2012, http://lbre.stanford.edu/realestate/research_park.

22.   Wellspring of Innovation, "Wellspring Home," October 18, 2011, accessed July 22, 2012, http://www.stanford.edu/group/wellspring/.

23.   John Swan, email communication with author, April 10, 2012.

24.   John Battelle, "The Birth of Google." *Wired,* August 13, 2005, accessed July 21, 2012, http://www.wired.com/wired/archive/13.08/battelle.html?tw=wn_top head_4.

25.   Luis Mejia, phone conversation with author, April 17, 2012.

26.   Lisa Krieger, "Stanford Earns $336 Million off Google Stock," *San Jose Mercury News,* December 1, 2005.

27.   Technology Licensing at Stanford University. *Technology Licensing at Stanford University,* Stanford University, 2011–2012, PowerPoint, 14.

28.   Ibid.

29.   Stanford University, "Stanford Facts: Research and Innovation," 2012, accessed July 19, 2012, http://facts.stanford.edu/research.html.

30.   Hans Wiesendanger, "A History of OTL Overview," Stanford University Office of Technology Licensing, 2000, accessed July 19, 2012, http://otl.stanford.edu /about/about_history.html.

31.   Ben Lauing, personal communication with author during a Stanford Science and Engineering quad (SEQ) tour, July 17, 2012.

32.   Stanford University, "Stanford Facts: Campus Life," 2011, accessed July 19, 2012, http://facts.stanford.edu/campuslife.html.

33.   Stanford University, "Undergraduate Research," 2012, accessed July 19, 2012, http://www.stanford.edu/dept/undergrad/cgi-bin/drupal/research.

34.   Diane Rogers, "Olmsted's Vision for Campus Advanced by Latest Design," *Inside Stanford Medicine,* May 10, 2010, accessed July 19, 2012, http://med.stanford .edu/ism/2010/may/lksc-olmsted-0510.html.

35.   Ibid.

36.   Ginny McCormick, "New Quad on the Block," *Stanford Magazine,* November/ December 1999, accessed July 23, 2012, http://alumni.stanford.edu/get/page /magazine/article/?article_id=40487.

37.   Stanford Engineering, "Science and Engineering Quad Services," accessed July 24, 2012, http://engineering-info.stanford.edu/stanford-engineering/deans-offi ce/facilities-planning-management/seq-operations.

38.   Stanford Engineering, "Departments and Programs," http://soe-oldwebserver .stanford.edu/departments/index.html; Stanford Engineering, "Stanford Engineering by the Numbers," Facts and Figures, 2011, accessed July 24, 2012, http://engineering.stanford.edu/about/facts.

39.   Stanford University School of Engineering, "Jen-Hsun Huang Engineering Center Self-guided Tour," Stanford University, accessed July 24, 2012, http://www .stanford.edu/dept/soe/downloads/huang_self_guided_tour.pdf, 2.

40.   Jonathon Levav, email communication with author, September 4, 2012.

41.   Author toured school on October 5, 2012.

42.   David Kelley, "How to Build Your Creative Confidence," TED presentation, Long Beach, CA: TED 2012, May 2012, accessed July 28, 2012, http://www .ted.com/talks/david_kelley_how_to_build_your_creative_confidence.html.

43.   Stanford Graduate School of Business, "Design Thinking Boot Camp: From Insights to Innovation," Programs, 2012, accessed July 22, 2012, http://www .gsb.stanford.edu/exed/dtbc/.

44.   d.school, "Our Team—Hasso Plattner Bio," 2012, accessed July 15, 2012, http: //dschool.stanford.edu/bio/hasso-plattner/.

45. Stanford University Parking & Transportation Services, "Bicycling at Stanford," accessed July 20, 2012, http://transportation.stanford.edu/alt_transportation /BikingAtStanford.shtml.

46. U.S. Census Bureau, "2010 Census Interactive Population Search: Santa Clara County," 2010, accessed July 22, 2012, http://2010.census.gov/2010census/pop map/ipmtext.php?fl=06.

47. Theresa Johnston, "These Old Houses," *Stanford Magazine,* November/December 2005, accessed July 15, 2012, http://alumni.stanford.edu/get/page/ma gazine/article/?article_id=33831.

48. Stanford University, "Stanford University Common Data Set," 2011–2012, accessed July 18, 2012, http://ucomm.stanford.edu/cds/2011.html#admission.

49. Stanford University, "Diversity at Stanford," August 14, 2012, accessed July 18, 2012, http://admission.stanford.edu/student/diversity/index.html.

50. "Farm Aid," *Stanford Magazine,* May/June 2008, accessed July 12, 2012, http://alumni.stanford.edu/get/page/magazine/article/?article_id=32301.

51. Stanford University, "Spotlight," Diversity at Stanford, accessed July 18, 2012, http://admission.stanford.edu/.

52. Richard Perez-Pena, "Mixed Returns for Endowments," *New York Times,* September 27, 2012, accessed July 20, 2012, http://www.nytimes.com/2012/09/28 /education/large-universities-report-mixed-year-for-endowments.html?_r=0.

53. Computer History Museum, "Silicon Graphics and MIPS Merge," *This Day in History*, accessed July 12, 2012, http://www.computerhistory.org/tdih/June /29/.

CHAPTER 4: A POPULATION OF HIGHLY MOTIVATED PEOPLE

1. Robert W. Merry, *A Country of Vast Designs: James K. Polk, the Mexican War and the Conquest of the American Continent* (New York: Simon and Schuster, 2009), 133, 452.

2. Ibid., 128.

3. Michael Beschloss and Hugh Sidey, "The Presidents of the United States of America," 2009, accessed July 28, 2012, http://www.whitehouse.gov/about /presidents/jamespolk.

4. Merry, *A Country of Vast Designs.*

5. Richard E. Snyder, *American Argonauts: Freedom and Order in the California Gold Rush* (Massachusetts: Brandeis University, 2000).

6. S.F Genealogy, "San Francisco Population," 2011, accessed July 30, 2012, http://www.sfgenealogy.com/sf/history/hgpop.htm.

7. Kevin Starr and Richard J. Orsi, *Rooted in Barbarous Soil: People, Culture, and Community in Gold Rush California* (California: University of California Press, 2000), 25.

8. Library of Congress, "Exploration and Settlement," July 22, 2010, accessed July 26, 2012, http://www.loc.gov/exhibits/british/brit-1.html.

9. Steve Garber, "Sputnik and The Dawn of the Space Age," National Aeronautics and Space Administration, October 10, 2007, accessed July 27, 2012, http:// history.nasa.gov/sputnik/.

10. Steve Garber, "National Aeronautics and Space Act of 1958," National Aeronautics and Space Administration, February 18, 2004, accessed July 27, 2012, http://history.nasa.gov/spaceact.html.

11. Garber, "Sputnik and the Dawn of the Space Age."

12. Jennifer Ludden, "1956 Immigration Law Changed Face of America," NPR, 2006, accessed July 15, 2012, http://www.npr.org/templates/story/story.php?storyId=5391395.

13. Sarah Starkweather, "U.S. Immigration Legislation Online," University of Washington, Bothell Library, accessed July 27, 2012, http://library.uwb.edu/guides/usimmigration/1965_immigration_and_nationality_act.html.

14. Ludden, "1956 Immigration law Changed Face of America."

15. U.S. Census Bureau, "The Foreign-Born with Science and Engineering Degrees," 2010, accessed July 23, 2012, http://www.census.gov/newsroom/releases/archives/education/cb11-tps46.html.

16. Mario Cervantes and Dominique Guellec, "The Brain Drain: Old Myths, New Realities," *OECD Observer,* January 2002, accessed July 21, 2012, http://www.oecdobserver.org/news/archivestory.php/aid/673/The_brain_drain:_Old_myths,_new_realities.html.

17. U.S. Census Bureau, accessed July 30, 2012, http://2010.census.gov/2010census/.

18. Kanwal Rekhi, phone conversation with author, April 10, 2012.

19. Julia Pitta, "The Venture Capitalist from Kanpur," *Forbes,* July 6, 1998, accessed April 15, 2012, http://www.forbes.com/forbes/1998/0706/6201162a.html.

20. TiE, "CM Benefits," accessed April 28, 2012, https://www.tie.org/page/charter-member-benefits.

21. Richard Springer, "Cetas: From Start-Up to VMware Acquisition in 18 Months," *India West,* June 18, 2012, accessed June 21, 2012, http://www.indiawest.com/news/5050-cetas-from-start-up-to-vmware-acquisition-in-18-months.html.

22. Vivek Wadhwa, "Silicon Valley is No Meritocracy," *The Kernel,* December 19, 2011, accessed June 20, 2012, http://www.kernelmag.com/features/essay/160/silicon-valley-is-no-meritocracy/.

23. Vivek Wadhwa, "The Face of Success, Part 1: How the Indians Conquered Silicon Valley," *Inc.,* January 13, 2012, accessed April 9, 2012, http://www.inc.com/vivek-wadhwa/how-the-indians-succeeded-in-silicon-valley.html.

24. Ibid.

25. AnnaLee Saxenian, *The New Argonauts: Regional Advantage in a Global Economy* (Massachusetts: Harvard University Press, 2007), 82; 121.

26. AnnaLee Saxenian, phone and email conversations with author, June 5–July 30, 2012.

27. Raj Desal, interview with author at TiE, July 20, 2012.

28. Mike Swift, "Blacks, Latinos and Women Lose Ground at Silicon Valley Tech Companies," *San Jose Mercury News,* November 8, 2011, accessed April 28, 2012, http://www.mercurynews.com/ci_14383730.

29. Wadhwa, "The Face of Success, Part 1."

30. Pitta, "The Venture Capitalist from Kanpur."

CHAPTER 5: THE CYCLE OF INNOVATION

1. Jay Yarrow, "A Day in the Life of Elon Musk, The Most Inspiring Entrepreneur in the World," *Business Insider,* July 24, 2012, accessed June 24, 2012, http://www.businessinsider.com/elon-musk-day-in-the-life-of-the-tesla-and-spacex-ceo-2012-7.

2. Michael Belfiore, *Rocketeers: How a Visionary Band of Business Leaders, Engineers, and Pilots Is Boldly Privatizing Space* (New York: HarperCollins, 2008).

3. Ibid., 166–195.

4. Josh Friedman, "Entrepreneur Tries His Midas Touch in Space," *Los Angeles Times,* April 22, 2003, accessed April 28, 2012, http://articles.latimes.com /2003/apr/22/business/fi-spacex22.

5. CrunchBase, "Elon Musk," June 07, 2012, accessed January 31, 2013, http:// www.crunchbase.com/person/elon-musk.

6. SpaceX, "Dragon Overview," 2012, accessed October 9, 2012, http://www .spacex.com/dragon.php.

7. Tony Dokoupil, "Elon Musk Shoots for the Stars with SpaceX," *Newsweek,* May 21, 2012, accessed June 12, 2012, http://www.thedailybeast.com/news week/2012/05/20/elon-musk-shoots-for-the-stars-with-spacex.html.

8. Tesla Motors, "Roadster," accessed October 9, 2012, http://www.teslamotors .com/roadster/technology.

9. Vivek Wadhwa, email with author, August 21, 2012.

10. Tesla Motors, "Model S," accessed October 9, 2012, http://www.teslamotors .com/roadster/models.

11. Seth Masia, "A Family Business Leads the Installer Universe," *Solar Today,* May 2011, accessed October 9, 2012, http://www.solartoday-digital.org/solar today/201105/?pg=22#pg22.

12. "Rocket Man," *R&D,* 2007, accessed October 9, 2012, http://www.rdmag .com/articles/2007/09/rocket-man.

13. "The 75 Most Influential People of the 21st Century," *Esquire,* accessed October 9, 2012, http://www.esquire.com/features/most-influential-21st-century -1008#slide-39.

14. Luisa Kroll, "Forbes World's Billionaires," *Forbes,* March 7, 2012, accessed October 9, 2012, http://www.forbes.com/sites/luisakroll/2012/03/07/forbes -worlds-billionaires-2012/.

15. *Merriam-Webster.com,* s.v. "Innovation," accessed June 20, 2012, http://www .merriam-webster.com/dictionary/innovation.

16. Ibid.

17. Garry Kasparov, Max Levchin, and Peter Thiel, *The Blueprint: Reviving Innovation, Rediscovering Risk, and Rescuing the Free Market* (New York: W. W. Norton & Company, 2013).

18. Paul Dean and Mack Reed, "An Electric Start: Media Billboards, Website Herald Launch of the EV1," *Los Angeles Times,* December 6, 1996, accessed May 19, 2012, http://articles.latimes.com/1996-12-06/news/mn-6275_1_electric-start.

19. "Driving the Future," *The Economist,* June 25, 2010, accessed May 28, 2012, http://www.economist.com/blogs/newsbook/2010/06/gms_new_electric_car.

20. "The Apple Connection," *Computer History Museum,* 2012, accessed June 29, 2012, http://www.computerhistory.org/revolution/input-output/14/348.

21. PARC, "Xerox PARC History," accessed October 9, 2012, http://www.parc .com/about/.

22. Dan Farber, "Apple in the Courtroom: 25 Years of Defending the Crown Jewels," *CNET* August 10, 2012, accessed August 13, 2012, http://news.cnet.com /8301-13579_3-57489319-37/apple-in-the-courtroom-25-years-of-defending -the-crown-jewels/.

23. Computer Museum, author took a tour, April 14, 2012.

24. Dafydd Neal Dyar, "Under the Hood: Part 8," *Computer Source Magazine,* November 4, 2002, accessed May 25, 2012, http://web.archive.org/web/2006 0901182630/http://www.computersourcemag.com/articles/viewer.asp?a=695.

25. James Wallace and Jim Erickson, *Hard Drive* (Michigan: Wiley, 1992).

26. IDEO, "Our Approach: Design Thinking," About IDEO, accessed June 15, 2012, http://www.ideo.com/about.
27. Ibid.
28. Adrian Wooldridge, "Think Different," *The Economist,* August 6, 2011, accessed June 20, 2012, http://www.economist.com/node/21525350.
29. Carmine Gallo, *The Innovation Secrets of Steve Jobs: Insanely Different Principles for Breakthrough Success* (Ohio: McGraw-Hill Professional, 2011), 1.
30. Bruce Upbin, "The Innovators Premium: A FAQ," *Forbes,* August 05, 2011, accessed December 06,2012, http://www.forbes.com/sites/bruceupbin/2011/08/05/the-innovators-premium-an-faq/.
31. KPMG, "Mobilizing Innovation: The Changing Landscape of Disruptive Technologies," KPMG Technology Innovation Survey, 2012, accessed May 27, 2012, https://www.kpmg.com/US/en/IssuesAndInsights/ArticlesPublications/Documents/mobilizing-innovation-evolving-landscape-of-disruptive-technologies.pdf.
32. Ibid., 24–25.
33. Andrew Hessel, lecture, author attended Singularity executive program, April 13, 2012.
34. Andrew Hessel, phone conversation with author, July 14, 2012.
35. Frank Spencer, many conversations with author, 2012.
36. Foresight and Innovation at Stanford University, "Center for Foresight and Innovation," 2012, accessed May 28, 2012, http://foresight.stanford.edu/.
37. Spencer, personal conversations with author, 2012.
38. Mallun Yen, multiple interviews and email exchanges with author, September 9, 2012.
39. *Berkeley Technology Law Journal,* University of California, Berkeley School of Law, Boalt Hall 27, 2012, http://btlj.org/data/articles/27_2/BTLJ%202012%20AR%20Full%20Volume.pdf.
40. Seth Besse, email to author, RPX Research and the *United States Patent and Trademark Office,* October 9, 2012.
41. Ibid.
42. "Patently Absurd?" *The Economist,* June 21, 2001, http://www.economist.com/node/662374.
43. Besse, email to author, RPX Research.
44. Ibid.
45. Ibid.

CHAPTER 6: THE UNIQUE PROFILE OF THE SILICON VALLEY ENTREPRENEUR

1. Dr. Richard Swanson, phone interview with author, June 6, 2012.
2. SunPower, "History," 2012, accessed October 11, 2012, http://us.sunpowercorp.com/about/history/.
3. Swanson, phone interview with author.
4. Dane Stangler, "The Coming Entrepreneurship Boom," *Ewing Marion Kauffman Foundation,* June 2009, accessed August 17, 2012, http://www.kauffman.org/uploadedfiles/the-coming-entrepreneurial-boom.pdf.
5. Laurie Segall, "War of Words Breaks Out Over Silicon Valley Diversity Debate," *CNN Money,* October 28, 2011, accessed October 11, 2012, http://money.cnn.com/2011/10/27/technology/silicon_valley_diversity/index.htm/.
6. Vivek Wadhwa, Raj Aggarwal, Krisztina "Z" Holly and Alex Salkever, "The Anatomy of an Entrepreneur," *Kauffman The Foundation of Entrepreneurship,* July 2009, accessed August 22, 2012, http://www.kauffman.org/uploadedfiles

/researchandpolicy/thestudyofentrepreneurship/anatomy%20of%20entre%20 071309_final.pdf.

7. Paul Saffo, quoted in Dean Takahashi, "For Silicon Valley Entrepreneurs, Failure Is an Option," *VentureBeat,* October 27, 2009, accessed November 20, 2012, http://venturebeat.com/2009/10/27/for-silicon-valley-entrepreneurs -failure-is-an-option/.

8. *Merriam-Webster.com,* s.v., "Passion," accessed November 27, 2012, http:// www.merriam-webster.com/dictionary/passion?show=0&t=1354044149.

9. *Merriam-Webster.com,* s.v., "Authenticity," accessed November 27, 2012, http://www.merriam-webster.com/dictionary/authenticity.

10. Bill Barnett, "Where Are the Authentic Entrepreneurs?" *Bill Barnett on Competition,* November 4, 2012, www.barnetttalks.com/2012/11/where-are-authentic -entrepreneurs.html.

11. *Merriam-Webster.com,* s.v., "Idea," accessed November 27, 2012, http://www. merriam-webster.com/dictionary/idea.

12. *Merriam-Webster.com,* s.v., "Risk," accessed November 27, 2012, http://www. merriam-webster.com/dictionary/risk.

13. *Merriam-Webster.com,* s.v., "Trust," accessed November 27, 2012, http://www. merriam-webster.com/dictionary/trust.

14. *Merriam-Webster.com,* s.v., "Resilience," accessed November 27, 2012, http:// www.merriam-webster.com/dictionary/resilience.

15. Cisco Corporation, "2011 Annual Report," accessed August 23, 2012, http:// www.cisco.com/assets/cdc_content_elements/docs/annualreports/media/2011 -ar.pdf.

16. Cisco Corporation, "Acquisitions Summary," acquisition by year, accessed September 1, 2012, http://www.cisco.com/web/about/doing_business/corpo rate_development/acquisitions/ac_year/about_cisco_acquisition_years_list .html.

17. Cisco Corporation, "Cisco Presents the Human Network Effect Campaign," *Cisco's Technology News Site: The Network,* September 22, 2008, accessed October 11, 2012, http://newsroom.cisco.com/dlls/2008/prod_092208.html.

18. Marguerite Reardon, "Cisco Buys Flip Video Maker for $590 Million," *CNET News,* March 19, 2009, accessed October 11, 2012, http://news.cnet.com/8301- 1023_3-10199960-93.html.

19. Cisco Corporation, "Cisco Presents the Human Network Effect Campaign."

20. Christina Brodbeck, interview with author, June 28, 2012.

CHAPTER 7: WHAT MAKES SILICON VALLEY BUSINESS MODELS DIFFERENT

1. Andy Reinhardt, Joan O'C. Hamilton and Linda Himelstein, "What Matters Is How Smart You Are," *Business Week Silicon Valley,* August 25, 1997, accessed January 31, 2013, http://www.businessweek.com/1997/34/b35414.htm.

2. Adam Lashinsky, "Remembering Netscape: The Birth of the Web," *CNN Money,* July 25, 2005, accessed July 27, 2012, http://money.cnn.com/magazines /fortune/fortune_archive/2005/07/25/8266639/.

3. "A Netscape Moment," *The Economist,* February 10, 2010, accessed July 27, 2012, http://www.economist.com/node/15464481.

4. John Markoff, "Microsoft Trying to Dominate the Internet," *New York Times,* July 16, 1996.

5. "Growing Up, Slowing Down: Netscape," *The Economist,* January 8, 1998, accessed August 21, 2012, http://www.economist.com/node/110465.

6. "Innovation: When AOL Bought Netscape," *Business Insider,* YouTube, 2009, accessed August 21, 2012, accessed July 25, 2012, http://www.youtube .com/watch?v=pi263_9QrD8.

7. Miguel Helft, "Tech's Late Adopters Prefer the Tried and True," *New York Times,* March 12, 2008, accessed July 28, 2012, http://www.nytimes .com/2008/03/12/technology/12inertia.html?pagewanted=all.

8. Eric Ries, phone conversation with author, July 17, 2012.

9. Somini Sengupta, Nicole Perlroth, and Jenna Wortham, "Behind Instagram's Success, Networking the Old Way," *New York Times,* August 13, 2012, accessed July 18, 2012, http://www.nytimes.com/2012/04/14/technology/instagram -founders-were-helped-by-bay-area-connections.html.

10. Ibid.

11. Ibid.

12. Randy Komisar, quoted in Steve Lohr, "With a Leaner Model, Start-ups Reach Further Afield," *New York Times,* December 5, 2011, accessed July 20, 2012, http://www.nytimes.com/2011/12/06/science/lean-start-ups-reach-beyond -silicon-valleys-turf.html?pagewanted=all.

13. Tim O'Reilly, *What Is Web 2.0?* (California: O'Reilly Media Inc., 2009).

14. Eric Silver, "The three P's of a Pivot," *Venture Beat,* September 1, 2012, accessed September 3, 2012, http://venturebeat.com/2012/09/01/the-three-ps-of-a-pivot/.

15. Lizette Chapman, "Pivoting Pays Off for the Entrepreneurs," *Wall Street Journal,* April 26, 2012, accessed July 18, 2012, http://online.wsj.com/article /SB10001424052702303592404577364171598999252.html.

16. Eric Ries, phone conversation with author, July 17, 2012.

17. Google, "Our Culture," accessed September 3, 2012, http://www.google.com /about/company/facts/culture/.

18. Jonathon Strickland, "How the Googleplex Works," August 4, 2008, accessed August 3, 2012, HowStuffWorks.com, computer.howstuffworks.com/google plex.html.

19. Google, "Locations," accessed September 3, 2012, www.google.com/about/jobs /locations/mountian-view/.

20. Jordan Newman, phone interview with Jamie Danno, research assistant, July 20, 2012.

21. Caitlin Kelly, "O.K. Google, Take a Deep Breath," *New York Times,* April 28, 2012, accessed August 9, 2012, http://www.nytimes.com/2012/04/29 /technology/google-course-asks-employees-to-take-a-deep-breath.html?page wanted=all.

22. Mark Bercow, email with author, September 5, 2012.

23. Google, "Green," accessed August 10, 2012, www.google.com/green/effciency /oncampus/#eating.

24. Ibid.

25. "Inside Google's Kitchens," *Gourmet Live,* March 3, 2012, accessed August 10, 2012, http://www.gourmet.com/food/gourmetlive/2012/030712/inside-googles -kitchens.

26. Lauren Drell, "The Perks of Working at Google, Facebook, Twitter, and More," *Mashable Business,* October 17, 2011, accessed August 08, 2012, http://mash- able.com/2011/10/17/google-facebook-twitter-linkedin-perks-infographic/.

27. Bercow, email with author.

28. Claire Cain Miller, "In Google's Inner Circle, a Falling Number of Women," *New York Times,* August 22, 2012, accessed August 25, 2012, http://www

.nytimes.com/2012/08/23/technology/in-googles-inner-circle-a-falling-number-of-women.html?_r=1&pagewanted=all.

29. J. P. Mangalindan, "Google: The King of Perks," *CNN Money*, January 30, 2012, accessed August 25, 2012, http://money.cnn.com/galleries/2012/technology/1201/gallery.best-companies-google-perks.fortune/2.html.

30. Ibid.

31. Drell, "The Perks of Working at Google, Facebook, Twitter, and More."

32. Bercow, email with author.

33. Google, "Green."

34. "Google, Bank of America Offer Hybrid Credit," *CNN Money*, June 7, 2006, accessed August 24, 2012, money.cnn.com/2006/06/07/news/companies/bofa_hybrid/.

35. Tatiana Chapira, email with author, September 6, 2012.

36. Google, "Benefits and Perks," *Life at Google*, accessed August 24, 2012, www.google.com/intl/en/jobs/students/lifeatgoogle/benefitsperks/.

37. Owen Thomas, "Google Daycare Now a Luxury for Larry and Sergey's Inner Circle," *Gawker*, June 12, 2008, accessed August 24, 2012, http://gawker.com/5016355/google-daycare-now-a-luxury-for-larry-and-sergeys-inner-circle.

38. Andrew Loh, "Reggio Emilia Approach," *Brainy Child*, December 2006, accessed August 23, 2012, http://www.brainy-child.com/article/reggioemilia.shtml.

39. Strickland, "How the Googleplex Works."

40. David Louie, "Google Hosts 'Bring Your Parents to Work Day,'" *ABC 7 News*, accessed August 3, 2012, http://abclocal.go.com/kgo/video?id=8610338#.

41. Rob Quinn, "Google Offers . . . Really Generous Death Benefits," *Newser*, August 9, 2012, http://www.newser.com/story/151745/googles-vaunted-benefits-go-to-the-grave.html.

CHAPTER 8: THE INVESTORS OF SAND HILL ROAD

1. Draper Fisher Jurvetson, "About DFJ Growth," accessed June 2012, http://www.dfj.com/about/index.php.

2. DFJ Frontier, "Synthetic Genomics," 2012, accessed June 2012, http://www.dfjfrontier.com/cgi-portfolio/artman/publish/syntheticgenomics.shtml.

3. Draper Fisher Jurvetson, "About DFJ Growth," 2012.

4. Tim Draper, interview with author, April 3, 2012.

5. Draper Fisher Jurvetson, "What is Viral Marketing?" May 1, 2000, accessed April 15, 2012, http://www.dfj.com)/news/article_25.shtml.

6. Adam L. Penenberg, "PS: I Love You. Get Your Free Email at Hotmail," *Viral Loop: From Facebook To Twitter, How Today's Smartest Businesses Grow Themselves*, October 18, 2009, accessed April 20, 2012, http://techcrunch.com/2009/10/18/ps-i-love-you-get-your-free-email-at-hotmail/.

7. Draper Fisher Jurvetson, "The Riskmasters," 2005, accessed October 12, 2012, http://www.dfj.com/20th_anniversary/DFJ_ANNIVERSARY_BOOK.pdf.

8. Draper, interview with author.

9. Alfred P. Sloan, "They Made America," *PBS: WGBH History Unit*, 2004, accessed April 8, 2012, http://www.pbs.org/wgbh/theymadeamerica/whomade/doriot_hi.html.

10. IDS News Service Staff, "Digital Equipment Corp. Co-founder Ken Olsen Dies at Age 84," *PC World*, February 7, 2011, accessed October 13, 2012, http://www.pcworld.com/article/218952/digital_equipment_corp_cofonder_ken_olsen_dies_at_age_84.html.

11. "The Origins of Venture Capital," *Life Science Foundation Magazine,* Fall 2011, accessed October 13, 2012, http://www.lifesciencesfoundation.org/magazine -The_Origins_of_Venture_Capital.html.

12. Chong-Moon Lee, William F. Miller, Marguerite Gong Hancock, and Henry S. Rowen, *The Silicon Valley Edge,* (California: Stanford Press, 2000), 235.

13. Ibid., 235–237.

14. Ibid., 237.

15. "Most Expensive Office Spaces: Sand Hill Road Named Priciest Commercial Real Estate in North America," *Huffington Post,* September 9, 2011, accessed October 13, 2012, http://www.huffingtonpost.com/2011/09/09/most-expensive -office-space_n_955709.html.

16. Lee, et al., *The Silicon Valley Edge,* 282.

17. Bob Pavey, interview with author, March 27, 2012.

18. William Draper III, *The Startup Game: Inside the Partnership Between Venture Capitalists and Entrepreneurs* (New York: Macmillan, 2011), 75–76.

19. Rod Turner, "Venture Capital As We Know It Is History," *Venture Beat,* May 15, 2012, http://venturebeat.com/2012/05/15/venture-capital-as-we-know-it-is -history/, April 25, 2012.

20. Matt Marshall, "VCs Learning New Tricks to Weather the Downturn," *San Jose Mercury News,* August 1, 2002, accessed December 6, 2012, http://vent ureconcept.com/management/Fairness%20in%20investing.htm.

21. Fenwick & West, "Silicon Valley Venture Survey," August 23, 2012, accessed June 25, 2012, http://www.fenwick.com/publications/pages/silicon-valley-ven ture-survey-second-quarter-2012.aspx.

22. Kauffman Foundation, "We Have Met the Enemy . . . and He Is Us," May 2012, accessed June 26, 2012, http://www.kauffman.org/uploadedFiles/vc-enemy-is -us-report.pdf.

23. John Hudson, interview with author, July 2, 2012.

24. "U.S. Private Equity Venture Capital Funds Handily Outperformed Public Equi- ties in 2011, According to Cambridge Associates Benchmarks," June 11, 2011, *Cambridge Associates,* accessed July 10, 2012, http://www.marketwire.com /press-release/us-private-equity-venture-capital-funds-handily-outperformed -public-equities-2011-according-1667658.htm.

25. Miguel Helft, "Ron Conway Is a Silicon Valley Startup's Best Friend," *CNN Money,* February 10, 2012, accessed July 15, 2012, http://tech.fortune.cnn .com/2012/02/10/ron-conway-sv-angel/.

26. Rusel DeMaria, "10 Tips for Raising Money on Kickstarters," *Mashable,* March 28, 2012, accessed July 12, 2012, http://mashable.com/2012/03/28 /raising-money-kickstarter/.

27. John Patrick Pullen, "Kickstarter: How Crowdsourcing Went Mainstream," *CNN Money,* June 7, 2012, accessed July 03, 2012, http://tech.fortune.cnn .com/2012/06/07/kickstarter-how-crowdsourcing-went-mainstream/.

CHAPTER 9: THE SERVICES

1. Regis McKenna, "About," 2003, accessed May 2012, http://www.regis.com /about/.

2. "The First Lady of Computers," *Entrepreneur,* October 10, 2008, accessed Oc- tober 12, 2012, http://www.entrepreneur.com/article/197656#.

3. Deborah Gage, "Silicon Valley Pioneer Sandra Kurtzig Back in Start-Up Game with Kenandy," *Wall Street Journal,* August 29, 2011, accessed

October 12, 2012, http://blogs.wsj.com/venturecapital/2011/08/29/silicon-valley -pioneer-back-in-start-up-game-with-new-company-kenandy/.

4. Sandra L. Kurtzig and Tom Parker, *CEO: Building a $400 Million Company from the Ground Up* (Massachusetts: Harvard Press, 1994).

5. Chong-Moon Lee, William Miller, Marguerite Hancock, and Henry Rowen, *The Silicon Valley Edge* (California: Stanford University Press, 2000), 378.

6. Ibid., 379.

7. Larry Sonsini, interview with author, June 19, 2012.

8. Ibid.

9. Carrie Merritt, email with Jamie Danno, research assistant, August 24, 2012.

10. Ibid.

11. Silicon Valley Bank, "About Silicon Valley Bank," accessed July 30, 2012, http://www.svb.com/about-silicon-valley-bank/.

12. Silicon Valley Bank, "About Silicon Valley Bank," accessed July 27, 2012, http://www.svb.com/about-silicon-valley-bank/.

13. KPMG Technology Innovation Center, "Mobilizing Innovation: The Changing Landscape of Disruptive Technologies," KPMG Technology Innovation Survey, 2012, accessed August 3, 2012, https://www.kpmg.com/US/en/IssuesAnd Insights/ArticlesPublications/Documents/mobilizing-innovation-evolving -landscape-of-disruptive-technologies.pdf, 38.

14. Patricia Rios, interview with author, July 27, 2012.

15. Michael Dorsey, confirmed research via email, August 24, 2012.

16. GrowthPoint Technology Partners, "GrowthPoint Announces Opening of a London Office," July 20, 2012, accessed August 20, 2012, http://www.gptpart ners.com/tag/offices/.

17. Ibid.

18. Laurie Yoler, interview with author, August 24. 2012.

19. Lindsey Zouein, IDEO research, August 1, 2012.

20. IDEO, "About," accessed October 10, 2012, http://www.ideo.com/about/.

21. Stacy Gray, verified research through email with the author, October 10, 2012.

22. IDEO, "Fact Sheet," accessed October 11, 2012, http://www.ideo.com/images /uploads/home/IDEO_Fact_Sheet.pdf.

23. *Merriam-Webster.com*, s.v., "Incubator," accessed November 27, 2012, http:// www.merriam-webster.com/dictionary/incubator.

24. Y Combinator, "Demo Day," accessed August 8, 2012, http://ycombinator .com/dday.html.

25. Ryan Mac, "Top Startup Incubators and Accelerators: Y Combinator Tops with 7.8 Billion in Value," *Forbes*, April 30, 2012, accessed August 8, 2012, http:// www.forbes.com/sites/tomiogeron/2012/04/30/top-tech-incubators-as-ranked -by-forbes-y-combinator-tops-with-7-billion-in-value/.

26. Laurie Segall," Breaking the 'Young White Male' Tech Founder Mold," *CNN Money,* November 11, 2011, accessed August 8, 2012, http://money.cnn.com /2011/11/11/technology/diversity_accelerators/index.htm.

27. Billy Gallagher, "Paul Graham Says Y Combinator Companies Have Raised More Than $1 Billion," *Tech Crunch,* July 25 2012, accessed August 10, 2012, http://techcrunch.com/2012/07/25/paul-graham-y-combinator-companies -have-raised-over-1-billion/.

28. Martha Josephson, interview with research assistant, August 1, 2012.

29. Lindsay Trout, interview with research assistant, July 30, 2012.

CHAPTER 10: THE MEETING PLACES

1. "Demographic Profile Bay Area Census," *U.S Census Bureau,* 2010 accessed October 10, 2012, http://www.census.gov/.
2. Jamis MacNiven, interview with author, March 23, 2012.
3. Mark Zetter, "Unofficial Mayor of Silicon Valley Jamis MacNiven Talks Pancakes, Steve Jobs, Startups and Pouring Millions into Idea," *Venture Outsource,* January 15, 2012, accessed October 14, 2012, http://www.ventureoutsource.com/contract-manufacturing/mayor-silicon-valley-jamis-macniven-pancakes-steve-jobs-startups-pouring-millions-ideas-videos.
4. Churchill Club, accessed June 22, 2012, "http://www.churchillclub.org/History.aspx.
5. Ibid.
6. Karen Tucker, email with author, January 27, 2013.
7. Ibid.
8. Kirsten Vernon, interview with Jamie Danno, research assistant, August 2, 2012.
9. "AlwaysOn OnDemand 2012," *AlwaysOn,* 2010, accessed August 04, 2012, http://www.alwayson-network.com/AOEvents/OnDemand-2012/Contact-Us.
10. Rachel Braun Scherl, Alley to the Valley DC summit, 2011.
11. Angie Chang, email with Jamie Danno, research assistant, September 09, 2012.
12. Ben Davidson, "TiE Testimonials," *TiE,* July 16, 2012, accessed September 02, 2012, https://sv.tie.org/testemonial/i-love-tie.
13. Raj Desai, interview with author, July 20, 2012.
14. CEO Summit, "China and Technology's Impact on the Global Economy," *HYSTA,* 2011, accessed August 26, 2012, http://www.hysta.org/ceosummit2011/home.
15. "Best Business Bars," *Entrepreneur,* June 21, 2010, accessed October 14, 2012, http://www.entrepreneur.com/article/207194-2.
16. Peter Rudolph, interview with Jamie Danno, research assistant, July 20, 2012.
17. Cynthia Liu, "Woodside Chef's Cuisine Rooted in Boutique Ranch," *SF Gate,* September 23, 2005, accessed July 26, 2012, http://www.sfgate.com/bayarea/article/Woodside-chef-s-cuisine-rooted-in-boutique-ranch-2606497.php.
18. Dmitry Elperin, "Team," *The Village Pub,* accessed July 28, 2012, http://www.thevillagepub.net/about/team/dmitry_elperin.
19. Greg Stern, interview with research assistant, August 29, 2012.
20. Jane Knoerle, "New Owner for the Dutch 'Goose,'" *The Almanac,* October 5, 2005.
21. Jean Paul Coupal, interview with Jamie Danno, research assistant, August 28, 2012.
22. Tomio Geron, "Coupa Café: Where Startups Meet, Work And Test Products," *Forbes Magazine,* December 5, 2011, accessed August 28, 2012, http://www.forbes.com/sites/tomiogeron/2011/11/16/coupa-cafe-where-startups-meet-work-and-test-products/.
23. Jules Maltz, quoted in Geron, "Coupa Café."
24. Lawrence Chu, interview with author, July 25, 2012.

CHAPTER 11: THE LIFESTYLE

1. Fern Mandelbaum, interview with author, May 28, 2012.
2. Ibid.

3. Ibid.
4. Ibid.
5. Bill Davenhall, "Your Health Depends on Where You Live," January 2010, *TED Partner Series,* accessed July 23, 2012, http://www.ted.com/talks/bill_davenhall _your_health_depends_on_where_you_live.html.
6. Morton, email with author, June 7, 2012.
7. *National Oceanic and Atmospheric Administration,* accessed August 31, 2012, http://www.noaa.gov/.
8. Miguel Miller, "Climate of San Jose," *National Weather Service,* April 1999, accessed July 30, 2012, http://www.wrh.noaa.gov/mtr/sfd_sjc_climate/sjc/SJC _CLIMATE3.php.
9. Morton, email with author.
10. Jessica Guynn, "Silicon Valley Is Getting Healthy, Crunching Abs, Not Just Apps," *Los Angeles Times,* May 11, 2012.
11. Jordan Newman, interview with Jamie Danno, research assistant, August 23, 2012.
12. Jennifer Myers, "Canadian Lured by Silicon Valley's 'Risk Mentality,'" *Globe and Mail,* August 23, 2012, accessed June 25, 2012, http://m.the globeandmail.com/report-on-business/small-business/sb-growth/canadian -lured-by-silicon-valleys-risk-mentality/article600131/?service=mobile.
13. Stanford University, " Commute Club," *Stanford University Parking and Transportation Services,* accessed June 26, 2012, http://transportation.stanford.edu /alt_transportation/Commute_Club.shtml.
14. Mark Jones, "Sunny Skies Spur Thousands to Celebrate Bike to Work Day," *Metropolitan Transportation Commission,* May 10, 2012, http://www.mtc .ca.gov/news/current_topics/5-12/btwd.htm.
15. Regional Open Space, "Open Space Preserves," Midpeninsula Regional Open Space District, accessed September 6, 2012, http://www.openspace.org/preserves/.
16. Alto Velo Bicycle Racing Club, accessed September 3, 2012, http://www.alto velo.org/, accessed September 03, 2012.
17. Kelly and Jonathan Knowles, *Big Basin Redwoods State Park,* 2010, accessed September 6, 2012, http://www.bigbasin.org/.
18. *Little Basin,* 2012, accessed September 6, 2012, http://littlebasin.org/.
19. *Spring Down,* accessed September 6, 2012, www.springdown.com.
20. *Sequoia Yacht Club,* accessed September 7, 2012, http://www.sequoiayc.org/.
21. "Early Winter Swells Anticipated for Mavericks International," *Mavericks International,* July 24, 2012, accessed September 6, 2012, http://mavericks invitational.com/2012/07/earlywinter/.
22. "Jeff Rowley Goes Left at Mavericks," *Surfer Today,* March 15, 2012, accessed September 6, 2012, http://www.surfertoday.com/surfing/7070-jeff-rowley-goes -left-at-mavericks.
23. Mark Conley, "Mavericks Surf Contest Adds Kelly Slater's Name Back to List," *San Jose Mercury News,* November 05, 2010.
24. Tamara Warta, "Surfing in San Fran," *Love to Know,* accessed September 8, 2012, http://sanfrancisco.lovetoknow.com/wiki/Surfing_in_San_Fran.
25. Thom Elkjer, *Fodor's Escape to the Wine Country: California's Napa, Sonoma, and Mendocino,* (New York: Fodor's 1st edition, 2002).
26. North Star Tahoe, accessed September 6, 2012, www.northstarattahoe.com.
27. Joanna Lin, "California Leads Nation in Farmers Markets," California Watch, August 9, 2011, accessed September 7, 2012, http://californiawatch.org /dailyreport/california-leads-nation-farmers-markets-11965.

28. "Silicon Valley Leadership Group 2012–2014 Work Plan," *Silicon Valley Leadership Group,* 2011, accessed September 6, 2012, http:// svlg.org/about-us.

29. Jerry De La Piedra, "Water Use Efficiency Strategic Plan," Santa Clara Valley Water District, September 2008.

30. Collaborative Economics, "Silicon Valley Index," Joint Venture, 2012, http://www.jointventure.org/images/stories/pdf/2012index-r2.pdf, 50.

31. Rami Branitzky, "Using Coulomb Technologies ChargePoint System, SAP Labs U.S., Palo Alto Installs Electric Vehicle Charging Infrastructure," *Business Wire,* December 09, 2010, accessed September 6, 2012, http://www.businesswire.com/news/home/20101209005914/en/Coulomb-Technologies-Charge Point-System-SAP-Labs-U.S.

32. Leon Kaye, "The 10 Emerging Sustainable Cities to Watch in 2012," *Triple Pundit,* January 3, 2012, accessed September 6, 2012, http://www.triplepundit.com/2012/01/top-10-sustainable-cities-2012/.

CHAPTER 12: THE BENCH

1. Heidi Roizen, interview with author, July 31, 2012.

2. Ibid.

3. Anshul Samar, interview with author, July 16, 2011.

4. Channing Hancock, interview with author, July 17, 2012.

5. Rod Strickland, interview with author, July 17, 2012.

6. Pamela Ryckman, "The Risk-Taking Edge of West Coast Women," *New York Times,* November 10, 2012, accessed August 6, 2012, http://www.nytimes.com/2010/11/11/business/smallbusiness/11sbiz.html?_r=0.

7. Lisa Ling, *Our America with Lisa Ling, OWN,* featuring author's children, November 27, 2011.

8. Anne Beneventi, gifted specialist, evaluation documentation of Dominick Piscione, January 27, 2010.

9. Eleanor E. Maccoby, Stanford Psychology Department, "Welcome!" Bing Nursery School home page, accessed August 28, 2012, http://www.stanford.edu/dept/bingschool/.

10. Jennifer Winters, interview with author, August 28, 2012.

11. The Nueva School, http://nuevaschool.org/, accessed August 28, 2012.

12. The Nueva School, "Learning by Doing," Notably Nueva, accessed August 29, 2012, http://nuevaschool.org/notably-nueva/learning-by-doing/philosophy -and-overview.

13. The author's children attend The Harker School, lower campus.

14. Pam Dickenson, interview with author, October 9, 2012.

15. Lisa M. Krieger, "The It School for the Next Einsteins," *San Jose Mercury News,* March 13, 2011, accessed January 31, 2013, http://www.mercurynews.com/rss/ci_17606226.

16. Anita Chetty, interview with author, July 20, 2012.

17. Ibid.

18. Ibid.

19. Ibid.

20. Pam Dickenson, interview with author, October 9, 2012.

21. Krieger, "The It School for the Next Einsteins."

22. Tony Wagner, *Creating Innovators: The Making of Young People Who Will Change the World* (New York: Simon & Schuster, 2012), 12.

23. Tony Wagner, "Educating the Next Steve Jobs," *Wall Street Journal,* April 13, 2012, accessed July 20, 2012, http://online.wsj.com/article/SB100014240527 02304444604577337790086673050.html.

24. Michael Finnegan, interviews with author, May–July 2012.

25. Quantum Camp, "Our Faculty," accessed June 2012, http://www.quantum camp.com/aboutus/ourfaculty.

26. Ibid.

27. Samar, interview with author.

28. Hancock, interview with author.

29. Ibid.

30. Mike Cassidy, "Startup Stripe Is Living the College Degree Debate," *San Jose Mercury News,* September 1, 2011, accessed July 20, 2012.

31. Gary Goldman, interview with Laura Demming, *Daily Brink,* accessed July 19, 2012, http://www.dailybrink.com/?p=1990.

32. Jessica Leber, "Too Young to Fail," MIT *Technology Review,* February 3, 2012, accessed July 19, 2012, http://www.technologyreview.com/news/426789/too -young-to-fail/.

33. Cassidy, "Startup Stripe Is Living the College Degree Debate."

EPILOGUE: CAN SILICON VALLEY BE REPLICATED?

1. Mark Z. Jacobson, "Review of Solutions to Global Warming, Air Pollution, and Energy Security," accessed September 10, 2012, http://www.stanford.edu /group/efmh/jacobson/EnergyEnvRev1008.pdf, 4.

2. Hermione Way, "Silicon Valley Cannot Be Replicated," *Entrepreneur, The Next Web,* May 25, 2012.

3. It is interesting to note that Timothy B. Lee recently argued in *Forbes* magazine that the Bay Area would and should have an additional 4 million people if housing policies were not so restrictive—and that these policies are detrimental to the continued growth of Silicon Valley by limiting the inflow of additional talent. Timothy B. Lee, "Why the Bay Area Should Have 11 Million Residents," *Forbes,* May 10, 2012, accessed June 27, 2012, http://www.forbes .com/sites/timothylee/2012/05/10/why-the-bay-area-should-have-11-million -residents-today/.

4. Paul Graham, "How to Be Silicon Valley," May 2006, accessed June 29, 2012, http://www.paulgraham.com/siliconvalley.html.

5. Richard Florida, "How Startups Have Changed the Way American Business Thinks," *The Atlantic,* October 18, 2011, accessed October 10, 2012, http://www.theatlantic.com/technology/archive/2011/10/how-startups-have -changed-the-way-american-business-thinks/246850/.

6. "Les Misérables," *The Economist,* July 28, 2012, accessed June 29, 2012, http://www.economist.com/node/21559618.

7. Ibid.

8. Graham, "How to Be Silicon Valley."

9. Carlos Baradello, "Mining the Silicon Valley Mind—A Perspective," June 29, 2012, accessed June 30, 2012, http://carlosbaradello.com/2012/06/29 /mining-the-silicon-valley-mind-a-perspective/.

10. "Entrepreneur at a Glance," *OECD,* 2012, accessed June 29, 2012, http:// www.oecd.org/industry/entrepreneurshipataglance2012.htm.

11. "Doing Business Report," Copublication of the World Bank and the International Finance Corporation, 2012, accessed August 22, 2012, http://www

.doingbusiness.org/~/media/FPDKM/Doing%20Business/Documents/Annual -Reports/English/DB12-FullReport.pdf.

12.   KPMG, "Mobilizing Innovation: The Changing Landscape of Disrupting Tech-nologies," KPMG Technology and Innovation Survey, 2012, accessed July 8, 2012, https://www.kpmg.com/US/en/IssuesAndInsights/ArticlesPublications/Do cuments/mobilizing-innovation-evolving-landscape-of-disruptive-technologies .pdf.

13.   Donna Petkanics, interview with author, June 8, 2012.

14.   Council of Foreign Relations, endorsement of Dan Senor and Saul Singer, *Startup Nation: The Story of Israel's Economic Miracle* (New York: Twelve, 2011).

15.   Tal Barak Harif, "NASDAQ Loses 'Holy Grail' Status for Offerings: Israel Overnight," *Bloomberg News,* November 07,2011, accessed October 10, 2012, http://www.businessweek.com/news/2011-11-07/nasdaq-loses-holy-grail-status -for-offerings-israel-overnight.html.

16.   Shiri Habib-Valdhorn, "Perrigo Joins NASDAQ 100 Index," *Globes Israel's Business Arena,* December 6, 2011, accessed October 10, 2012, http://www .globes.co.il/serveen/globes/docview.asp?did=1000704046&fid=1725.

17.   Senor and Singer, *Startup Nation.*

18.   Gil Kerbs, "The Unit," *Forbes,* accessed July 2, 2012, http://www.forbes .com/2007/02/07/israel-military-unit-ventures-biz-cx_gk_0208israel.html.

19.   "China's 12th Five Year Plan," *APCO Worldwide,* December 10, 2010, accessed October 12, 2012, http://apcoworldwide.com/content/PDFs/Chinas_12th_Five -Year_Plan.pdf.

20.   KPMG, "Mobilizing Innovation Survey," KPMG Technology and Innovation Survey, 2012, accessed July 8, 2012, https://www.kpmg.com/US/en/IssuesAnd Insights/ArticlesPublications/Documents/mobilizing-innovation-evolving-land scape-of-disruptive-technologies.pdf.

21.   Jason Lim, "Why China Won't Be Innovative for at Least 20 More Years," *VentureBeat,* March 26, 2012, accessed July 10, 2012, http://venturebeat.com /2012/03/26/why-china-doesnt-innovate/.

22.   "Survey Report," *KPMG,* September 04, 2012, accessed October 13, 2012, http://www.kpmg.com/global/en/issuesandinsights/articlespublications /technology-innovation-survey/pages/china.aspx.

23.   An interesting recent development has been the government-led Zhongguancun Science Park's investment in an office park in the original Silicon Valley to at-tract tenants with an interest in the Chinese market, as well as Chinese startups looking to establish operations in the United States. Chinese provincial and municipal governments setting up representative offices in the United States are also seen as potential client bases for this office park, underscoring the sig-nificant role that Chinese government plays in the international expansion of Chinese business.

24.   Wang Yanlin, "China to Quicken Reform and Invest in Innovation," *People's Daily Online,* March 19, 2012, accessed July 1, 2012, http://english.people daily.com.cn/90785/7761701.html.

25.   "From Brawn to Brain," *The Economist,* March 10, 2012, accessed June 23, 2012, http://www.economist.com/node/21549938.

26.   Sunny Ye, "Weixin 4.0 Is Vintage Tencent and the Most Important Chinese Internet Product Since Weibo," *Techrice,* April 23, 2012, http://techrice.com /2012/04/23/weixin-4-0-is-vintage-tencent-and-the-most-important-chinese -internet-product-since-weibo/, accessed June 18, 2012.

27. Gordon Orr and Erik Roth, "A CEO's Guide to Innovation in China," *McKinsley Quarterly,* February 2012, accessed September 10, 2012, http://www.mckinseyquarterly.com/A_CEOs_guide_to_innovation_in_China_2919.

28. Andy Grove, "How America Can Create Jobs," *Bloomberg Businessweek,* July 1, 2010.

29. Vivek Wadhwa, "The Future of Manufacturing Is in America, Not China," *Foreign Policy,* July 17, 2012.

30. "The Program," *Start-Up Chile,* accessed October 10, 2012, http://startupchile.org/about/the-program/.

31. Vivek Wadhwa, "Want More Startups? Learn From Chile," *Bloomberg Businessweek,* April 11, 2012, accessed August 20, 2012, http://www.businessweek.com/articles/2012-04-11/want-more-startups-learn-from-chile.

32. Shani Shoham, "Can Silicon Valley Be Replicated?" *Shani's Business Review,* November 27, 2011, accessed June 28, 2012, http://shanishoham.wordpress.com/2011/11/27/can-silicon-valley-be-replicated/.

33. Graham, "How to Be Silicon Valley."

34. Nikola Danaylov, "Linda MacDonald Glenn on Singularity 1 on 1: Sentience Matters!" *Singularity weblog,* accessed October 14, 2012, http://www.singularityweblog.com/linda-macdonald-glenn-on-singularity-1-on-1-sentience-matters/.

INDEX